GHOSTS OF NO CHILD LEFT BEHIND

Studies in the
Postmodern Theory of Education

Shirley R. Steinberg
General Editor

Vol. 361

The Counterpoints series is part of the Peter Lang Education list.
Every volume is peer reviewed and meets
the highest quality standards for content and production.

PETER LANG
New York • Washington, D.C./Baltimore • Bern
Frankfurt • Berlin • Brussels • Vienna • Oxford

Joanne M. Carris

GHOSTS OF NO CHILD LEFT BEHIND

PETER LANG
New York • Washington, D.C./Baltimore • Bern
Frankfurt • Berlin • Brussels • Vienna • Oxford

KH

Library of Congress Cataloging-in-Publication Data

Carris, Joanne M.
Ghosts of No Child Left Behind / Joanne M. Carris.
p. cm. — (Counterpoints: studies in the postmodern theory of education; 361)
Includes bibliographical references and index.
1. Literacy—Social aspects—New York (State)—New York—Case studies.
2. Language arts (Secondary)—New York (State)—New York—Case studies.
3. Reading—Remedial teaching—New York (State)—New York—Case studies.
4. Youth with social disabilities—Education—New York (State)—New York—
Case studies. 5. Educational accountability—United States.
6. United States. No Child Left Behind Act of 2001. I. Title.
LC153.N48C37 379.2'60973—dc22 2009011333
ISBN 978-1-4331-0548-7 (hardcover)
ISBN 978-1-4331-0547-0 (paperback)
ISSN 1058-1634

Bibliographic information published by **Die Deutsche Nationalbibliothek**.
Die Deutsche Nationalbibliothek lists this publication in the "Deutsche
Nationalbibliografie"; detailed bibliographic data is available
on the Internet at http://dnb.d-nb.de/.

FSC
Mixed Sources
Product group from well-managed
forests, controlled sources and
recycled wood or fiber

Cert no. SCS-COC-002464
www.fsc.org
©1996 Forest Stewardship Council

Cover illustration by Copie

The paper in this book meets the guidelines for permanence and durability
of the Committee on Production Guidelines for Book Longevity
of the Council of Library Resources.

© 2011 Peter Lang Publishing, Inc., New York
29 Broadway, 18th floor, New York, NY 10006
www.peterlang.com

3/6/12

To the courageous and resilient students
who inspired this book

In loving memory of
Joe L. Kincheloe
(December 14, 1950 – December 19, 2008)
who made so much possible for so many

CONTENTS

Acknowledgments

Many people contributed to the realization of this book, and I am profoundly grateful. Their service ranged from being scholarly mentors, to allies within a troubled school system, to technical assistants, to sounding boards, to emotional supports.

I am eternally thankful to Joe Kincheloe, whose passion, wisdom, scholarship, and encouragement—both in body and in spirit—fueled this book. I know he is with us, celebrating its completion. I am grateful to Shirley Steinberg who provided indispensable scholarly guidance and insights, as well as writing the preface.

Family and friends kept me strong throughout the creation of this book—especially as I struggled with an unexpected health crisis. My profound gratitude. I would like to thank my mother for reading numerous drafts and making important suggestions. And, I am thankful to Pamela Joyce, who read chapters, encouraged me, and continually provided valuable input. My husband, Tim Shorter, was a calming force, which helped ground me during the writing process, and I tremendously appreciate his astute literary suggestions. I am deeply grateful to my parents, Joe Carris and Joan Carris, for their unconditional love that has supported and sustained me throughout all my endeavors.

Thank you to Copie Rodriguez for bringing to life the idea for the book cover with his exceptional artistry and to Pamela Joyce, Robert Carris, Marika

Bethel, Wesley Alexander, and Tim Shorter for their assistance in developing the conceptual image.

I greatly appreciate the emotional support that Karen Abrams-Gerber, Cynthia Carris-Alonso, Alicia Alonso, Jennifer Morris, Liza Finkelstein, Jennifer Finkelstein, and Donny Etheredge have all provided along this creative journey.

In addition to those already mentioned, several other family and friends have also been a tremendous source of inspiration, and I thank you all.

I am profoundly grateful to Guru Dev Singh who has assisted in guiding my spirit through personal and professional growth throughout the years. Finally, the book has materialized—soon the baby and tree will follow.

Thank you to Sophie Appel of Peter Lang Publishing, who was a great help throughout the production process, and my editors for their work. I would like to express my appreciation to Ian Steinberg for his typesetting, for the many logistical questions about publishing he answered as this book neared publication, and for his invaluable support and expertise.

I profoundly thank the assistant principal—who was at both schools where I worked—and the principal at each of these schools. To protect the privacy of all concerned, I will keep their names anonymous. Their genuine concern for children showed me that, within the larger education system, at the school level, there are ways to care for youth according to their academic and socio-educational needs. Their compassion and professionalism made it an honor to be a member of this team of visionary educators. My sincere thanks, as well, to all of my professional colleagues.

Finally, my deepest gratitude and appreciation to my students for our respectful exchange of knowledge and joy.

Reading the Worlds

Shirley R. Steinberg

Forgive me for prefacing this preface with the fact that I shouldn't be writing it. Joanne Carris was one of Joe Kincheloe's dearest, brightest, and most insightful students, and he should be here today writing for her. Joe died not long after Joanne defended her doctorate, but I can unequivocally say, he was confident she would become the scholar she is now. I beg your indulgence, as I will attempt to say what I feel, and what I know Joe felt about her important work.

Joanne's work comes from what many liberals call, the trenches. I interpret this pejorative phrase as discussing someone who is working with those kids who most people don't give a damn about. Joanne, however, gives a damn. This book reflects just how deep her concerns and research go in attempting to change the on-going notion that kids in those 'trenches' should be viewed as a deficit, both to society and to us, as educators: that they are a problem, and our work should be to solve them.

North American educational critics have not sought Band Aids to solve the ills of the public system; they have jumped over splints and casts, and proposed entire body bags in which to bury our kids. It began to hit the fan in full force in 1983 during the Commission on Excellence, *A Nation at Risk,* in which a group of non-educators created a mandate and pushed a national curriculum based on failing schools. The 90s ushered in *No Child Left Behind,* and the 2000s have brought *Race to the Top*. These are the body bags of educational solutions…zipped up by corporate interventions, management organizations (EMOs), and publishers, these bags have heralded in the national notion that children aren't learning, teachers are to blame, and non-educators need to solve the problems. What these "solutions" don't do is to contextualize the illiteracies of the students, understand the socio-economic nuances of their lives, and attempt to change the systems which perpetuate the deficits. Policymakers need to focus on teacher education, improving schools by lifelong teacher learning, improved sites of learning, and contextualized and authentic curricula. Obsessed with purchasing and implementing new programs, solutions for education and literacy learning have been limited to packaged, teacher-proof plans with the endorsement of the government and the lack of competitive examination or alternative programs. Employing the one-size-fits-all method of curriculum design, failed programs like *Success for All* and *Voyager* have padded the pockets of publishers, test makers, and running records fanatics and left America's children and youth less able to read, write, and count.

Using a critical pedagogical grounding, Joanne looks at the failures of literacy in North America. Reading the world of literacy, the business of literacy, she sheds light on the dirty little secrets of the first-world country with the lowest literacy rate in the world. This book will enhance and provoke discussions in teacher education classrooms about the nature of literacy, the politics of literacy, and the economics of literacy packaging. The research will inform those who are investigating the failure of the USA to create literate children...and the inability of the committees of the 80s, the sloganism of the 90s, and the neo-liberal attempts at education in the new millennium. This is serious stuff Joanne is dealing with, and it is time we, as teachers and citizens pay attention to a nation's failure to respect what became our childrens' legacy in Johnson's 1965 Education Act. This book is a call to action for us to engage in an informed conversation about the inability of America's children and youth to read, and the inability of a government to figure out what the hell the problem is. Joanne Carris has taken the words and pedagogy of Paulo Freire and Joe Kincheloe, to re-name and re-claim the right of all children to read the word, and the world.

— *Shirley R. Steinberg, Director, The Paulo and Nita Freire International Project for Critical Pedagogy, McGill University and Research Professor at the University of Barcelona*

ONE

Recognizing Non-reading Adolescents

Introduction

For a country that regards itself as a model of democracy for other countries around the world, the fact that the school system plays a role in the creation of a population of non-reading adolescents, many of whom were born in the United States, and excludes these youth from the educational process, represents a failure in purported democratic ideals. Presently, public school systems nationwide contend with a contingent of non-reading adolescents (generally defined, according to the school system's measures, as having reading abilities that fall within pre-primer through upper 2nd grade level equivalents). Given discriminatory practices within U.S. social institutions and limited economic opportunities, this population of adolescents who are in the emergent stages of literacy in New York City (and other urban areas) is predominantly comprised of black and Latino youth from low-income backgrounds. These students consist of U.S.-born children as well as those who have immigrated. Some are already labeled as special education students; some have been designated for ESL or bilingual services; and even a small percentage, although they qualify according to the educational system's definitions, have not, as of yet, been identified for special education services. Non-reading adolescents generally attend school with students who read at higher levels than they do. Such schools include mainstream schools, schools within juvenile detention centers, schools for court-involved youth in non-secure sites, schools for children under the supervision of the New York City Administration for Children's Services, and others.

Discourse among educational policymakers seldom pertains to this population of adolescents who read below a 3rd grade level equivalent—particularly the U.S.-born youth within this group of students. Consideration is given to implementing curriculum and pedagogy for those upper middle school and high school students who read two or more grade levels below their given age equivalents, as well as for those adolescents who read at a 4th grade level. National figures indicate that as many as 8.7 million 4th through 12th graders struggle with print literacy skills in school (Fletcher et al., 1999). However, those upper middle and high school students who are still learning the principles of letter/sound coordination are often forgotten in national discourse and policy decisions.

Sometimes, teachers of high school and upper middle school students do not anticipate that a student in these upper grades would read and write below a 3rd grade level equivalent. So, many of these teachers do not know that they have to look for signs from their students who need textual literacy instruction; nor do they even know what these signs may look like. For some of these teachers, often the student is labeled as, to name just a few terms, a "behavior problem," a "class-cutter," "lazy," or "disinterested." Yet, the teacher is unaware that these characteristics, in fact, result from the child's limited text knowledge amidst a class that requires advanced literacy skills.

As the academic and emotional needs of non-reading adolescents are not systemically addressed, these youth are often more likely to be left behind. Given the limited options within school and the society at large for youth who are classified as non-readers, some of these adolescents spend time in juvenile correctional facilities. Furthermore, as research indicates the link between limited academic attainment—which includes low reading abilities—and incarceration, educational policymakers, administrators, and educators must focus more attention on addressing this student population's need within the school system, beyond the confines of schools within juvenile detention centers (GAO, 2002; Gregory, 1996). Such action, among other benefits, could minimize non-reading adolescents' chances of winding up in jail.

However, in the current educational arena, as educational policy fueled by the No Child Left Behind Act of 2001—which was signed into law in January 2002 and is the contemporary version of the Elementary and Secondary Education Act (ESEA)—prioritizes high-stakes standardized assessment (the use of a single test score to make important educational decisions), instead of comprehensive, meaningful print literacy pedagogy, youth who struggle with reading (and the teachers who teach them) are increasingly subjected to the sole use of mandated reading programs that focus exclusively on the mechanics of reading and writing. No Child Left Behind's (NCLB's) emphasis on so-called scientifically researched reading programs and practices reduces literacy instruction to scripted reading programs—such as Voyager Expanded Learning and Success for All. These programs focus exclusively on the mechanics of literacy—the acquisition of skills for decoding and encoding written symbols. They, therefore, eliminate essential aspects of literacy—for example, social and creative elements as well as critical, higher level thinking.

Although states and school districts have poured millions of federal dollars into these reading programs, a population of non-reading adolescents persists, as these programs (a) do not root literacy development in meaningful practices that relate to students' lives and (b) cannot address the economic, social, and political forces at play in the creation of adolescents who read below a 3rd grade level equivalent. Additionally, economic and political motives have fueled the selection of reading programs promoted under No Child Left Behind's (NCLB's) Reading First program—the $1 billion per year program that provides grants to schools and districts to implement reading programs and practices in kindergarten through 3rd grade that, as indicated in Reading First, are grounded in "scientifically based reading research." Among numerous conflicts of interest that have influenced the programs policymakers have endorsed for the Reading First initiative, various members on the panel for selecting the programs also created some of the chosen programs—as in the case of Voyager. Also with Voyager—one of the main reading programs that George W. Bush's administration touted—the publisher of the program was one of the former president's major campaign contributors.

In addition to the detriments of NCLB's mechanistic approach to literacy instruction and underlying political and financial motivations that have shaped the particular literacy pedagogy promoted, NCLB's high-stakes accountability system has posed serious harm to scores of youth. In promoting high-stakes standardized assessments, youth who struggle with reading confront the threat of multiple grade retentions, as places such as New York City, have in recent years enacted single-test promotion policies. In light of studies showing that grade retention raises dropout rates and does not enhance student achievement over time, such policy creates a structure that "pushes out" non reading adolescents. Equally pernicious, the test-driven curriculum that accompanies the 3rd through 8th grade standardized tests, among other problematic consequences, denies non-reading adolescents textual literacy teachings that actually address their specific academic needs. Rather than allowing students to develop these skills at each child's specific pace, high-stakes standardized tests require all students to attain a pre-determined print literacy standard that policymakers have arbitrarily deemed developmentally appropriate for each grade level. Thus, due to test-driven curriculum those students in upper middle school and high school who read below a 3rd grade level equivalent generally do not even receive remedial print literacy, nor empowering contextual literacy (see below *Print Literacy/Textual Literacy and Contextual Litera-cy/Critical Literacy* for definition), instruction as NCLB's high-stakes assessments force teachers to "teach to the test" for each grade-level.

As Congress considers renewing the NCLB Act, it is unlikely that this federal legislation, although under-funded from the beginning, will be voted out of existence for at least a decade. It is more probable that NCLB will just undergo considerable revision for now—ideally changes with regard to assessment policy for special education and English Language Learners (ELLs), amidst other needed amendments. However, hopefully in time, NCLB, with its one-size-fits-all paradigm and punitive high-stakes test-driven accountability mandate, will ultimately be dismantled. In its place, policymakers could implement legislation that truly ensures high-quality education for all students within a genuine framework of high standards. Within such a context, assessment and accountability procedures would, for example, encompass the complexity of teaching and learning; allow students to learn according to their specific academic needs; embrace educational consequences of poverty and historical discrimination; reject single-test promotion and graduation policies; and employ authentic, multiple measurements of students' progress in ways that (a) support, rather than punish, students, teachers, and schools and (b) enable meaningful teachings and higher-order learning.

Situating the Issue within Current Literature

Focusing on urban areas in the U.S., current literature, including studies cited earlier, has addressed issues pertaining to the education, literacy, and incarceration of inner-city youth—who, given discriminatory procedures that have shaped urban planning, are predominantly black and Latino. Theorists, historians, and educational analysts within the critical tradition discuss prejudicial policies and practices leading to unequal outcomes for economically disadvantaged black and Latino youth.

Although Taylor and Dorsey-Gaines's (1988) study documents the resilience of many inner-city children in their successful acquisition of literacy, despite prejudicial structures, numerous studies reveal the structural inequities that operate in the lives of urban, low-income youth. In line with critical theorists' analyses, this research contextualizes the reality in which, due to discriminatory practices and policies, many inner-city youth struggle with reading and are over-represented in both special education classes and juvenile detention centers. Additional research highlights this correlation between low reading skills, special education placement, and incarceration (Leone et al., 2003). Such trends become all the more problematic in light of the proliferation of prisons.

With regard to print literacy, trend studies conducted by the National Assessment of Educational Progress (NAEP), which provide national statistics on 4th and 8th grade reading scores, indicate that approximately twice as many economically disadvantaged students scored below the basic proficiency level as compared to those students living above the poverty line (NCES, 2003). Research also documents the large population of incarcerated youth who read on a 4th grade level (Coalition for Juvenile Justice, 2001).

Numerous studies, therefore, highlight inequitable educational practices and policies that have historically marginalized low-income African American and Latino youth; emphasize the over-representation of inner-city youth in both special education classes and juvenile detention centers; and underscore the prevalence of lower reading abilities among economically disadvantaged and incarcerated youth.

Deficiencies of Current Literature

The available literature, however, does not include adequate discourse specifically about inner-city adolescents within both mainstream schools and schools within detention centers whose textual literacy abilities fall below 3rd grade limits—and are, thus, still learning the principles of letter/sound coordination. The absence of research, specifically about non-reading adolescents in the U.S. school system, has limited discussion of the social, political, and economic backdrop shaping these students' pedagogical lives. Consequently, policymakers have not provided comprehensive educational measures that actually address non-reading adolescents' particular academic, emotional, and social needs. Existing research, even research within the critical tradition, lacks qualitative inquiry that explores both the ways in which structural forces impact the contemporary socio-educational experiences of non-reading youth and what type of pedagogy can facilitate meaningful and empowering literacy curriculum and educational policy for them. Expanding on the current literature, my analysis will incorporate contemporary curricula theory—an interdisciplinary study of educational experience—to understand curriculum as political text, to create more just and democratic schooling for all students, particularly for non-reading adolescents in New York City.

The Importance of This Study and the Audience It Targets

A political understanding of curriculum within a critical context can lead to the synthesis of meaningful literacy pedagogy for non-reading adolescents—some of whom are incarcerated. To promote a more humane educational experience for these youth, this book, therefore, brings to light structural obstacles that non-reading adolescents in New York City face in their pedagogical experiences, given the historically rooted educational consciousness that continues to inform exclusionary policies and practices. This in-depth understanding, focused in New

York City, can offer educational policymakers, administrators, and educators an insight and stimulus for developing policy, practices, and curriculum that serve non-reading adolescents' needs and nurtures their well-being. This analysis can also inform the general public, particularly parents and educators, so that they may urge policymakers to reverse educational injustices perpetrated against non-reading adolescents by creating positive alternatives.

Perhaps, with greater public awareness and discourse about the existence of non-reading adolescents within mainstream and detention center schools as well as the impact of social, political, and economic conditions on their schooling experiences, policymakers and administrators will implement reform measures that are rooted in a transformatory model. Such educational reforms could (a) prevent the institutional circumstances that contribute to teenage illiteracy and (b) remediate the literacy abilities of non-reading adolescents, who have thus far been disenfranchised within the school system.

Despite efforts in some of the public schools within correctional facilities, and even some mainstream high schools, to develop the literacy abilities of non-reading adolescents through a curriculum that considers their academic needs, this book advocates for a more comprehensive and critical approach. It is imperative that policymakers:

a. Create designated upper middle and high schools specifically for adolescents who are still learning the principles of letter/sound coordination to provide them empowering and meaningful literacy pedagogy;

b. Employ these self-actualizing literacy programs for non-reading adolescents throughout schools within juvenile detention centers;

c. Implement an infrastructure and support system to provide textual literacy instruction in every grade (pre-kindergarten through 12th grade) that is tailored to each child's specific needs, thereby ensuring that all students, regardless of their age and the level at which they are performing, develop their ability to read and write print;

d. Abolish high-stakes testing procedures, which merely penalize non-reading adolescents (and other student populations) without providing literacy pedagogy to promote their textual, as well as contextual, literacy development.

This book, thus, calls attention to the need for discourse and action on these issues pertaining to the pedagogical lives of non-reading adolescents.

Definition of Terms

This section defines key terms used in this book. In particular, since various perspectives on literacy abound, I will briefly discuss several definitions pertinent to this study and explored throughout. These terms will provide useful grounding before embarking in the main chapters on an analysis of curriculum in its political context and the construction of empowering pedagogy for non-reading adolescents. While this book advocates critical literacy (to be explained further), a key point with regard to the teaching of literacy is that policymakers' underlying ideologies about the purposes of literacy shape the type of literacy pedagogy that is used, and education in general. The definitions are preceded by an overview of several different types of literacy.

Technical Literacy

In NCLB, the U.S. government views literacy within a technical framework. It, thus, prioritizes the mechanical, cognitive components of literacy—such as phoneme awareness, decoding, encoding, and comprehension. The Reading First section of NCLB defines literacy as:

> A complex system of deriving meaning from print that requires all of the following: (a) The skills and knowledge to understand how phonemes, or speech sounds, are connected to print; (b) The ability to decode unfamiliar words; (c) The ability to read fluently; (d) Sufficient background information and vocabulary to foster reading comprehension; (e) The development of appropriate active strategies to construct meaning from print; and (f) The development and maintenance of a motivation to read. (U.S. Department of Education, 2001, Section 1208 Part B subpart five)

Functional Literacy

Functional literacy places literacy within a technical and economic framework. The United Nations Educational, Scientific and Cultural Organization (UNESCO) describes the goal of functional literacy initiatives as programs designed to promote technical reading, writing, and arithmetic skills necessary for increased economic productivity.

Socially Situated Literacy

More encompassing definitions, which still, however, ignore the political component, view literacy as a social practice that extends to the larger purpose of life long learning. In 1992 and then again in 2003, the U.S. Department of Education conducted a nationally representative study of adult literacy among people who were age 16 and older. These two studies used the following definition for literacy:

> Using print and written information to function in society to achieve one's goals and to develop one's knowledge and potential. (NCES, 2007a, p. 24)

In 2003, UNESCO drafted a definition of literacy for countries to use for measurement purposes:

> Literacy is the ability to identify, understand, interpret, create, communicate and compute, using printed and written materials associated with varying contexts. Literacy involves a continuum of learning in enabling individuals to achieve their goals, to develop their knowledge and potential, and to participate fully in their community and wider society. (UNESCO, 2004, p. 13)

While these two latter definitions embrace the social component of literacy, they still fall short from recognizing issues of power related to literacy—a fundamental focus of critical literacy.

Critical Literacy

Critical literacy, in contrast to the aforementioned literacy perspectives and goals, goes beyond an understanding of literacy as just the acquisition of technical skills. It expands on the economic and social significance of literacy by embracing its political element. As such, it recognizes the ever-present power-laden dimensions of literacy. Therefore, critical literacy roots teaching, learning, and knowledge within the socio-economic and socio-cultural conditions of the learner to facilitate and encourage self and social transformation. Renowned educator Paulo Freire (1970, 1974, 1985) named this process critical consciousness, or *conscientization* (conscientização in Portuguese).

Although related to educational reformer John Dewey's earlier concept of reflective thinking, or critical thinking (see the next section), Freire's critical consciousness embodies the political notion of social change. For Dewey, critical thinking involved naming, defining, and solving experiential problems. Freire expanded on this notion in his socio-political concept of critical consciousness and added the component of intervention in society to transform conditions. While discussed briefly here, I will elaborate on the idea of critical literacy and its related terms, such as critical consciousness, later in this chapter and extensively throughout this book.

Reflective Thinking or Critical Thinking

John Dewey (1991, originally published 1910) defines reflective thinking as: "The active, persistent, and careful consideration of any belief or supposed form of knowledge in the light of the grounds that support it, and the further conditions to which it tends" (p. 6). Dewey further believed: "To maintain the state of doubt and to carry on systematic and protracted inquiry—these are the essentials of thinking" (p. 13). Within this context, Dewey, thus, posited that one gains knowledge through active questioning, previous experiences, interpersonal relations, and social practices. While Dewey embraced the intellectual, emotional, and social components of thinking, learning, and knowledge, and further argued that democratic education requires critical thinking, Freire's concept of critical consciousness employs these components, as well as the transformative, liberatory potential of education.

Critical Consciousness

In Freirean terms, critical consciousness signifies the awakening of one's critical awareness of power relations within an historical context in order to intervene against oppressive, dehumanizing forces and transform one's reality. This process of human agency is facilitated through praxis—critical reflection and action—and offers a liberatory education. Learning within a liberatory education challenges "what is" to create more humane structures, both for self and society. Ira Shor (1992) defines critical consciousness:

> …The desocialized thinking called critical consciousness refers to the way we see ourselves in relation to knowledge and power in society, to the way we use and study language, and to the way we act in school and daily life to reproduce or to transform our conditions. (p. 129)

Print Literacy/Textual Literacy and Contextual Literacy/Critical Literacy

In this book, I differentiate between print (or textual) literacy as opposed to contextual (or critical) literacy. Print and textual literacy, which I use interchangeably, involve solely mechanical aspects (e.g., decoding, spelling, punctuation, etc.) of the written word. However, contextual and critical literacy, also employed interchangeably as discussed earlier, situates literacy development in social, historical, and cultural conditions to cultivate learners' critical consciousness or conscientization. This experiential view of literacy, thus, goes beyond mere mechanical, technical teachings of reading and writing as it also facilitates critical literacy—critical thinking and action—to promote self and social transformation.

Use of Push-Out/Dropout

In an effort to counter establishment language that attempts to place the blame on students, contemporary critical writings often use the term "push-out," rather than "dropout." This usage of the phrase "push-out" emphasizes the structural dynamics enacted across "racial"/ethnic, class, gender, and other identity bound-aries that create an educational environment in which a student leaves school. However, I feel that the term "push-out" does not capture the student agency—the ability to act independently in the world—in the conscious choice for many students to leave school rather than participate in an educational system that per-petuates discriminatory structures present throughout societal institutions. I also believe that the term "dropout" does not encompass the prejudicial forces that push students out of the school system across socio-cultural, socio-economic, and gender boundaries.

I will, therefore, use the term "push-out/dropout" to include both the sys-temic structures of exclusion as well as the student agency present in what can, at times, be a conscious act of resistance. When using the word "dropout" in this book, I use it within a context that recognizes the institutionalized exclu-sion of students within the education system, and society at large, who are from economically disadvantaged and/or marginalized ethnic minority backgrounds.

Linguistic Minority vs. English Language Learner

The term "linguistic minority" refers to those people in the U.S. who speak a lan-guage other than English. In this book, this term implies those linguistic minori-ties who also come from historically discriminated ethnic groups within the U.S. and, therefore, experience heightened marginalization. Language abilities, how-ever, among linguistic minorities vary. For example, the language abilities among Latino students can include being bilingual, English- or Spanish-dominant. Some linguistic minorities, those who are not bilingual or English-dominant, are Eng-lish Language Learners (ELLs). I use this term to refer to a particular group of linguistic minority students. However, it bears noting that I believe the 21st cen-tury educational policymakers have conveniently adopted this phrase to serve as a strategic tool for downplaying first language preservation in bilingual programs and, instead, to promote English as a Second Language (ESL) programs that pri-marily teach English acquisition without maintaining the first language.

Non-reading Adolescent Population Described in This Book

This book centers on those non-reading adolescents in New York City who are not in District 75, the centrally operated, all-special education district designated for students who the school system has identified as severely physically and men-tally challenged. Many of the students have difficulty with reading (decoding) and spelling (encoding), often referred to as dyslexia, which generally results from problems (emerging from a myriad of causes beyond the scope of this book) at the phonological stage of language. Some of these youth have been identified for special education services, while some have not; and some are linguistic minorities. Many of these youth were born in the U.S., while others are immigrants. Some are monolingual English speakers, while others are from linguistic minority families. Among this latter group of students, as described in the previous section, their varying language backgrounds consist of those who are English-dominant, bilingual, or ELLs.

Of those designated for special education, their identification categories principally include what the system labels: learning disability, emotional disturbance, and mental retardation (see below *Concept of Disability and Special Education—Social Construction* for discussion on deficit lens of special education programs). However, I consider these categories to be socially constructed in that the dominant culture's belief system shapes the definitions of so-called normalcy. For example, students who struggle with reading may act in defiant ways, which leads to their identification as "emotionally disturbed"; thus, often, the imposition of the school system's pre-determined standards of what is developmentally "appropriate" for each grade level produces the frustration that causes students to "act out" and, subsequently, become identified as "emotionally disturbed."

Furthermore, numerous non-reading adolescents, despite institutionalized barriers, surmount societal limitations to create fulfilling, dynamic lives for themselves. Many raise children of their own. Through their resilience, many of these youth, for example, as young adults struggle to attain viable employment in order to financially care for themselves, their own child (or children), and/or other family members, including parents. Through supportive, loving relationships that they forge with others and their natural ingenuity, these youth construct positive structures even though their limited literacy abilities restrict societal opportunities. However, some within this population of non-reading adolescents cannot manage so well in the face of the heightened social dislocations accompanying poverty and textual illiteracy; among this group of non-reading adolescents, many spend time in jail as youth and/or as adults. This book includes those non-reading adolescents who have been incarcerated at one point in their youth and those who have not.

Concept of Disability and Special Education— Social Construction

The language used in the educational system for students who have difficulty in mastering the knowledge that school and, thus, the dominant culture, values reflects the deficit mindset surrounding special educational services. These special educational services are guaranteed through the Individuals with Disabilities Education Act (IDEA)—the federal law that directs how states and public agencies deliver early intervention, special education, and related services to people with disabilities from birth to 21 years of age. The National Dissemination Center for Children with Disabilities (2002) outlines the 13 "disability" categories:

- autism
- deaf-blindness
- emotional disturbance
- hearing impairment (including deafness)
- mental retardation
- multiple disabilities
- orthopedic impairment
- other health impairment
- specific learning disability
- speech or language impairment
- traumatic brain injury
- visual impairment (including blindness)

Many of these special education identifications—particularly those categories based on subjective clinical judgment (such as "mental retardation," "learning disability," and "emotional disturbance")—reflect the exclusionary consciousness informing the school system. Only those categories based on biologically verifiable conditions (such as visual or hearing impaired) are free from prejudicial evaluation.

This system also promotes success or failure for students by ranking and sorting them according to the dominant class's definitions of valued cognitive skills, physical ability, and behavioral patterns. Such a deficit orientation places the source of the problem on attributes of the individual student, rather than the school structure, which, reflecting prejudices within the larger society, discriminates against those whose cognitive and/or physical abilities, behavior, ethnicity, language, and other identity factors vary from the dominant class's norms. Thus, instead of viewing difference among students as natural variation among humans, the school system imposes a culturally informed "standard" that stigmatizes those students who do not conform.

In this book, I discuss special education programs with a profound recognition of their deficit mindset and discriminatory placement process. Yet, I also believe that until a transformation of the school system abolishes the "deficit" model shaping the system on the whole and its accompanying exclusionary, punitive structure, the provision of special education services provides a means, albeit a fragmented approach, for struggling readers to gain extra support.

Geographic Place-based Perspective

To understand the social, political, and economic circumstances impacting non-reading adolescents in this book, I employ Kincheloe and Pinar's (1991) contemporary curriculum theory of "place." This technique positions curricula as a form of social psychoanalysis and links various strands of critical curriculum theory—an interdisciplinary study of curriculum from a critical perspective to understand overt and covert sociopolitical influences. Kincheloe and Pinar root their theory in Habermas's (1970) emphasis on social psychoanalysis as a means for methodical critical reflection on society and a similar literacy theory of "place." In Habermas's approach, just as therapists use psychoanalysis to facilitate a patient's self-reflection for exposing previously hidden issues to the patient's conscious mind, social psychoanalysis explores the impact of past events and circumstances on contemporary life to grasp the root causes of an issue. Social psychoanalysis, thus, serves as a powerful means for social critique and understanding curriculum as political text (i.e., curriculum in its political context). By bringing the understanding of causal connections to the surface, social psychoanalysis can uncover the complexities of institutionalized pathologies in order to address them and create more just structures.

By focusing this study on New York City, this distinctiveness of "place" enables critical reflection (or social psychoanalysis) on the influence of historical social and political forces on the particular as well as the general. Thus, it facilitates critical analysis of the pedagogical lives of non-reading adolescents in the city, itself, and the nation at large. Examining the specific attributes of "place" aims to avoid disconnected generalizations. Employing the curricular concept of "place" as social psychoanalysis within this study, furthermore, highlights educational themes specific to "race"/ethnicity, class, and gender in the urban setting of New York City.

Thus, after initially unraveling inequitable dynamics, policies, and practices within the larger school structure that impact non-reading adolescents, among other student populations, I subsequently position an understanding of curriculum geographically in New York City. This geographic focus underscores how historically situated social, political, and economic conditions play out in the contemporary socio-educational lives of non-reading adolescents in New York City and how a pedagogy emerging from students' language and lived experiences can transform literacy curricula into a liberatory educational experience for these particular students.

Critical Pedagogy and Freire's Critical Pedagogical Model

Insights of Paulo Freire, the father of critical pedagogy, provide the backbone of an empowering education for non-reading adolescents. As such, an initial description of critical pedagogy and his critical pedagogical model serves to position the theoretical underpinnings of this book. Elaborating on both critical pedagogy and Freire's critical approach underscores concepts such as liberatory education, lived experiences, and the role of critical reflection. It, furthermore, offers a lens for examining structures involved in the heightened exclusion of non-reading adolescents, and other marginalized student populations, within the educational system.

A critical pedagogical model—unlike that which has been historically practiced within the U.S. school system—values the humanity of all students by providing a transformatory education that includes all students from diverse backgrounds. It, additionally, encourages students to move beyond possible positions of marginalization and attain their fullest human potential. As critical pedagogy embraces social, cultural, economic, and political components of education, it acknowledges that schooling is not neutral, but rather a political sphere. As such, educators of critical pedagogy engage students in teachings that analyze power relations and, in particular, ways in which power dynamics are enacted across identity markers, such as "race"/ethnicity, class, gender, and nationality, within social institutions, including schools.

Through critical dialogue within a horizontal teacher–student relationship, instruction explores how these forces impact each individual student. Teachings, therefore, center on the role power plays both in constructing consciousness and in privileging particular groups, while subordinating others. Instruction is also student-centered, examining students' lived experiences and language as the starting point for generating knowledge. Within a critical pedagogical framework, since diverse ideologies are integral to the educational process, it provides possibilities for all students to explore and attain their highest human potential—not just a select group of the privileged few. Critical teachings intrinsically center on critical multicultural perspectives and the inclusion of multiple voices; for, as instruction is generated from each student's diverse lived experience, it naturally situates students in the center of their own scholarship. Such a critical multilogical paradigm, thus, celebrates difference and unravels inequitable institutionalized power dynamics.

Through a critical analysis, teachers facilitate students' reflection on and understanding of their particular positionality within the social web, thereby fostering a student's ability to move through and beyond possible societal limitations. As previously discussed, Freire refers to this critical awareness, this understanding of power relations to ultimately transform one's reality, as conscientization (conscientização). Conscientization—which, as Freire (1974) explains, "represents the development of the awakening of critical awareness" (p. 15)—aims to engender a more heightened consciousness through reflection and action, or human agency (the transformative capacity for an individual to act in the world). Freire (1970) describes this transformation process in further detail:

One of the gravest obstacles to the achievement of liberation is that oppressive reality absorbs those within it and thereby acts to submerge men's consciousness. Functionally, oppression is domesticating. To no longer be prey to its
force, one must merge from it and turn upon it. This can be done by means of
the praxis: reflection and action upon the world in order to transform it. (p. 36)

An exploration of Freire's critical pedagogy model—which he explains must
be repositioned and adapted to different historical, cultural, and political contexts—provides a deeper understanding of the transformatory nature of critical
pedagogy, which continues to influence progressive educators throughout the
globe. Freire's dialogical educational pedagogy and political literacy project, which
are rooted in a postcolonial discourse, grew from his work—prior to the military
coup of April 1, 1964—in adult literacy with economically impoverished Brazil-
ians who were unable to read and write.

For Freire (1985), education is either dehumanizing and domesticating or
humanistic and liberating:

Education of a liberating character is a process by which the educator invites
learners to recognize and unveil reality critically. The domestication practice tries
to impart a false consciousness to learners, resulting in a facile adaptation to
their reality. (p. 102)

Freire's theory of political literacy aims (a) to debunk what he refers to as the
"culture of silence"—which he describes as "a response that lacks a critical quality" (Freire, 1974, p. 21)—and (b) to facilitate a liberatory education, one in which
learners examine reality critically for self and social empowerment. His concept
of political literacy, or critical literacy, in which the learner "reads the word and
the world" offers a theoretical and practical framework for facilitating an empowering literacy instruction and curriculum not just for non-reading adolescents, but
also for all students in the U.S. schools.

In Freire's critical theory of literacy, literacy is not just the acquisition of
technical skills but a vehicle for human agency. As such, it provides learners a
means for developing literacy skills to decode and comprehend print while simultaneously stimulating critical social inquiry. This critical analysis of the status
quo—the initial "texts" Freire believes learners must "decode"—strives to foster
self-awareness and understanding of positionality within the social web to ultimately encourage learners to move beyond current obstacles, thereby enacting
self and social transformation. Such pedagogy, while essential for all students,
has especially significant meaning for non-reading adolescents in New York City
in mainstream and detention center schools—given their heightened status of

marginalization. (chapters four, five, and six will further explore the impact of Freire's critical pedagogical approach with non-reading adolescents).

Freire developed his critical pedagogy in reaction to and as an alternative for what he referred to as a "banking system" of education. According to Freire, within this "banking" concept, the educator deposits knowledge into the students, who are merely "receptacles to be filled" (1970, p. 58). For Freire, the "banking system" of education serves as a pedagogy of social control and domestication. This "banking system" prevails within the U.S. educational system. On the whole, teachings within schools are based on a Eurocentric curriculum that is then re-inforced and tested through standardized assessments, which in the contempo-rary educational system have become high-stakes standardized tests—the policy practice of using one test to determine important educational decisions (this is-sue will be covered further in chapters three and four). Students are viewed as "receptacles" into which this standardized information is to be transferred so as to perpetuate the status quo. As Freire emphasizes, such a structure serves to preserve the dominant culture's ideologies and attempts to minimize students' critical consciousness, conscientization, and ultimately their personal transforma-tion. Freire (1970) writes:

> The more that students work at storing the deposits entrusted to them, the less they develop the critical consciousness which would result from their interven-tion in the world as transformers of that world. (p. 60)

While this central critical pedagogy notion that "banking" education is de-signed to domesticate students according to dominant ideology has profound im-plications for all students within the U.S., it is particularly pivotal in theoretically positioning the increased exclusion of particular groups. The banking system serves as a mechanism for subjecting those within socially subordinated positions to heightened structures of social control and simultaneously attempting to stifle their social critique. As the "banking system" impacts particular groups more profoundly, it represents an integral part of the dominant group's larger domes-tication effort manifested in such social realities as: the over-representation of those from historically discriminated ethnicities and economically impoverished backgrounds, who are imprisoned and/or unable to read and write; the creation of a population of non-reading adolescents; and the proliferation of juvenile prisons.

My Personal Frame of Reference

After attaining a master's degree in bilingual special education in 1998, I worked in New York City Department of Education schools as a Literacy Specialist with a license in Bilingual Special Education until 2009. This book stems from my professional knowledge that was nurtured through these years and beyond. My work focused on literacy development with non-reading adolescents within both an alternative high school as well as schools within secure and non-secure facilities for children involved in the court system. Students did not receive a grade for this literacy support. While the administrations within these schools that I worked genuinely prioritized curriculum that supported non-reading adolescents' academic needs, the macro school structure imposed policies and practices, such as high-stakes standardized tests and a deficit model of learning differences, that often demoralized and damaged the self-esteem of these youth as well as impeded transformatory pedagogy.

While learning to decode and encode to comprehend print represents a crucial component of literacy, I view literacy teaching and learning within a more holistic, socially situated, and political perspective. I believe that literacy instruction must incorporate social, cultural, and critical aspects of reading and writing. I maintain that while being able to read and write is essential for economic survival and emotional well-being in a literate society, it is also a powerful means for enhancing critical, analytic capacities, and engaging imagination.

Paulo Freire's critical theoretical teachings of transformation and emancipatory pedagogy, thus, have guided me tremendously throughout my personal formal education studies and literacy development work with inner-city non-reading adolescents. Repositioning Freire's critical pedagogy within contemporary postmodernist discourse, it, in essence, teaches the whole child within a context of "racial"/ethnic, class, gender, and other identity markers to provide a liberatory educational experience for all students. In keeping with his pedagogical beliefs, I maintain that the instruction of the mechanics of literacy must be taught within a framework of critical literacy so that students learn to "read the word and the world" (Freire, 1974, 1985; Freire & Macedo, 1987). Literacy teachings must therefore foster students' critical reflection on self and society to encourage self-actualization.

I have seen the excitement, dedication, and joy in the majority of teenagers with whom I have worked as they gain skills necessary for access to the world of print, a process that had previously been obstructed. It is my belief that, with the exception of some children with what mainstream society refers to as severe developmental delays, every child (including many who have been identified as having an autism spectrum disorder) can learn to read and write print, if given the proper instruction. For many of the youth with whom I have worked, I have seen a shift in their level of self-confidence and independence as they acquire a skill—which they themselves view as important—and develop new ways of making meaning and seeing themselves in the world. It was Paulo Freire's writings that initially inspired me 20 years ago to study and, ultimately, facilitate critical literacy development pedagogy with older learners.

Socially Situating Myself in Relation to This Book

This book, like all social research, is admittedly not neutral. My own personal experiences, position within the social matrix, and reflections on facilitating literacy development with non-reading adolescents have shaped my choice of topic and the perspective represented within it. I present a brief autobiographical overview so that the reader may understand the evolution of the analysis presented in this book and keep in mind my own perceptions, conscious and unconscious, influencing my research lens.

While my parents always showered me with unconditional love and support in the choices I made with my life—a pattern that continues to this day—home-life chaos during my youth propelled me to grow up quickly. A childhood characterized by my family's own brand of pathology—which I now view as a gift—led me to regularly choose to seek refuge outside of the house, beginning when I was six years old. Frequenting friends' homes, video arcades, parks, and other locations, to avoid my house during my elementary school years, exposed me to the vast cultural diversity that typifies New York City. I am grateful for this experience as it planted in me an appreciation of difference among human beings and a curiosity about human relations. As my "nomadic-ways" and interest in human activity continued through my older years, it evolved in the academic arena into an undergraduate social science major. The combination of this social science major and financial difficulties led me to study for a period of time at a university in the Dominican Republic—which showed me directly the challenges involved in doing academic level work in a language other than one's first language.

Also as an undergraduate student, while reading Paulo Freire, my concern with equality and justice—which, despite instability at home, my family's values and teachings nurtured early in my life—and my desire to enter the educational field merged as I became increasingly interested in literacy development work with adults who were unable to read and write. However, in years to come, while fulfilling my student teaching requirement during my master's studies, I worked at a high school in the South Bronx in New York City. This professional experience exposed me to the reality of the seldom-discussed student population comprised of adolescents who read below a 3rd grade level equivalent. From that time forward, in addition to other roles within the educational field, as previously mentioned, I facilitated literacy development with non-reading adolescents in schools that were the exception, rather than the norm, in that they addressed these students' print literacy needs.

This work subsequently instilled in me a desire to understand the larger context involved in the existence of non-reading adolescents attending schools outside of District 75. This critical questioning, thus, inspired me to learn more about this issue through an academic frame within a Ph.D. program, culminating in subsequently writing this book. Now, I turn to a discussion of my positioning within the social web.

Although I may identify with certain identity categories more than others—particularly depending on the environment in which I find myself—among various identity markers, I am a white, non-practicing Jewish female from an upper middle-class background who was born and raised in New York City within a so-called "broken-home." As an educator and researcher, I am continually aware of the ways in which my social position influences what I can see and what I cannot. While sharing commonalities with non-reading adolescents, such as certain experiences that accompany growing up in New York City, when considering our social differences, our lives vary tremendously. On account of my higher social position, attributed by virtue of my class and skin color, my challenges outside of school, and even my slight reading difficulties, were not compounded by structural restrictions that limited opportunities.

Given that non-reading adolescents, as a collective, and I occupy different social positions, I have, consequently, intentionally situated my analysis as an exploration of institutional forces that have contributed to the creation of a non-reading adolescent population; for, as an educator within the school system, I have observed firsthand discriminatory policies and practices perpetuated against this group of students. Therefore, the analysis in this book only presents a part of the social reality. It represents my perspective as an educator and an academic—one who comes from a privileged social position and does not have the same class and cultural background as the students described, but who shares similarities rooted in experiences intrinsic to all human beings and derived from growing up in New York City. An expanded analysis of the socio-educational experiences of non-reading adolescents, however, would include, for example, their personal narratives centered on their lived experiences in relation to literacy and school.

Purpose of the Study

In light of the reality of adolescents who only have emergent print literacy levels, numerous questions arise which have profound implications for future educational measures: How did children become teenagers without learning to read and write? What are the diverse societal, familial, and organic reasons children can become adolescents and still be in the emergent literacy stages? And, what are measures that can be taken to remediate and reverse this trend? The purpose of this book, therefore, is to (a) understand institutionalized dynamics and pedagogical structures that have contributed to the creation of a population of non-reading adolescents in New York City's public schools and (b) grounded in this understanding, reconceptualize literacy curriculum to facilitate empowering and meaningful literacy pedagogy for non-reading adolescents in New York City.

Removing barriers inhibiting meaningful pedagogy and transforming schools into democratic sites requires an understanding of institutionalized forces that foster inequities in order to, instead, provide educational experiences that nurture the intellect and soul. This study, therefore, offers educators, policymakers, administrators, and the public, in general, an opportunity to reflect on:

a. Underlying assumptions that have and continue to guide educational policies and practices;

b. The ensuing detrimental impact of these notions on the educational lives of non-reading adolescents, in particular;

c. The manner in which these youth negotiate structural inequities;

d. New educational approaches that provide students, who are classified as non-readers, meaningful and empowering literacy curricula.

I do not present this book as a panacea to the prevention of an adolescent population who read, according to the school system's definitions, within an early elementary grade level equivalent. Such a feat would require a cessation of discriminatory practices perpetrated across identity categories, such as "race"/ethnicity, class, gender lines and other identity markers, throughout U.S. social institutions. These practices, subsequently, create conditions of poverty and promote the miseducation of targeted youth according to ethnic and class backgrounds. However, through an understanding of curriculum as political text within a socio-historical view, this analysis presents a deconstruction of the ideology that perpetuates the status quo and Western privilege (which furthers Western culture). It, furthermore, exposes the simultaneous exclusion from the educational system of the voices, cultures, and experiences of historically marginalized populations. Understanding curriculum within a critical and political lens highlights contemporary socio-educational and socio-political forces that inform lived experiences of non-reading adolescents. This perspective enables educators to understand experiences of these students in order to provide a transformatory, self-actualizing literacy curriculum and, ultimately, school experience.

The research field profoundly requires more studies highlighting the numerous success stories of inner-city youth who counter oppressive forces and social dislocations to achieve high academic performance. I also feel, however, that, in light of the grave injustice facing non-reading adolescents in the education system, this book serves a critical need as well.

Rooting Illiteracy in Its Political Origins: Socio-Historical Perspective of Structures Underlying Textual and Contextual Illiteracy

The hegemonic mindset (ruling group's means for domination) that denies literacy to marginalized groups has persisted throughout the ages and embodies an entrenched aspect of the U.S. socio-political fabric. For example, recognizing the social power of literacy, during the period of institutionalized slavery in the U.S., the white power structure made it illegal for enslaved blacks to know how to read and write and also to teach them to read and write. While the white power structure continued to impede African Americans' print literacy knowledge after emancipation, African Americans vigorously resisted, on individual and collective levels, throughout the decades. This struggle has evolved today in the fight for equitable educational outcomes. This theme of power and literacy acquisition also continues among some immigrants to the U.S. who come from subjugated social positions. Some have experienced a history within their home country in which ruling elites—often with the support of the U.S., given its history of colonialism and imperialism—created institutionalized forces that obstructed these immigrants' textual literacy development. Such socio-historical perspectives situate present-day textual illiteracy dynamics in the U.S. within long-standing structural trends.

The legacy of this institutional impediment to print literacy for subordinated populations, primarily those positioned in lower economic classes, has contributed to the inability to read and write among some in the U.S. today from economically marginalized backgrounds. While those from historically discriminated "racial"/ethnic populations within the U.S. continue to combat forces of oppression, this book will explore contemporary structures that operate in obstructing literacy development for, in particular, low-income black and Latino youth in New York City.

While the previously described dynamic delineates a frequent structural interference to textual literacy for those within marginalized social positions, the technical literacy framework employed within the school system and its accompanying instrumentalist approach (which limits literacy teachings to solely mechanical skills) inhibits contextual literacy for all students. This instrumentalist approach gears literacy teachings and all pedagogy to the standardization of information and knowledge—as exemplified in the current use of high-stakes testing and test-driven curriculum. It further prevents critical literacy—one that can facilitate self-actualization—and hinders an emotional, subjective engagement with literacy.

Ultimately, these high-stakes assessments embraced within the instrumentalist literacy vision informing the educational system (a) enable a transfer of the dominant culture's knowledge without any possibility for critical analysis; (b) negate profound aspects of education—such as critical thinking, recognizing interconnections of seemingly disconnected pieces of information, and engaging the imagination and creative awareness; and (c) ignore the way in which social, economic, and political factors impact students' educational lives. Thus, we see examples of the close interplay of contextual literacy and power within the school system impacting all students. Subsequent chapters will expand on these ideas as well as highlight literacy issues specific to non-reading adolescents.

Conclusion

As non- reading adolescents represent a population of children who, except within a small number of schools, generally have been dismissed and ignored within the educational system as well as mainstream society on the whole, this book aims to: encourage discourse about this population of students; unravel structural obstructions in their educational process; and present a literacy curriculum model that offers non-reading adolescents empowering, meaningful pedagogy.

On a larger scale, it is my hope that this analysis may encourage educational policymakers and administrators to:

1.   Develop self-actualizing literacy curriculum;

2.   Implement literacy intervention programs that are built into the infrastructure of the school system, including schools within detention centers, in grades pre-K–12 and that do not operate on punitive policy, such as high-stakes testing;

3.   Establish specific schools for non-reading adolescents that provide critical literacy pedagogy.

In addition to promoting literacy development for struggling readers at every grade-level, thereby mitigating the creation of a non-reading adolescent population, such comprehensive literacy measures could, perhaps, minimize the incarceration and high recidivism rates of adolescents with remedial level reading abilities.

Overview of Chapters

Chapter two (a) roots discriminatory U.S. educational policies, practices, and research within an historical lens and (b) situates this book within existing literature regarding the miseducation of low-income, urban youth within the U.S. This analysis underscores the systemic prejudicial practices that have contributed to the creation of a population of non-reading adolescents. In highlighting the historical structural disadvantages impacting inner-city children, the literature reviewed reveals and contextualizes the disproportionately high push-out/dropout rates among this student population and their over-representation in both special education programs and juvenile detention centers. As this chapter presents issues concerning inequitable outcomes for inner-city youth and the role of power in relation to language and literacy, it lays the foundation for a critical political understanding of curriculum so as to promote transformatory literacy pedagogy for non-reading adolescents in New York City.

While laying down elements involved in providing a meaningful pedagogy for non-reading adolescents, chapters three and four describe how the contemporary social, political, and cultural backdrop shapes the socio-educational experiences of these youth. These chapters explore such pedagogical questions as: What is the role of school in a democratic society? What is the nature of learning? What constitutes good teaching? What are alternative forms for evaluating quality education? And, how do these issues influence the pedagogical lives of non-reading adolescents? This analysis highlights the impact on non-reading adolescents of recent antidemocratic educational practices and policies—predominantly fueled through NCLB mandates. Conversely, it presents democratic alternatives that offer a complex understanding of teaching, learning, and knowledge. While chapter three examines educational policy to unravel the harmful consequences for non-reading adolescents of various NCLB mandates, chapter four positions non-reading adolescents' school experience within a social and cultural context—illustrating the detriments of, in particular, NCLB's focus on high-stakes assessments and its accompanying test-driven curriculum.

Chapters five and six involve the design of a critical literacy curriculum for non-reading adolescents in New York City. By engaging their textual and contextual literacy development, it nurtures their critical consciousness. It centers on students' participation in constructing the curriculum, language, and lived experiences, as well as critical reflection to encourage self and social transformation. This critical literacy curriculum integrates direct phonics instruction and whole language approaches within a critical literacy context. It develops students' mechanical skills involved in reading and writing, promotes their ability to generate meaning with text, stimulates their creative spirit, and fosters their critical social inquiry to facilitate self-awareness and to affect change. Within this focus of chapters five and six, chapter five also describes the way in which this critical literacy curriculum additionally encourages critical self-awareness for non-reading adolescents' teachers. It positions them as researchers who seek to understand the imprints of power in their professional experiences and their students' socio-educational lives so that these educators may provide empowering pedagogy that tailors teachings to the specific needs of each student.

Chapter seven, the conclusion, revisits issues covered in the book; discusses their importance and implications; reiterates positive alternatives for transforming restrictive, antidemocratic literacy curriculum, instruction, policies, and, ultimately, the consciousness informing the school system; and suggests future avenues for research. The chapter concludes with a policy position that advocates for an educational structure and literacy pedagogy, which ensures democratic education for non-reading adolescents and all students.

Unlike teachings embodied within the critical literacy framework, pedagogy that inhibits critical inquiry of society and understanding of one's social position within it and the world denies a transformatory educational experience. This book, therefore, serves as a call for changing the educational system to (a) provide more humane and inclusive structures that ensure print literacy acquisition for non-reading adolescents and other struggling readers, regardless of their grade level and (b) ensure the implementation of critical literacy curriculum so that all students may attain their greatest human potential.

TWO

Contextualizing Non-reading Adolescents within Historical Educational Structures and Literature

This chapter presents an initial historical overview of the exclusionary paradigm that has informed the educational system for over a century. It situates the subsequent analysis of current literature pertaining to educational and related inequalities specific to inner-city youth. The structural forces within the education system that are highlighted here have played a significant role in the creation of a population of non-reading adolescents. This chapter, therefore, provides a backdrop for understanding the socio-educational experiences specific to non-reading adolescents explored in later chapters.

Critical Historical Overview: An Ideology of Social Efficiency

Since the turn of the 19th century, educational policymakers have prioritized socially efficient purposes of schooling, which have, in turn, operated to maintain and perpetuate the social order. These frameworks, initially put into place within the U.S. educational system during the early stages of the progressive reform era (at the end of the 19th to the beginning of the 20th century), continue to influence school policy and practices and, in essence, educational consciousness. During this time period, driven by an ideology of "social efficiency," the purpose of education became social control, rather than intellectual growth. For over a century, social efficiency's utilitarian vision essentially has relegated students to a fixed status within the social order—predetermined by their present socio-economic positions.

During the second half of the 19th century, in the wake of social transformation, engendered through the Industrial Revolution and heightened immigration patterns, a new consciousness evolved. It centered on what knowledge was most worthwhile for learning in school. Many reformers contended that, in light of the societal transformation, the theory of mental discipline—which viewed the mind as a muscle that could be strengthened through monotonous drills, stern disciplinary measures, and mindless recitation—no longer seemed appropriate.

Therefore, at the close of the 19th century, amidst an atmosphere of rapid social and economic change, brought on by the Industrial Revolution, the future course of curriculum and pedagogy was a crucial topic on the political and social reformers' agenda. Under the progressive reformers' ideological banner of the common school, which professed "education for all," schooling was becoming more widespread. As attendance in public high schools soared, American education leaders continued to vehemently contest the purposes and approaches of these schools. Distinct interest groups clashed over what curricula content would be most beneficial. However, since the early 20th century, proponents of the social efficiency curriculum have proven to be the most forceful of all the interest groups in implementing their vision.

Ravitch (2000) notes the burgeoning trend in schooling at this time. She explains that although progressive reformers in the Committee of Ten in 1893 had recommended that all students be given the same quality humanist education, regardless of their occupational pursuits, other progressive reformers staunchly challenged such a belief. Ravitch highlights how these other reformers preferred a curricula differentiation, depending on the student's future employment possibilities. Rooted in social eugenics theories and believing in, as Ravitch documents, the racial superiority of "the Nordic group over all other racial groups" (p. 145), social efficiency theorists, therefore, encouraged a differentiated curriculum.

This differentiated curriculum led some students to "academic studies" and, ultimately, college, while relegating others to vocational education and a predetermined place in the job market. Tyack (1974) explains that these efficiency reformers—who were a body of policy elite, comprised predominantly of white men whom he refers to as "administrative progressives"—initiated the centralization and bureaucratization of schools. This process replaced the previous decentralized rural pattern of schooling. Tyack delineates in great detail the process in which, imbued with positivism's presumed authority of scientific "understanding," these efficiency proponents developed a school system that reflected and perpetuated social inequities within U.S. society.

Tyack describes that administrative progressives' scientific management of the schooling process was part of their larger social engineering effort, which centered on issues of social control. He states how administrative progressives constructed this differentiated school structure so as to sort children according to the destinies that this administrative body deemed appropriate for each child. As such, Tyack reports that their system generally favored those within the higher socio-economic sector of the dominant culture and negatively impacted those across "racial"/ethnic, class, nationality, linguistic, and gender identities.

The progressive ideologies of democratic education and "equal opportunity" were, therefore, redefined to mean that children of the masses would get vocational and industrial training so as, in the views of reform leaders, to serve society more effectively. Tyack points out that policymakers decided whether to place a child in the higher vocational tracks, which provided academic curriculum, or the lower vocational tracks, according to the child's current socio-economic status. Tyack further notes the intentional institutional exclusion within such a school structure of African American students, specific immigrant populations, and children from economically disadvantaged backgrounds.

According to Tyack, as the administrative progressives—in the early 20th century—created a system that intrinsically disregarded the diversity of the culturally and linguistically pluralistic U.S. school population, additional measures furthered their social engineering efforts. He describes that the process of "Americanization"—an imposed assimilation to the dominant Anglo culture's morays and ideologies—served to preserve the status quo. (I will expand upon this concept of "Americanization" and its impact on Bilingual Education later in this chapter.) Tyack also documents that the implementation of increasingly effective compulsory education laws, initially enacted between 1900 and 1920, made it mandatory that all children attend school. Such legislation, therefore, ensured that all youth would encounter the sorting process of the differentiated curriculum design.

Lazerson (1983) too provides a critical perspective on social engineering and the creation of special education practices. Lazerson documents how administrative progressives embraced special education—which became the lowest track within the differentiated curriculum structure—and its accompanying use of IQ testing as an appealing reform for containing and constraining particular groups of children. Lazerson explains that special education served as a means for separating those students whom the administrative progressives considered particularly problematic for society—a practice, which he highlights, remains entrenched in current school practices.

Lazerson describes that, as the socio-political climate has changed, such pernicious measures have targeted different ethnic groups. However, he adds that, given the prejudicial practices and ideologies determining track placement, special education has had especially injurious ramifications for children from low-income backgrounds, immigrant students—particularly from working class positions and those of darker phenotype—and African Americans. As Lazerson points out, beginning around World War I, "special education originated and remained a class and racially based system; it was not to change" (1983, p. 33).

A Critical Perspective on Psychometric Testing and Its Use in Furthering Social Efficiency

The development of psychometric testing (e.g., IQ tests and standardized assessments) and its growing role of importance arose within the prevailing focus on social efficiency. In line with the administrative reformers' methods of scientific management, intelligence testing emerged during the early part of the 20th century as the "scientific" means for assessing a child's ability. According to these test results, students were placed in their differentiated curricula and, additionally, those students "requiring" special education programs were identified. Tyack and Lazerson, among others, document that the use of intelligence testing has been embedded in scientific racism and has perpetuated social class and "racial"/ethnic inequities (Kincheloe, Steinberg, & Tippins, 1999; Macedo, 2006).

These critical pedagogues emphasize how psychometric testing measures give value to and promote the dominant culture's knowledge, while discriminatorily deeming inferior that of subordinated groups. They describe that since the production of knowledge and philosophies of science are intricately tied to politics, those in positions of power determine who is or is not accorded access to making and defining a culture's system of knowledge. Subsequently, decisions about institutionalized knowledge and intelligence criteria are dependent upon the dominant culture's specific interests, as power relationships underlie their use.

Therefore, the perspectives and presumptions of those who create any tool for measuring a human phenomenon influence the validity and neutrality of such an instrument. As such, the assessment measures that psychometricians, who have traditionally been members of the dominant culture, have implemented throughout the generations are intrinsically flawed. Morris (2004) offers a frame of reference that highlights the inaccuracies of psychometric assessments, such as IQ and standardized achievement tests:

> Psychometricians often deny that the subjectivity of the researcher, the prejudices of the researcher, are built into the test. Testing is not innocent. (p. 160)

With the rise of social efficiency ideology, these evaluation methods first appeared in the education system in the early 20th century. Steeped in social eugenics philosophy and believing that intelligence was purely a biological function, American Psychologists, Henry C. Goddard and Lewis Terman, distorted the mental testing studies of French psychologist, Alfred Binet. Goddard and Terman revised and applied Binet's scale to supposedly measure an innate, set quantity of intelligence. Driven by a positivist ideology, which asserts the notion that if knowledge exists it can be both measured and quantified, Goddard and Terman initiated the wide-scale implementation of IQ tests. The use of intelligence testing proliferated within the public education system through the 1940s. As policymakers disregarded the culture- and class-based nature of intelligence tests, they implemented these assessments to erroneously justify the disproportionate placement of low-income, immigrant, and African American students within the lower tracks and special education.

Through the use of what critical theorists reveal as flawed intelligence tests to construct social class– and culture-based tracking systems, policymakers set the stage for an educational system that has reflected and perpetuated rather than ameliorated social class and "racial"/ethnic inequalities within U.S. society. Tyack and Cuban (1995) describe how by the mid 20th century what the administrative progressives viewed as progress within the educational system was actually leaving many groups behind and creating major disparities in educational opportunities. In chapter three, I will return to the issue of the standardization of information and knowledge as well as highlight the way that the instrumentalist approach—which standardizes information and is furthered in the contemporary No Child Left Behind (NCLB) policy initiative—jeopardizes non-reading adolescents, in addition to other students from historically marginalized backgrounds.

Beginning in 1954, with the *Brown vs. Board of Education* case, Congress passed Civil Rights legislation that aimed to provide educational equality for historically discriminated groups. Inequities, nevertheless, have persisted. Since the genesis of the progressive movement and the reign of social efficiency, the idea of educating all students has in practice meant a varied quality of education depending on one's position within the social hierarchy. Tyack and Cuban emphasize these limited educational improvements, despite Civil Rights Acts: "The enduring but unsatisfactory compromise represented in school trends was a simple exchange— open access in return for differentiated instruction" (1995, p. 54).

In response to the educational system's alienation of, in particular, those groups positioned outside the dominant culture's configurations, Macedo (2006) additionally argues:

> Large groups of people, including the so-called minorities, were never intended to be educated….How else can we explain why we sit idly by and tolerate dropout rates of minorities that exceed 60 percent in many urban cities, with New York City at 70 percent? (p. 36)

The fact that, throughout urban areas nationwide, public schools presently contend with a contingent of adolescents who read below designated 3rd grade level equivalents, who are also predominantly from historically subjugated social groups and low-income backgrounds, further supports Macedo's position.

Ethnic disparities within juvenile detention center populations (to be detailed later in this chapter) also reflect these racial-economic inequities pervasive throughout schools and other social institutions. As Foucault (1977, 1980) argues, penal institutions serve as essential apparatuses for the ruling class' control within a network of power formations, or relations of domination. In light of high push-out/dropout rates (to be discussed in depth in chapters three and four), compulsory education laws and special education programs no longer appear to maintain the social order, as educational policymakers had originally envisioned.

In line with Foucault's analysis, I would therefore add that the recent expansion of juvenile detention centers, thus, functions as the contemporary solution for domination and social control of those students who do not fit in or assimilate to the dominant culture's morays and ideologies. Juvenile prisons seem to provide such a function, as children in New York City juvenile detention facilities, for example, are disproportionately inner-city African American and Latino youth who (a) have been placed in special education programs and (b) have below grade-level literacy abilities, which includes those who are classified as non-readers. We now turn to these issues to contextualize specific disproportionate representations of these two student populations, resulting from discriminatory patterns, within such institutions as schools and the justice system.

Reviewing Literature on the Schooling of Inner-City Youth

Examining existing literature and studies related to the education of low-income, urban youth within the U.S. highlights systemic prejudicial practices that have contributed to the makings of a population of non-reading adolescents. As described earlier, due to discrimination within the U.S. social institutions and resulting limited economic opportunities, these non-reading adolescents within urban areas predominantly consist of black and Latino youth from low-income backgrounds. These youth, who are an often-disregarded group of students, are in mainstream public high schools and also represent a high percentage of those in schools within juvenile detention centers. Some are U.S.-born and others immigrated to the U.S. Among those born in the U.S. and abroad the students' language abilities vary including English dominant, bilingual, and English Language Learners (ELLs).

Reviewing the literature accentuates socio-educational forces impacting inner-city youth. This understanding provides the grounding for later chapters, which illuminate the ways in which these forces specifically affect non-reading adolescents and present alternatives for countering such trends to promote empowering literacy pedagogy for non-reading adolescents. Critical theorists, historians, and educational analysts have extensively documented the miseducation of economically disadvantaged black and Latino youth in the U.S. These education theorists and researchers reveal how institutionalized discriminatory policy and practices—which are played out across social class, "racial," and gender lines and are systematically perpetuated within public schools—impact these children. As Kantor and Brenzel (1992) inform, many of these students are segregated from other student populations through the spatial arrangements of urban planning which have confined these children to inner-city schools. Additionally, although these students individually and collectively resist oppressive structures, statistics reveal that inner-city youth have disproportionately high push-out/dropout patterns and are over-represented, both in special education classes and in juvenile detention centers.

A review of the literature highlights historical forces that have denied students within these communities equal opportunities and resources and have, ultimately, contributed to the production of a group of inner-city adolescents, who have reading abilities that range within kindergarten through upper 2nd grade limits. The literature review's first section outlines the structural miseducation of urban, low-income African American and Latino students. The following section emphasizes particular inequitable schooling practices that specifically have impacted children from linguistic minority groups. The third and fourth sections, respectively, show how these discriminatory policy and practices have led to both disproportionately high push-out/dropout rates among low-income black and Latino children and their over-representation in special education placement. The fifth section contextualizes these biased special education procedures within a historical account.

The sixth section illustrates how on the structural level the over-representation of economically disadvantaged African American and Latino students in juvenile detention centers is (a) another manifestation of discriminatory practices perpetrated against these youth and (b) intricately related to their miseducation within the school system. The seventh section delineates the link between low reading levels, special education, and incarceration. The last section will discuss issues of power related to language and literacy. While available literature does not include adequate discourse specifically about urban adolescents both within mainstream schools and schools within detention centers whose textual literacy abilities fall below 3rd grade limits, a literature review highlights disparities within the U.S. school system impacting the educational outcomes of inner-city youth.

This backdrop contextually positions chapters three, four, five, and six, which highlight:

- Damages of paradigmatic assumptions that continue to guide educational policy and practices impacting the socio-educational lives of non-reading adolescents, in particular;

- Ways in which these youth negotiate harmful and inequitable structures;

- New forms of education that, in contrast to current trends, offer students who are classified as non-readers the potential for meaningful literacy curricula that facilitate self-affirming and self-actualizing pedagogy.

Analysis of these issues, therefore, expands on the literature so as to create more just and democratic schooling for all students, especially for non-reading adolescents.

Miseducation of Inner-City Youth

Even more than 50 years after the *Brown vs. Board of Education* ruling, economically disadvantaged children within urban schools—who are predominantly black and Latino students—are generally provided a persisting separate and unequal education. Inequitable distribution of funds has led to profound "racial"/ethnic disparities within the school system. While some gains in educational access have been attained through the struggles of historically dispossessed groups, educational opportunity and quality still remain unequal for low-income black and Latino youth. A myriad of education historians and analysts within the critical theoretical tradition discuss these inequitable educational practices that operate against low-income African American and Latino youth most dramatically.

Tyack (1974), as detailed earlier, highlights the deliberate institutional exclusion of African Americans, particular immigrant populations, and students from economically disadvantaged backgrounds within the construction of the school system. As noted previously in the historical discussion of social efficiency, according to Tyack, during the first part of the 20th century, the original architects of the school structure, the "administrative progressives," designed a system that offered a differentiated curriculum. This differentiated curriculum favored those from higher social positions, in order to maintain the social order and perpetuate the status quo. The compulsory education laws that the administrative progressives additionally enacted, subjected all students to this social engineering mechanism.

Such a theory supports Asante's (1991) argument that the U.S. educational system has provided a Eurocentric curriculum and perspective, which is based on white supremacist notions. Although in itself exclusionary, Asante's call for an Afro-centric perspective, one that places African Americans as the major subjects of the world, draws attention to his contention of both the institutionalized racism operating within the school system and the need for more inclusive teachings and perspectives.

Many critical educational theorists echo and expand on Asante's view. They, too, stress the need for a curriculum and an overall school structure that goes beyond the current Eurocentric, scientific framework designed to validate particular experiences, defined by "race"/ethnicity, class, and gender, while invalidating others. However, these critical pedagogues additionally promote the creation of an educational system that is based on critical multicultural and multilogical frameworks. They argue that by valuing the voices of students from diverse backgrounds and social positions, such an educational structure intrinsically offers an inclusive educational experience to those students from historically marginalized groups.

Kozol (1991) highlights the "savage inequalities" of a school system that, as Fine (1991), Fine and Weiss (1993), and Trueba (1989) describe, systematically "silences" the voices of students across "racial"/ethnic, class, and gender lines, particularly low-income African American and Latino youth. Ogbu (1978) and Fordham (1988) further describe that the status of particular minority groups— which is maintained through institutionalized economic and social discrimination combined with the internalization of inferior status attributed to them by the dominant group—often engenders academic failure disproportionately for economically disadvantaged African American and Latino students.

hooks (1994) and Kincheloe and Steinberg (1997) discuss the tacit, or sometimes even blatant, subordinating cultural messages of the school system that are inscribed in prejudicial practices and ideologies. Illich (1971) refers to these discriminatory practices, which hinder certain members while privileging others, as the "hidden curriculum." Inequities, according to hooks, Kincheloe, and Steinberg, which are part of a larger mechanism designed to maintain and perpetuate the status quo, are evidenced in culturally and class-biased standardized tests and the common use of Eurocentric curricula. For Foucault (1980), this interplay of power and control within the assessment process serves as a technology of power, in which practices such as standardized testing act as hegemonic vehicles for the ruling classes.

While the "cultural messages," "hidden curriculum," and "technologies of power" operate to restrict educational opportunities and marginalize students across "racial"/ethnic, class, and gender lines, the status quo diverts responsibility. hooks, Kincheloe, and Steinberg, among many others (Darder, 2002; Trueba, 1989), argue that often dominant discourse places the blame of "academic failure" on students from particular ethnic and class backgrounds, rather than on a school system that alienates students across "racial"/ethnic and class lines (among other identity boundaries). Needless to say, such a tactic has impacted low-income African American and Latino youth most profoundly.

Foster (1997) notes the irony of "racial" integration. She describes that on the one hand it was a pivotal step in the struggle for "racial" equality. However, in comparison to teachings delivered in desegregated schools, African American students received more ideologically empowering teachings within their segregated all black schools from their black teachers, despite the meager funding and limited resources of all black schools during the years of segregation. According to Foster and other critical analysts (Brandon, 2002; Delpit, 1995), as African American students were integrated into white schools, they were subjected to a different systematic exclusion: prejudicial attitudes of many white teachers and discriminatory school practices and procedures perpetrated a new form of segregation. Macedo and Bartolomé (1999), Villanueva (1993), and Zentella (1997) also outline how, despite bilingual education legislation (beginning in 1968)—which in theory attempted to ensure "educational access for all"—the linguistic and cultural needs of language-minority students continue to be disregarded.

These theories that focus on the structural miseducation of low-income African American and Latino youth help explain how the reading grade level equivalents of many of these inner-city youth are disproportionately below that of their actual age grade levels. In an April 14, 2004 *New York Times* article, Tamar Lewin reports that, as a result of the reading lag in inner-city schools, there are at least twice as many 9th graders as 12th graders—a pattern that continues in many urban schools. Balfanz, McPartland, and Shaw (2002) additionally highlight that in high-poverty urban schools, approximately 50% of the students entering 9th grade read on a 6th or 7th grade level.

Additional statistics on reading assessments on the national level indicate that economic impoverishment negatively impacts a student's academic performance. National statistics on 4th and 8th grade reading scores from trend studies conducted by the National Assessment of Educational Progress (NAEP) illustrate the link between poverty and literacy [National Center for Education Statistics (NCES), 2003, 2007b]. Results on the NAEP's reading assessment, given to students in 4th grade and 8th grade, indicate that those students who live below the poverty line—nationally defined as those who live near or below the poverty line and are, therefore, eligible for free or reduced-price lunch—score significantly lower in reading than other students in the sample. In the *Nation's Report Card: Reading 2003* study, for example, approximately twice as many economically disadvantaged students scored below the basic proficiency level as compared to those students living above the poverty line—a pattern that has been consistent throughout the years (NCES, 2003, 2007b).

On the state level, the overall scores for the New York 4th and 8th grade reading scores on NAEP's *Nation's Report Card: Reading 2007* study correlate with patterns of national statistics. In 2007, 4th grade students who were eligible for free/reduced-priced lunch had an average score that was 28 points lower than students who did not receive the free lunch. Similarly, 8th grade students who qualified for free/reduced-priced lunch scored 25 points lower than students who did not qualify (NCES, 2007b). Again, these results—which will be further explored in chapter three—were in accordance with trends from prior years (NCES, 2003, 2007b).

These statistics clearly reveal the consequence poverty can have on a student's academic achievement. Additionally, however, while neither apparent from the NAEP reading assessment scores, nor sufficiently analyzed within contemporary writing, educational inequities are even more pronounced as some inner-city youth have reading levels that fall within kindergarten to upper 2nd grade limits, even though they are teenagers. As a result of limited societal options, as discussed earlier, some of these youth spend time in juvenile detention centers.

Dominant theories throughout existing literature do, in fact, provide a historical framework for understanding socio-economic forces impacting low-income African American and Latino students' educational experiences as compared to other student populations. Several scholars describe the grave funding disparities between inner-city schools and those in economically privileged areas. These scholars, furthermore, illustrate how children within these inner-city schools often receive instruction of differential quality and watered-down teachings of content material in comparison to other students who are in public schools within economically privileged neighborhoods. As a result, student achievement in inner-city schools often lags behind national norms and push-out/dropout rates are exceedingly high.

While many inner-city youth have overcome these institutional obstacles, very often these procedures have paved students' way for what the dominant culture has referred to as "academic failure." In all too many cases, inner-city students have chosen the inevitable decision to drop out, or opt out, of high school, instead of participating in an exclusionary school system. As these inner-city schools are under-funded, many students within them are prepared ineffectively and are, therefore, not afforded the necessary tools for success within mainstream society. Such systematic discriminatory measures, coupled with, among other oppressive structures, prejudicial practices within the mainstream job market (Wilson, 1996) and racial–economic bias in arrest and incarceration patterns (Oliver & Yocom, 2004), contribute to a reality in which the majority of youth in New York City juvenile detention facilities come from these substandard inner-city schools (Leone et al., 2003).

Bilingual Education

In addition to the previously discussed inequitable schooling practices aimed at low-income African American and Latino children within U.S. urban public schools, there are a myriad of other negative educational factors that are specific to children from historically discriminated linguistic minority groups. An analysis of several theories and studies related to the education of Latino students—those who are Spanish dominant, English dominant, or bilingual—reveal these specific prejudicial schooling procedures.

Many non-reading Latino adolescents—including those who have been detained in detention centers—were enrolled in bilingual education programs within the U.S. school system. These bilingual programs, however, were never given the proper resources due to political conflict. As Baca and Cervantes (1989), Crawford (1991), Macedo and Bartolomé (1999), Trueba (1989), Villanueva (1993), Zentella, (1997) and others discuss, the majority of these bilingual programs were not afforded an opportunity to flourish. These scholars note that although legislation throughout the 1970s mandated the implementation of bilingual programs to address the academic and language needs of linguistic minority children, an agenda of politics rather than pedagogy has sabotaged these programs from their inception.

As literature has documented, the contention that American English reflects American nationalism and constitutes being a "good American" has historically fueled the political controversy over the use of languages other than English for instruction. Giroux (1997) points out that other languages and multiculturalism have represented an ideological threat to the concept of being American. The move toward Anglo-conformity attempted to deny linguistic minorities' language and, therefore, erase their cultural identity. Anglo-conformity, subsequently, became the pedagogical focus.

Freire (1970, 1985), among others (Bruner, 1996; Gramsci, 1971), further contextualizes this political controversy in his discussion of the intrinsic relation between language and culture. Freire delineates the structural dimensions of power that can operate within such a relationship, as evidenced in the dominant culture's use of language politics as a means for subordinating linguistic minorities. Such a reality affirms Bakhtin's (1973, 1981) sociolinguistic assertion that language is always ideological and, therefore, intrinsically related to issues of power.

In the wake of the initial Bilingual Act of 1968, Title VII, educational policymakers embraced "Americanization" beliefs. The political controversy over bilingual education, one deeply rooted in the very nature of language itself, mushroomed. As a result, varying models of bilingual programs emerged with limited resources. Furthermore, maintenance programs—those programs that taught English while maintaining a child's native language—were generally sabotaged. As Crawford (1991) explains, in order for the government to give native-language maintenance programs preference over other bilingual programs, such as immersion programs, its effectiveness needs to be proved through adequate evaluation measures. However, Crawford explains that according to Rudolph Troike, professor of education at the University of Illinois, of the $500 million Congress appropriated for bilingual programs in the first decade of Title VII, only one-half of 1% actually went to research. Therefore, as a result of the hindered research on these native-language maintenance programs, which Crawford delineates, they seldom received Title VII grants.

Additionally, Crawford documents how advocates of native-language in-struction have claimed that national evaluation of federally funded bilingual pro-grams have generally employed faulty research methods. He sites an evaluation conducted by the American Institutes for Research (AIR) in 1977–1978, which was the first evaluation of Title VII ever completed. The AIR study concluded that programs using native-language instruction had shown no significant impact on the education of English Language Learners. As Crawford explains, however, critics of AIR claimed that the methodology of the study was flawed because instead of testing an ideal instructional model, AIR had examined a myriad of programs labeled "bilingual." Therefore, opponents of the study believed that AIR had quantified their overall results without controlling for a multitude of variables.

As inadequacies of AIR's study were being disputed, in a 1978 monograph for the National Clearinghouse for Bilingual Education, Troike (1978) identified a dozen evaluation studies that documented the effectiveness of well-designed bilingual programs using native-language instruction. Ultimately, as Crawford (1991) concludes, despite Troike's findings, due to political motivations, research of questionable quality and validity has focused on what he refers to as the "sim-plistic" (p. 89) question of whether bilingual programs have worked. Crawford concludes that if politics were not part of the equation, instead of the narrow fo-cus of comparing program models, more research could study what Hakuta and Snow (1986) describe as the linguistic and psychological, and I would add social, processes in the development of bilingual children to actually enhance effective classroom practices. Macedo and Bartolomé (1999) further argue that in the con-troversy over bilingual education sound research (Cummins, 1991; Hakuta, 1986) confirming its effectiveness is dismissed and the research that is valued often ignores the crucial issue of social inequities that inform bilingual programs.

Crawford highlights that many educational policymakers argued for English-only programs, as other languages were perceived as an ideological threat to the concept of being American. Thus, prejudicial language policy obstructed pro-grams with potential to provide effective bilingual pedagogy, which could both teach students English while maintaining the child's home language and also pro-mote a natural progression of literacy acquisition from the student's highly devel-oped oral first language base.

Since the 1978 reauthorization of the Bilingual Education Act (which was initially signed into law in 1968) policymakers have embraced policy that repro-duces the dominant ideology by placing many linguistic minorities in English immersion programs, such as English as a Second Language (ESL). In so doing, they have subverted empowering pedagogy that could build on and incorporate linguistic minorities' cultural and linguistic knowledge—an educational decision that has far-reaching negative psychological and academic ramifications. According to Cummins' (1991) research, the use of linguistic minority students' home language facilitates academic success by (a) preventing home–school linguistic mismatch, (b) enabling transfer of knowledge, (c) fostering English language acquisition, and ultimately (d) including a student's identity through home language preservation. His "linguistic mismatch" theory suggests that the switch between the language of the home (L1) and the language of the school (L2) can produce academic troubles. However, bilingual programs that maintained the child's first language, attempting to address this "linguistic mismatch" issue, were, and continue to be, strategically subverted.

Crawford points out that despite the intentions of the initial Bilingual Act of 1968, the failure to implement effective bilingual education programs over the years, due to political motives, has resulted in persisting problems of exorbitant dropout rates and poor academic performance among linguistic minorities. Therefore, since many linguistic minority adolescents, including those who are incarcerated, have been caught in the middle of educational decisions framed by politics, many, in particular among those from economically disadvantaged backgrounds, have not been effectively taught to read and write. In Tamar Lewin's April 14, 2004 *New York Times* article, she documents that in a predominantly Latino populated high school in Phoenix, approximately two-thirds of the incoming 9th graders read below grade level, a trend in reading levels that she indicates is mirrored in most large cities and has continued through the years. While many Latino students excel, despite structural barriers, the Education Trust (2003) reports that on the national level as many as 57% of Latino 4th graders have not reached the basic level of proficiency in reading and that by the end of high school a substantial percentage of Latino students' reading skills are comparable to those of white middle school youth.

Trueba (1989), in accordance with the critical pedagogues previously referenced, contends that the differential academic achievement of Latino students has been a result of the systematic silencing of their voices in the public school system and mainstream society at large. Trueba's historic account of bilingual education outlines (a) the legislative landmarks affecting the educational experiences of language minority students; (b) the backlash of local political groups who have aimed to restrict the use of languages other than English; and (c) the federal government's "laissez-faire" attitude toward bilingual schooling, which has relegated the decision as to which type of bilingual model should be implemented to the individual states. Such an analysis as well as the previous overview of the bilingual education debate accentuates structural dynamics, forces built into the system, which are involved in the differential academic performance of Latino students.

These perspectives, thus, highlight the political controversy, rather than pedagogical focus, involved in the education of "linguistic minority" students.

Push-Out/Dropout Rates

High school push-out/dropout rates among inner-city black and Latino youth are alarmingly high. Fine (1991) argues that since public schools were never designed for economically disadvantaged students of color [see Du Bois, 1903 (reprinted in 1953); Tyack, 1974], the dropout patterns among inner-city youth are dramatically higher than those in economically privileged positions within the social ladder. Scholarly writings indicate that, due to prejudicial policy and practices, U.S. public schools are characterized by dramatically different patterns of pushing out/dropping out by social class, "race"/ethnicity, and gender.

Gersten and Woodward's (1994) findings demonstrate how these rates of dropping out play across ethnic boundaries. In 1994, their figures revealed that in New York City the Latino population—which has rapidly increased in light of immigration patterns—was in the greatest risk category for dropping out with African American students following close behind. According to their statistics, 51% of Latinos age 21 and over possessed a high school diploma, compared with 63% for African Americans and 77% for non-Latino, whites.

Figures from the U.S. Census Bureau conducted in October 2001 reveal the persisting high school completion discrepancy amongst ethnicities. The 2001 Census Bureau records the following dropout figures disaggregated by ethnicity: African Americans represent 15.2% of the entire student population and 6.3% drop out; Latinos represent 12.5% of the entire student population and 8.8% do not finish high school; and white, non-Latinos represent 67.1% of the entire student population and 4.1% do not graduate high school. According to the Census Bureau, this gap has remained stable since 1970. The Census Bureau further records that in the 1-year period between October 2000 and September 2001, students living in low-income families (defined as the bottom 20% of all family incomes) were six times more likely to drop out of high school than their peers in high-income families (the top 20% of all family incomes). According to the Census Bureau, low-income students represent 12% of the total student population and approximately 10.7% drop out; middle-income students (between 20% and 80% of all family incomes) make up 58.8% of the total student population and approximately 5.4% do not graduate high school; and high-income students represent 29.1% of the total student population and approximately 1.7% drop out of school (U.S. Bureau of the Census, 2001).

The Census Bureau does not provide statistics disaggregated by ethnicity within each socio-economic category. Therefore, their statistics do not offer direct information on the dropout patterns of inner-city youth. However, statistics presented by Fine (1991) indicate that 40% to 60% of low-income, urban African American and Latino students drop out of high school—a trend that has continued at comparable rates throughout the years.

Orfield, Losen, Wald, and Swanson (2004) offer even more precise data on graduation patterns. They report that formulas which states use to determine graduation rates, such as that of the National Center for Education Statistics (NCES) and the U.S. Census Bureau's Current Population Survey (CPS), underestimate dropout figures. Within findings from NCES, students who have left school but are older than mandatory attendance age in their high schools are not counted as dropouts. With the CPS data, since it relies on self-reports from a young adult population, rather than on data from public schools, respondents may misrepresent their educational attainment. Furthermore, statistics from both NCES and CPS do not include incarcerated students who do not graduate. Therefore, these calculations underestimate push-out/dropout rates among black and Latino students, given their disproportionately high incarceration rates.

Orfield et al. present national statistics, which they argue represent more accurate measures of high school graduation rates, based on the actual enrollment data that every district provides annually to the nation's Common Core of Data. Their calculations indicate that in 2001 only 50% of all black students, 51% of Native American students, and 53% of all Latino students graduated from high school, while 76.8% of all Asian/Pacific Islander students and 74.9% of white students graduated. In addition to disaggregating their measures by "race"/ethnicity, they also offer figures broken down by gender, highlighting lower graduation rates among males: among black students, 42.8% males and 56.2% females graduated; among Native Americans, 47% males and 51.4% females graduated; among Latinos, 48% males and 58.5% females; among Asian/Pacific Islander students, 72.6% males and 80% females; and among white students, 70.8% males and 77% females (Orfield et al., 2004).

Orfield et al. provide more specific figures for students within the larger school districts, highlighting low academic outcomes for blacks and Latinos. Within the predominantly black districts of Oakland and Atlanta, black students graduate at rates of 30.4% and 39.6%, respectively; and, within the predominantly Latino school districts of New York City and Houston, graduation rates are 38% and 40%, respectively. Orfield et al. additionally report on the existence of particular patterns across the nation relating to characteristics of districts with low graduation rates. They inform that low graduation rates are more prevalent within high poverty districts, located in central urban areas, with high percentages of students classified as having disabilities, or with high percentages of English Language Learners (Orfield et al., 2004).

The disproportionately high dropout rates among African American and Latino students and among those students from low-income backgrounds, particularly inner-city youth, clearly indicate that the locus of the problem is structural, situated within the segregationist educational system and other societal institutions. Critical pedagogues explain how these disproportionate dropout rates across social class, "racial," and gender identity markers reflect how schools reproduce and perpetuate oppressive practices and ideologies that originate in the wider society. These educational analysts discuss numerous discriminatory school policy and practices. Some of these educational measures are (a) the implementation of general education curriculum that does not accommodate cultural and linguistic diversity and (b) culturally and class-biased standardized tests and assessment procedures that track students into ability groups, including special education placement (discussed extensively in chapters three and four). Critical theorists, therefore, argue that, while several low-income black and Latino urban youth triumph over structural limitations, prejudicial school procedures gear many for school failure.

The dropout rates are evidence that, as many within the critical theoretical tradition argue, the civil right of equal opportunity is institutionally subverted by the guarantee of unequal outcomes across identity boundaries. Furthermore, as several of these critical theorists note, through rhetoric, such as "academic failure" many in positions of power have blamed the below grade-level academic performance of large groups of students within inner-city schools on the students, their parents, their poor environment, their lack of motivation, and what perniciously has been referred to as their "culture of poverty" (Lewis, 1965) and "verbal and cultural deprivation" (Bereiter & Engelmann, 1966).

Blaming the individual student deflects attention away from institutionalized inequities such as unbalanced school financing, curriculum differentiation, and culturally biased assessment measures, to mention only a few. Therefore, as critical theorists indicate, many within the dominant culture view the students and their parents as the culprits, rather than recognizing systemic socio-economic imbalances and discriminatory cultural forces at play in miseducating economically disadvantaged urban youth.

Systematically Biased Special Education Procedures

The literature illustrates that prejudicial school practices, which reproduce those specifically aimed at African American and Latino groups throughout societal institutions, are also perpetuated through special education identification and grade retention. Consequently, as Voltz (1996) points out, instead of participating in the separate special education programs in which, all too often, these students inappropriately have been placed, many of them may choose dropping out as a viable option. For many youth, therefore, dropping out, and even acts that lead to incarceration, can often be conscious or unconscious forms of protest and resistance against structures of social and cultural reproduction. Graduation rates are low for special education identified students. Among this student population only approximately 32% graduate (Orfield et al., 2004).

A considerable body of literature discusses how institutionalized biases reflected in special education referral and assessment procedures disproportionately designate economically disadvantaged black and Latino youth for special education classes. Again, rather than attributing these students' academic difficulties to a function of how the school may be reflecting the power relations present within the larger society, students are blamed and often identified as "learning disabled."

Latinos and African Americans are overrepresented in particular disability categories within special education. Voltz (1996) informs that, as a result of faulty special education assessment tools, Latino children—those who are either English dominant, English Language Learners, or bilingual—are over-represented in classifications for language, speech, and hearing impairment; and, African American students are disproportionately identified as mentally delayed, neurologically impaired, learning disabled, and emotionally disabled.

Results of an extensive study of patterns of representation in special education enrollment conducted by Robertson, Kushner, Starks, and Drescher (1994) further highlight these prejudicial practices. With regard to special education placement for Latino linguistic minority students, Robertson et al. find that ELL students are placed in the categories of specific learning disabilities and trainable mental retardation more often than non-ELL students. However, as Robertson et al. note, in many of these cases the child is not necessarily learning disabled, but rather the student is experiencing academic difficulties that are merely a reflection of normal second language learning development.

For the special education disability categories of African Americans, Robertson et al. (1994) also conclude that black students are disproportionately identified as emotionally disturbed. These researchers, as well as others (Cummins, 1991; hooks, 1994), note that such over-representation of black students in this special education category often reflects the students' response to the school's reproduction of the dominant culture's ideology and resulting inability to include culturally relevant curriculum for these students.

The inappropriate identification and subsequent over-representation of inner-city Latino and African American youth in special education is, as the aforementioned scholars have discussed, proof that the general education system has not been able to accommodate students' cultural and linguistic diversity. These disproportionate classifications merely reflect the broader social and economic inequalities that often afflict these students in the U.S. Like all labels that the dominant culture uses to discriminate, the socially negotiated nature of the special education labeling process is yet another mechanism used to marginalize and control subordinate cultures. The over-representation of African Americans and Latinos in the respective special education categories further illustrates the school system's prejudicial design that places the problem solely within the individual, instead of the systematic mechanisms that produce such results.

Cummins (1991) and others (Fordham, 1988; Macedo & Bartolomé, 1999) maintain that considerable research reveals that for so-called minority groups who experience disproportionate levels of "school failure," the degree to which students' language and culture are integrated into the schooling process constitutes a significant predictor of academic success. However, as abundant literature has noted, the denial of such culturally relevant curriculum for inner-city African American and Latino students and the use of culture-, class-, and language-based special education classification practices ensure their over-representation in special education programs. While the path from educational disadvantage to incarceration is by no means inevitable, the disproportionate representation of this student population in juvenile correctional facilities can, therefore, also be attributed to the inequitable school policy and practices that create high push-out/dropout rates and biased special education identification.

Contextualizing Special Education within a Historical Lens

As noted earlier in this chapter, according to Lazerson's (1983) historical account of the origins of special education programs, special education has served, since the beginning of the 20th century, as the system's answer for those students who do not fit the limited definition of "regular" education. Lazerson further highlights that during the early 20th century special education programs emerged as "socially efficient" ways of sorting the children that educational administrators—the body of policymakers who Tyack (1974) refers to as "administrative progressives"—deemed "rebellious" or "deviant" (Lazerson, 1983, p. 18) from the so-called normals (p. 18). The motivating factor behind the emergence of special education classes was, therefore, to separate students across social class and ethnic boundaries. As such, it has provided the ruling class a systemic means for segregating, in particular, economically disadvantaged students and those from discriminated "racial"/ethnic groups.

Implemented in 1975, Public Law 94-142 (P.L. 94-142)—a federal policy that called for a "free appropriate public education" (FAPE) for all students with disabilities, previously named the Education for All Handicapped Children Act and currently known as Individuals with Disabilities Education Act (IDEA)—attempted to reverse prejudicial assumptions and practices pervasive in special education since its inception (to be discussed further in chapter three). Additionally, the Regular Education Initiative, which the Office of Special Education and Rehabilitation Services launched in 1986, intended to reverse the previous segregation practices within special education by integrating general and special education into one system. Despite efforts, beginning with Public Law 94-142, to improve special education, discriminatory measures continue.

Current literature within the critical theoretical tradition underscores that, in addition to culturally, linguistically, and class-biased special education classification procedures that have persisted, in most cases, the quality of instruction in special education programs does not compare to that provided for the general population. Critical theorists further emphasize that to this day, among other injustices within special education practices, the school system's response to the miseducation of so-called "racial" and linguistic minorities has been to channel these youth into special education programs.

However, since high push-out/dropout rates have minimized the ability for special education programs to maintain the social order and serve as a safety valve for the system's miseducation of particular student populations, juvenile detention centers have played an increasing role. Revisiting Foucault's (1977, 1980) analysis, detailed previously in this chapter, and relating it to special education, situates the modern-day proliferation of juvenile detention centers. His description of penal institutions as an integral component of the ruling class' technologies of power accentuates the development of juvenile detention centers as the contemporary means for repressing students across class and "racial"/ethnic boundaries. The over-representation in juvenile detention centers of inner-city youth who have been identified for special education programs, including adolescents who read below a 3rd grade level equivalent, reflects this phenomenon. Thus, as more and more students from subordinated groups who are classified for special education drop out of school, thereby bypassing direct institutional power over them, juvenile detention centers have evolved as the modern-day mechanism for controlling these youth.

Juvenile Incarceration

As a result of societal limitations, many non-reading adolescents, a large percentage of whom have been identified for special education, spend time in juvenile correctional facilities. The disproportionate representation of low-income black and Latino youth in juvenile detention centers is yet another indication of the denial of equal outcomes for those within specific social positions. Statistics provided by the Correctional Association of New York indicate that the majority of youth within juvenile facilities come from low-income backgrounds. Statistics gathered in 2002 further indicate that 63% of youth in state custody were African American, 23% were Latino, and 16% were white (Correctional Association of New York, 2005). Between January and March 2007, approximately 64% of youth in state custody were African American and only 13% were non-Latino whites (Correctional Association of New York, 2009a). These racial disparities reflect the racial–economic inequities prevalent throughout society, as well as the ensuing discriminatory arrest and incarceration patterns within the justice system (Oliver & Yocom, 2004; Males & Macallair, 2001).

Researchers, outside of the traditional body of critical theorists, have noted the correlation between the miseducation of socio-economically disadvantaged black and Latino youth, their limited employment opportunities, and incarceration. As a result of the ineffective educational practices maintained in many inner-city public schools, Chambliss (1994) informs that inner-city children seem to be increasingly prepared for only low wage jobs, the military, and/or incarceration. Leone et al. (2003) argue that the failure of the educational system to provide inner-city youth effective teachings is creating an underclass of youth.

Gregory (1996) notes that the cumulative effect of prejudicial school policy and practices makes it more likely that low-income African American and Latino students drop out of school and, therefore, increase their vulnerability for involvement with juvenile corrections. A review of Educational Services in Juvenile Justice Residential Facilities from the Office of Program Policy Analysis and Government Accountability (1998) concluded that over 66% of youth admitted to correctional facilities had not been attending school regularly at the time of their admission.

Several studies have shown a strong correlation between not graduating high school and the possibility of spending time in prison. A 2002 report by the U.S. General Accounting Office (GAO) indicated that a disproportionate percentage of those who are in prison did not finish high school (GAO, 2002). Additional statistics on adult prisoners provide an indication of patterns for juvenile offenders. In their study, *Dropout Statistics*, the National Dropout Prevention Network (2000) reported that 80% of adult prisoners in the U.S. in 2000 had not completed high school. According to an analysis conducted by Western, Schiraldi, and Ziedenberg (2005), in 2005 two-thirds of adult prison inmates had not finished high school.

As Leone et al. (2003) explain, when youth leave school early, they are unable to find meaningful work, which places them at higher risk for possible involvement with juvenile courts and corrections. Kantor and Brenzel (1992) and Anyon (1997) explain that prejudicial structures within mainstream society decrease employment opportunities for inner-city youth. A study conducted by the National Center on Education, Disability, and Juvenile Justice also indicates that discriminatory practices within the mainstream job market have further contributed to the over-representation of low-income black and Latino youth in prison (Leone et al., 2003). Wilson (1987, 1996) highlights that, due to the combination of macrostructural economic and cultural constraints placed on inner-city youth, the availability of viable mainstream jobs for these juveniles continues to decrease.

As a result, Wilson concludes that such a dynamic compounds their resulting social dislocations and, therefore, heightens their chances for involvement with detention centers.

Low Reading Level, Special Education, and Incarceration Connection

Several studies have also noted the correlation of remedial level literacy abilities, special education placement, and incarceration. As previously noted, special education students represent a disproportionate percentage of those youth who are incarcerated. According to a study conducted in 2000, 49% of youth in the care of Office of Child and Family Services (OCFS)—the state agency responsible for the placement of youth in the juvenile justice system—were identified for special education programs (Correctional Association of New York, 2004a).

Furthermore, within numerous juvenile detention centers nationwide, the literacy levels of students both within general and special education classifications are low. Figures from the Office of Program Policy Analysis and Government Accountability (1998) record that nearly 80% of juveniles entering correctional facilities scored 1 year or more below the grade level appropriate for their age. Additional statistics provided by the Coalition for Juvenile Justice in 2001 indicate that the average reading level for 9th grade youth in detention facilities is 4th grade. Given the connection between low print literacy levels and incarceration, some states factor 3rd grade reading scores into the formula for determining the need for the future construction of prisons.

Within a particular New York City juvenile detention center, the majority of students' ages range from 13 to 16 years old—with those who are 15 years old representing 43.5% of the population (New York City Department of Juvenile Justice, 2007). A program intake analysis of print literacy levels in January 2007 from the school housed within this detention center reveals that 91% of the students in grades 4–8 and 54% of students in grades 9–12 read below a 6th grade level (New York City Department of Education, 2007a). Additional literacy figures, provided in the 2007 Yearly Principal's Report, show that approximately 50% of the students read on or below 4th grade equivalents (New York City Department of Education, 2007b). Since the majority of the student population is in 7th grade or beyond, the latter statistic is particularly alarming. These numbers also correlate with national statistics.

Existing studies and literature include limited discourse, however, about the population of incarcerated adolescents who read on or below a 2nd grade level equivalent. Yet, the 2007 Yearly Principal's Report from this school further indicates that approximately 25% of the students read below a 2.5 grade level equivalent (New York City Department of Education, 2007b). Prior to their incarceration, these students were the responsibility of the mainstream school system.

Literacy and Power

In the tradition of critical literacy, Gramsci's (1971) political analysis of literacy as a social practice exposes the contradictory nature of literacy. On the one hand, literacy serves as a means for the ruling class to dominate and perpetuate repressive social relations. Such an analysis situates the instrumentalist nature of U.S. literacy instruction (which will be contextualized within contemporary literacy policy in chapter three). However, on the other hand, Gramsci believed that literacy could also be used as a means for self and social empowerment. Gramsci, therefore, envisioned an oppositional politics potential in literacy that could be activated, enabling people to understand and transform oppressive structures. Giroux's (1988) and Freire's (1985) descriptions of critical literacy embody Gramsci's view of literacy as a social practice that is historically tied to knowledge and power as well as a political and cultural struggle over discourse and narrative.

In line with Gramsci's view of literacy as a social practice that is intricately connected to a political and cultural struggle over language, knowledge, and experience, Freire (1985) discusses, as initially presented in chapter one, the ways in which illiteracy is a political creation. He writes, "Illiteracy is one of the concrete expressions of an unjust social reality" (p. 10). Freire describes that educators who view illiteracy as a "'disease' that's contagious and transmitted to others" (p. 7) often implement a mechanistic approach to facilitate literacy. This mechanical view of literacy, he maintains, has social control as its goal and often teaches literacy through primers. Freire explains that these primers serve the needs of a "banking system" as they "are instruments for 'depositing' the educator's words into the learners" (p. 8). Freire stresses that just as "scientific neutrality does not exist" (p. 117) education is not neutral.

In countering "banking" education, Freire advocates a critical literacy, or political literacy, approach to provide learners a liberatory pedagogy that enables what he refers to throughout his writings as "reading and writing of the word and world" (1970, 1974, 1985). As such, it embraces the learner's life experiences within a problematical vision—which explores the root causes of one's circumstances—and facilitates critical thinking, as it places literacy within a cultural, social, and historical context. Freire positions this act of reading the word and the world within a framework of culture, power, and liberation. As Freire emphasizes, critical thinking is essential for understanding the hidden forces of power that can often interfere with societal advancement of dominated groups. According to Freire's vision, critical literacy contributes to the learner's process of liberation, or transformation, through conscientization as it "associates the learning of reading and writing with a creative act" (1985, p. 17). Within this critical literacy, learners are able to enact their agency and transform their reality. They acquire tools that assist them in (a) exposing the dominant culture's myths and (b) transcending societal barriers.

Freire (1974) explains in detail literacy acquisition from a critical literacy perspective. He describes this critical pedagogical approach to literacy so eloquently and poignantly that his words merit inclusion in their entirety:

> To acquire literacy is more than to psychologically and mechanically dominate reading and writing techniques. It is to dominate these techniques in terms of consciousness; to understand what one reads and to write what one understands; it is to *communicate* graphically. Acquiring literacy does not involve memorizing sentences, words, or syllables—lifeless objects unconnected to an existential universe—but rather an attitude of creation and recreation, a self-transformation producing a stance of intervention in one's context. Thus the educator's role is fundamentally to enter into dialogue with the illiterate about concrete situations and simply to offer him the instruments with which he can teach himself to read and write. (pp. 42–43)

Although Freire originally designed this literacy pedagogy for disenfranchised adults in Brazil who were unable to read and write, Giroux (1988) describes that, regardless of one's socio-economic background, such literacy pedagogy provides "a narrative for agency as well as a referent for critique" (p. 155) that empowers both students and teachers. Giroux argues that within the liberal's and right-wing's functionalist literacy framework "illiteracy is not merely the inability to read and write, but also a cultural marker for naming forms of difference within the logic of cultural deprivation theory" (p. 149). Giroux (1988) and Macedo (2006) contend that the functionalist approach to literacy instruction disserves students of all socio-economic backgrounds. Macedo explains that it "prevents the development of the critical thinking that enables one to 'read the world' critically and to understand the reasons and linkages behind the facts" (p. 16). Giroux adds that by inhibiting critical reflection the functionalist literacy approach, in fact, produces a societal illiteracy; it prevents citizens of all socio-economic backgrounds from reading the world and ultimately denies critical democracy.

Conclusion

The unjust circumstances pertaining to the miseducation of inner-city youth and their resulting unequal outcomes demand a shift in the consciousness informing the long-standing paradigm framing U.S. educational practices and policies. Among other atrocities, as these inequities have produced a population of non-reading adolescents, who are rarely directly discussed in the literature or in policy, it becomes all the more crucial for social action to reverse this current trend. This action must address the academic needs, and ultimate well-being, of adolescents who read below a 3rd grade level equivalent—some of whom are in mainstream schools and some of whom are in schools within juvenile detention centers. The social consequences for those who have been denied textual literacy and their positionality within the social matrix reveals (a) the educational impact of discriminatory practices prevalent throughout societal institutions and (b) the ramifications of a flawed educational system and literacy pedagogy in its most pernicious manifestation.

Chapters three and four will now explore how contemporary socio-political and socio-cultural forces impact the pedagogical experiences of non-reading adolescents. Such an analysis simultaneously unravels existing antidemocratic educational structures in the socio-educational lives of these youth and highlights democratic alternatives rooted in critical pedagogy and a holistic understanding of teaching, learning, and knowledge. Chapters five and six will subsequently describe a critical literacy curriculum for non-reading adolescents that facilitates their critical consciousness to ultimately "read and write the word and world."

THREE

The Perils of Contemporary Educational Policies for Non-reading Adolescents

Introduction

As chapter two has highlighted, the school system generally provides a persisting separate and unequal education for inner-city children. A hidden curriculum exists in which school policies and practices favor some groups over others. Additionally, the curriculum for all students often requires regurgitation of predetermined, fragmented information, which is then "measured." The educational system's design, thus, intrinsically attempts to stifle human possibility. It, furthermore, subverts one's understanding of self within society, the world, and the cosmos. This restrictive structure, which aims to perpetuate the current socioeconomic order, ultimately infringes upon the well-being of students.

While educational pathology rests in the prevailing paradigm that has shaped school practice and policy since the turn of the 19th century, it afflicts non-reading adolescents in one of its most dysfunctional manifestations. In addition to constricting school policy and practices that affect all students and the miseducation inflicted on inner-city students, in general, those adolescents whom the school system classifies as non-readers occupy heightened positions of marginalization. The education system produces academic failure for non-reading adolescents at basically every level of the school process—with the possible exception of their art and physical education classes, if their schools even have the resources and facilities to provide these classes. Since these adolescents do not have textual reading skills, they cannot keep up with lessons in their content area classes, nor can they pass required grade-level standardized tests that, more detrimentally, often determine grade promotion—as was recently the case in New York City (to be discussed further).

This chapter will highlight contemporary policy, in large part initiated through No Child Left Behind (NCLB) mandates, which perniciously impact the educational lives of non-reading adolescents—many of whom are special education identified and/or linguistic minorities. Chapter four will subsequently place this socio-political analysis of non-reading adolescents' school experience within a social and cultural context, as I discuss the ways in which the emphasis on standardized testing fails to take into account the complexity of learning, knowing, and teaching.

Literacy Paradigm Guiding U.S. Schooling: A Restrictive Lens

An analysis of federal policy informing literacy practices and policy within the school system provides a context for the subsequent discussion of the damage that such literacy pedagogy presents for non-reading adolescents. For over a century, a prevailing paradigm of rationalization, standardization, and fragmentation has guided reading instruction practices and policy—and pedagogy in general—within the public school system at the national and state levels. Shannon (1989) describes that by 1960 this reductionist vision—one that reduces literacy pedagogy to a constricted view—and the accompanying implementation of what policymakers have referred to as "scientific measures" transformed reading instruction. It changed it into a technocratic discipline achieved through the use of (a) basal readers—which Freire (1974) refers to as tools of a domesticating education—and (b) standardized assessments. Such a practice placed basal publishers and so-called reading specialists as the arbiters of classroom teachings. Teachers and students became subjected to these external dictates and control measures. Shannon further explains the presumed goals of this rationalistic reading instruction and assessment as well as the behaviorist psychology framing these educational structures:

> ...Standardized tests objectively and scientifically arbitrated which students were making the most progress under what program, and teacher's guidebooks presented the proper stimulus to evoke the correct response from teachers while they used the basal technology during their reading instruction. (p. 42)

This adaptation of scientific management to reading instruction has had profound implications for literacy pedagogy that have had an enduring influence. First of all, as emphasized previously, this instrumentalist perspective has reduced literacy to the acquisition of quantifiable mechanical skills, and it has dismissed the crucial affective and imaginative elements involved in reading and writing. Secondly, as instrumentalist literacy ignores the social and cultural components of reading and writing, it has obscured the power-laden aspects embedded within literacy to, in the words of Freire (1985), "reinforce the learner's 'false consciousness'" (p. 102). As such, this technical framework guiding literacy instruction in the school system has consistently denied a critical literacy—a liberatory pedagogy for all students that enables reading and writing of the word and world (Freire, 1974, 1985; Freire & Macedo, 1987). (To be discussed in detail in chapters four, five, and six.)

The Contemporary Focus on Standards through No Child Left Behind and the National Reading Panel: Another Version of Social Efficiency

While the primary use of basal readers in contemporary education has subsided, technocratic, external mandates, to this day, often control and monitor literacy instruction, as well as all other academic subjects. This domesticating approach to reading and writing instruction continues in the 21st century through the No Child Left Behind Act (NCLB) and the research findings of the National Reading Panel (NRP)—which provided the reading research that was articulated in NCLB and that has shaped federal literacy policy. Despite continuing rhetoric of democratic education and "education for all," the century-old "scientific" methods of social efficiency influence these national, contemporary educational reform initiatives.

The present-day educational stress on standards, as defined by the dominant culture, and the reinforcement of this institutionalized knowledge through standardized tests has provided a modern positivistic means for scientific management and maintenance of the socio-economic structure. Ohanian (1999) further explains that this staunch emphasis on standards, which increased momentum in the 1990s, originated from the uproar created in 1983 by *A Nation at Risk*. This government report described how the school system had failed in producing a viable workforce and, thus, the U.S. had faltered in its competition on the international stage. As a result, since U.S. President Ronald Reagan's administration, the solution to such an educational issue has increasingly become a technical focus on top-down standards and standardized testing.

The No Child Left Behind Act of 2001 and the findings of the National Reading Panel, released in 2000, reflect this instrumentalist pedagogical trend. Instilled with the alleged power of science, NCLB purports to rely on the "objective data" and "achievement data" of standardized tests to measure whether a student meets or exceeds the standards (U.S. Department of Education, 2001). Just as NCLB relies on the supposed power and objectivity of science for legitimacy, these rationalistic principles guide the NRP as well. Overall, the report of the NRP—which referred to struggling readers, but did not include discourse on non-reading adolescents—advanced an instrumentalist literacy approach. It concluded that scientifically researched reading instruction and professional development, in combination with ongoing standardized assessments to ensure accountability, increase literacy achievement abilities for all students (National Reading Panel, 2000).

With the purported goal of raising standards and an accountability system based on standardized assessments to gauge students' attainment of these standards, NCLB and the NRP, in keeping with literacy policy in the 20th century, place literacy teachings within a "banking" framework centered on the acquisition of quantifiable basic skills. While standards, no doubt, must be set high, NCLB and NRP actually impede high standards as they negate pedagogy that facilitates an understanding of connections behind received information—the relationships underpinning knowledge that is taught—and a critical reading of the world. Contrary to actually raising standards, the constricted literacy curriculum they encourage furthers social regulation, suppression of critical consciousness, and ultimately reproduction of dominant ideology.

In NRP's narrow perspective, it delineated five specific literacy skills that all children must master in order to read: phonemic awareness, phonics, fluency, vocabulary, and comprehension. The panel highlighted the necessity of systematic phonics instruction, and stressed that phonics skills must also be "integrated with the development of phonemic awareness, fluency, and text reading comprehension" (National Reading Panel, 2000, p. 10). Nowhere does the NRP's report analyze the benefits of critical literacy—reading the word and the world—nor does it position literacy within its social, emotional, and power inscribed contexts.

In addition to the importance the NRP report places on testing measures, its restriction of literacy discourse to these purely technical boundaries has ultimately facilitated the continuation of standardized and fragmented literacy policies and practices. As NCLB employed the findings of the NRP, this mechanistic focus on literacy teaching has informed educational initiatives at federal and state levels. As such, it has inhibited the potential for literacy as (a) a means for creative exploration of one's imagination and (b) a tool for critique to encourage self and social empowerment. (To be discussed further in chapters four, five, and six.)

Furthermore, in NCLB's alignment with functional literacy—which emphasizes the necessity of being able to read for economic survival within society—it intrinsically embraces the mechanics of reading and writing without acknowledgment of the critical and affective components of literacy. Viewing literacy as primarily a cognitive process, a functionalist framework (see chapter two), ignores social and ideological contexts of literacy learning in which relationships between language and power play a major role. Macedo (2006) explains that functional literacy serves "the basic literacy demand of an industrialized society" (p. 18). As detailed in chapter two, Giroux (1988), echoing Gramsci's (1971) contention that literacy can be used as a tool of the ruling class to dominate and repress, describes the functionalist literacy framework as an ideological mechanism for the transmission of the dominant culture's discourse, values, and narrative. The design of NCLB's *Reading First* program, which aims to raise students' reading skills in the early years of school, ensures this transmission of the dominant culture's knowledge and ideology.

Within the *Reading First* program, NCLB mandates that states must measure progress of students' reading skills for children in grades 1–2 as well as implement annual reading tests for students in grades 3–8. The implementation of these class and culturally biased standardized reading tests to measure student progress and program effectiveness, ultimately maintains the status quo. It directs teachings in the U.S. school system toward Western cultural and scientific frameworks that are then reinforced and tested through class and culturally bound standardized assessment practices. This process brings us to a discussion of the heightened damage that educational policy in the 21st century presents for students from subjugated groups, particularly non-reading adolescents.

Deconstructing Standardized Testing: No Child Left Behind's Exclusion of Children from Historically Subordinated Groups

As policy initiatives such as NCLB and NRP have shaped the contemporary delivery of pedagogy and maintained the vestiges of the 20th-century scientific management and standardization procedures—which have subjected all students to a watered-down, technocratic educational experience—historically marginalized student populations have been impacted all the more perniciously. Despite the intrinsic flaws, as initially discussed in chapter two, of standardized tests, which are centered on the dominant culture's heritage and language and deny the cultures and indigenous knowledges of subjugated social groups, these assessment practices continue to define and determine the academic progress of all students.

As was the trend throughout the 20th century, those students whose histories do not coincide with the cultural standpoints represented in the tests are fundamentally at a disadvantage in these exams. NCLB's reliance on standardized testing, therefore, perpetuates the hindrance of academic achievement for select student populations—those children from identity groups that are already marginalized within the larger society. The privileging of the dominant culture's system of knowledge and the ensuing exclusion of differing cultural perspectives continue to provide a constricted educational system that tends to credential students according to their positions within the social web.

Revisiting Freire's (1970), Macedo's (2006), and Shor's (1992) analyses, underscores the social efficiency goals underlying the standardized testing mandated in

NCLB. They argue that standardization of information and knowledge functions as a pedagogy of social control. As such, standardized testing serves as an instrument for "banking education" by forcing educators and students to both think and keep discourse within certain fixed parameters; these boundaries are within a set system of knowledge that those in positions of power in the social hierarchy have deemed acceptable. Shor discusses the way in which standard knowledge reinforces and maintains the status quo:

> Any material imposed by authority as doctrine stops being knowledge and becomes dogma. Critical learning and democratic education end where orthodoxy begins. (p. 34)

This authoritarian orthodoxy prevails through NCLB's standardized testing, as the dominant culture enforces pre-packaged information deemed to be "fact." Within such a practice, teachings are designed according to the material that is tested in the class and culturally biased achievement tests. As such, through NCLB's "banking" measures, critical reflection on, for example, "race"/ethnicity, class, and gender within the classroom is, consequently, often silenced.

As previously examined in chapter two, student scores on the National Assessment of Educational Progress (NAEP) reading tests, as well as math tests, reveal the culturally and class-biased nature of standardized assessments and their resulting exclusion of particular groups of students. Due to the tests' inherent cultural and socio-economic biases, since the 1970s—when the National Center for Education Statistics (NCES) initially began to generate assessment statistics—Native Americans, African Americans, Latinos, and economically disadvantaged students have on average scored lower than Caucasian students. In 2003, for example, on the 8th grade reading test, white students had an average score that was 28 points higher than black students and 27 points higher than Latino students (NCES, 2003). Continuing this trend, on the 8th grade reading test in 2007 white students had an average score that was 27 points higher than black students and 25 points higher than Latino students (NCES, 2007b). Additionally, in both 2003 and 2007, students from low-income backgrounds scored approximately 25 points lower than their peers (NCES, 2003, 2007b). These gaps in scores have been consistent throughout the years.

Such statistics indicate the ethnic and class biases of standardized exams as well as the impact of instrumentalist literacy practices. Yet, as Zentella (1997) points out, despite leading anthropologists' sound methodological and theoretical research to refute prejudicial myths explaining the disproportionate educational failure of "racial"/ethnic minorities, such pernicious notions persist. In rebuking these discriminatory views, such as "cultural deprivation," disproportionate testing scores, in fact, reflect social inequities that engender them.

With the focus on standards and standardized testing, NCLB provides a modern day school mechanism for eradicating multiple ideologies and maintaining the status quo. From a critical standpoint, Kincheloe (2001a) argues that school measures, such as standardized testing, promote mono-cultural ideals and interests to reinforce the current social order. He additionally concludes:

> The creation of a one-dimensional national interest is one strategy employed to win the consent of the people—a national interest, it must be added, that often excludes black, Native American, Latino, female and other minority communities. (pp. 617–618)

Harding (1998) as well describes the purpose of educational policymakers' focus on standards, as championed in NCLB, and its effects on consciousness:

> The dominant discourses, their institutions, practices, favored conceptual frameworks, and languages, restrict what everyone is permitted to see, and shape everyone's consciousness. (p. 158)

Kincheloe's and Harding's assertions frame the educational reality that unravels the rhetoric behind claims of providing democratic education. As they, as well as other critical theorists, argue, the monological ideals presented in school curriculum and accompanying psychometric testing practices contribute to the alienation of particular groups of students.

Such measures have strategically excluded cultures and perspectives placed outside a Western, Eurocentric scientific framework. As information inscribing curriculum and standardized tests is generated through an upper-middle class, Eurocentric historical lens, those students from different social positions are placed at a fundamental educational disadvantage. The voices of students from these diverse backgrounds are silenced, as multiple historical and cultural perspectives are disregarded within knowledge covered in the curriculum and measured on these psychometric tests. Therefore, with their prescribed focus, prevailing school curriculum and accompanying standardized tests validate particular experiences, defined by "race"/ethnicity, class, gender, and other identity markers, while invalidating others.

Standardized tests are additionally faulty in that they are designed to prioritize verbal modes of processing and expressing knowledge, rather than assessing how students view the interconnectedness of relationships. Pedagogy that has been historically steeped in a language-based means of receiving and producing knowledge has relegated many students, who favor non-verbal modes of processing and producing information, to special education. Such a fragmented, exclusionary approach to both pedagogy and, ultimately, the measurement of the so-called standards to be attained, often inhibit an empowering education—which Shor (1992) describes as "a critical-democratic pedagogy for self and social change" (p. 15).

As NCLB maintains the educational legacy of social efficiency and its guiding positivistic framework, which favors culturally and class-biased practices, it is not surprising that the students who have been denied teachings that ensure textual literacy acquisition—not to mention contextual literacy—are primarily those from lower socio-economic positions, especially those within historically discriminated "racial"/ethnic groups. Ultimately, as the analysis presented here indicates, since non-reading adolescents are predominantly from economically disadvantaged backgrounds, they are unable to read and write as a result of unequal social relations that have limited economic opportunity as well as quality educational experiences for them. NCLB's focus on standards and standardized testing, while especially harmful to students placed outside of the dominant culture, fundamentally dismisses the educational needs of non-reading adolescents.

Penalizing Non-reading Adolescents through Testing Policies

The goals of an education based on social engineering are accomplished as contemporary literacy policy alienates many non-reading adolescents from the educational process. As the previous section delineates, in an embrace of NCLB—which prioritizes standards that reflect the ruling class' discourse and ensures the maintenance and continuation of their ideology through standardized testing—non-reading adolescents have very limited options for legitimate learning within the mainstream school system. Non-reading adolescents must contend with a school system that imposes uniform standards that are, in fact, unattainable for these youth by virtue of the fact that these students do not have the print literacy skills, as of yet, to even decode the graphemes, the letters, within the standardized tests that measure the acquisition of these standards.

Although non-reading adolescents—whether or not they are identified for either special education or bilingual/English as Second Language (ESL) services—do not have the textual literacy required for grade-level standardized tests, they are, nevertheless, subjected to the frustration of having to "take" the test. As opposed to other students within inner-city schools, it is therefore not just the class and culturally biased nature of standards and their accompanying standardized assessments that jeopardize non-reading adolescents. In the case of non-reading adolescents, it is the cruelty of this schooling practice in which they are forced to show up for grade-level standardized tests requiring advanced reading and writing abilities, even though these youth are still learning the principles of letter/sound coordination.

Further cause for alarm, educational policymakers—steeped in their traditional cognitive psychology perspective—increasingly employ high-stakes testing as they use a single standardized assessment to determine important educational decisions about students, teachers, and schools. Within a high-stakes paradigm, if students receive a low grade on these standardized tests, they could be retained in the same grade (as was the case recently in New York City) or prevented from graduating high school, regardless of a student's achievement on other variables; and, students' low scores on high-stakes testing could also mean that schools are shut down. If an adolescent can only read and write on a level that falls below a 3rd-grade limit, then how can this individual possibly take a grade-level standardized test and pass it? Without the textual literacy to pass, for example, the English Language Arts (ELA) exam—the state assessment that NCLB currently mandates must be administered each year to all public school students throughout the nation in 3rd through 8th grades—students who struggle with decoding and encoding print have often been held back, sometimes several times throughout their schooling careers.

Furthermore, graduation relies heavily on standardized testing, as failure to pass the mandated standardized tests results in failure to graduate, regardless of whether a student has attained the required course credits and attendance record. At the high school level in New York City, for instance, the New York State Education Department (NYSED, 2008) states in Section 100.5 of the Regulations of the Commissioner of Education that general education students who enter 9th grade in 2008 and are not able to pass the five Regents exams with a score of 65 or above will not graduate with a Regents Diploma—which qualifies a student to go to college. Advocates for Children of New York (2008c) additionally delineates that this diploma requirement even applies to English Language Learners (ELL) in the general education population. Only the group of ELL students who enter the U.S. in 9th grade or later and take the test within 3 years of entrance may take the exams, except for the English Regents, in their first language.

In terms of students identified for special education, in Section 100.5 of the Regulations of the Commissioner of Education the NYSED (2008) allows those who enter 9th grade in or after 2001 and before 2010 and cannot pass the Regents exams with a score of 65 or above the possibility of receiving a local diploma through other criteria. These special education classified students may (a) pass the Regents with a score of 55 or above or (b) pass the Regents Competency Tests (RCTs)—less challenging standardized tests than the Regents. Yet, there is no comprehensive literacy intervention throughout the school system at the high school level to support non-reading adolescents so that they may develop the necessary textuality for passing even the RCT exams.

For students in special education who cannot pass these standardized testing options, the NYSED (2008) stipulates in Section 100.9 of the Regulations of the Commissioner of Education that this student population may receive an Individualized Education Program (IEP) diploma. However, this diploma, which colleges do not accept, simply certifies that a student attended high school and met their IEP goals. Indeed, these dynamics reveal the way in which technologies of power, such as high-stakes standardized testing, sort and classify adolescents who read below 3rd grade limits, English Language Learners, and other student populations.

High-stakes evaluation measures have a profoundly negative psychological impact on the formation of non-reading adolescents' self-esteem and often produce frustration, shame, and anger, among other emotions. As students repeatedly do not pass designated grade-level state assessments, they can develop feelings of inadequacy—particularly when this standardized test determines promotion to the next grade. Extensive research shows that retention can lead to heightened anxiety and behavior problems among youth (Roderick, 1995; Xia & Glennie, 2005). Furthermore, as a result of being retained, particularly multiple retentions, students can become disengaged and disinterested with school. For many, retreating from school activities is preferable to partaking in an experience that undermines their positive sense of self.

In this era of high-stakes testing, non-reading adolescents must endure what for many of them represent humiliating educational experiences. Rather than allowing educators to provide teachings according to the level at which each child performs and enabling him/her to develop according to his/her own pace— which would promote positive self-esteem and create opportunities for school success—high-stakes standardized tests enforce predetermined standards for each grade level that negate such supportive teachings. As such, they position students for academic failure. This dynamic often damages these students' self-image. While each individual adopts a different coping mechanism response, some may become withdrawn and quiet and others may assume a defiant and aggressive stance. Instead of punishing non-reading adolescents for their emergent print literacy level, a more just school system would assume the responsibility of providing these youth with instruction tailored to their specific textual literacy level without stigmatizing them.

Within an educational system rooted in a humane structure that does not penalize students for variations in learning style, pedagogical policies and practices would also emphasize each student's unique strengths, while building on their particular academic weaknesses at the child's required pace. Therefore, students of all ages, who are still learning how to decode and encode print, no matter if they are 7 or 15 years old, would receive the instruction necessary to develop their textual literacy within the general education context. Within such a supportive educational paradigm policymakers would reject high-stakes standardized assessments. Additionally, decisions with regard to promotion or retention, and, above all, the concept of "grade-level" knowledge (knowledge that educational policymakers, steeped in their class and culturally bound notions, have arbitrarily deemed developmentally appropriate according to age) would not exist in educational discourse. I will return to this subject of humane educational alternatives throughout this chapter and in chapters four, five, and six.

Situating High-Stakes Testing in New York City

A focus on educational policies in New York City beginning in the 2003–2004 school year and lasting until 2008 reveals the school system's increased reliance during that time on a single standardized exam for determining important educational decisions. It, additionally, underscores the pernicious impact that such a policy had on non-reading adolescents, among other student populations. In New York City, testing policies became more severe in the 2003–2004 school year. In March 2004, under the leadership of Mayor Michael Bloomberg and School Chancellor Joel Klein, the New York City Department of Education (NYC-DOE) established a new promotion policy, purportedly designed to end what policymakers refer to as "social promotion"—a policy wherein students continue to pass to the next grade with their peers without satisfying mandated academic requirements or performance indicators for each grade.

The new procedure based the decision for 3rd grade promotion on the sole criteria of a student's performance on the standardized ELA and math tests. The New York City school system retained those 3rd grade students who did not score Level 2 or above on this standardized assessment. Subsequently, this single test promotion program expanded as the NYCDOE adopted the same policy for 5th graders in September 2004, for 7th graders in August 2005, and for 8th graders in January 2008. Grade 8 students were ultimately spared from the single-test promotion policy, due to a June 2009 reform. However, beginning in the 2005–2006 school year and lasting until June 2009, students' performance on the 3rd, 5th, and 7th grade standardized state ELA and math assessment served as the sole indicator for the NYCDOE's decision to promote or retain students in these particular grades. It bears mention that the 2005–2006 school year also marked an expansion of the use of standardized tests in general, as the New York State Regents—in compliance with NCLB—mandated the administration of a standardized state test to grades 3–8, rather than the previous practice of just a 4th and 8th grade standardized state assessment.

As of the start of the 2008–2009 school year, the single-test promotion policy in New York City applied to 8th graders (Advocates for Children of New York, 2008a). Yet, Advocates for Children of New York (2008a) further informed in their July 2008 report that in addition to scoring a 2 or above on the math and ELA assessments, 8th grade promotion included the added criteria that students pass all their classes in the major subject areas—English, math, social studies, and science. Within this policy, all students who had not achieved both requirements would be able to have an automatic appeal in June 2009. They would have the opportunity to attend summer school and retake the standardized ELA and/or math test or failed courses. If they were able to meet promotion standards in August, they would be promoted. The policy for 8th graders underwent changes toward the end of the school year, as promotion policy shifted for all students.

In June 2009, the New York City Department of Education altered their promotion policy, yet again. Fortunately, in June 2009 they reversed their long-standing single-test promotion policy. While this new policy is quite extensive, in part, it has returned to a policy of "social promotion" for overage 8th graders without systemically providing literacy remediation for either them or for those students who are retained. After first analyzing the flaws of the single-test promotion policy that existed from the 2003–2004 school year until 2008, I will discuss the policy that is currently being enacted. Although this newer development has promise, in terms of providing a less punitive educational process for students, it (a) still fails to address students' academic and socio-emotional needs, (b) disregards comprehensive literacy intervention for struggling students, and (c) cannot erase the damaging legacy of Mayor Bloomberg and School Chancellor Klein's previous single-test promotion policy, which damagingly impacted a significant number of students.

Single-Test Promotion Policy in New York City

The single-test promotion policy that was originally adopted in the 2003–2004 school year did not address struggling readers academic issues, as it did not structurally ensure that students would get the academic help they needed. Equally disturbing, it merely penalized them for not having the academic skills mandated for their grade level. Recent budget cuts, furthermore, reduced the likelihood that the NYCDOE would provide a system-wide intervention program for struggling readers and for those who could not pass the standardized tests.

Despite an appeals process in the NYCDOE's previous single-test promotion policy—which required the review of student work and teacher recommendations for those students designated for retention, due to their test score—this policy of using high-stakes testing for determining promotion/retention decisions had detrimental implications for providing meaningful and empowering pedagogy. On the whole, it rendered essential indicators of academic growth virtually irrelevant, such as a student's attitude toward learning or his/her performance throughout the school year on class work, tests, and projects. As administrators often required educators in New York City (and elsewhere) to gear curriculum to material covered in the standardized state exam, the high-stakes test also served as a means for controlling instruction. Furthermore, since teachers were not (and still are not) even given the opportunity to see their students' responses to each question on the standardized tests, these assessments do not even provide teachers valuable information for helping their students improve their print literacy skills.

With the expansion of the single-test promotion policy to 8th graders, in the beginning of the 2008–2009 school year—albeit an initiative that had the potential of increasing the already growing population of overage middle school students—the NYCDOE included a necessary provision for students in special education—which, in fact, presently continues. However, to the detriment of scores of non-reading adolescents and other students, this provision was previously omitted. According to the policy enacted at the beginning of the 2008–2009 school year, Individuals with Disabilities Education Act (IDEA)-eligible students (those classified for special education) could have the possibility of being held to a different promotion standard than students in general education. As Advocates for Children of New York (2008a) specifies this revised policy, therefore, afforded all IDEA-eligible students the flexibility of having modified promotion criteria and taking alternate tests, if designated on the Individualized Education Program (IEP)—which is a legal document that delineates a specialized educational plan for each student identified for special education services. If an IDEA-eligible student's IEP team viewed participation in the standardized grade-level state exam for purposes of promotion as inappropriate, then this assessment would not determine advancement to the next grade.

Decisions on the appropriateness of the grade-level state assessment rested with the child's IEP team, and the child's parent(s)/guardian(s) had the final decision-making power. As is always the protocol with IDEA-eligible students, the IEP team automatically consisted of the student's parent(s)/guardian(s), special education teacher, one general education teacher, and school psychologist. It could also include school administrators, school counselor, school nurse, speech therapists, occupational therapist, or advocates chosen by the district and/or parent(s)/guardian(s). If appropriate, the student could also be part of the IEP team. On a yearly basis, the IEP team would decide the child's promotion standard and whether the student would take the standard grade-level assessment or an alternate assessment.

While the single-test promotion policy prior to the 2008–2009 school year subjected every student, including IDEA-eligible students, to high-stakes testing, it severely jeopardized non-reading adolescents. However, the revised policy enacted at the start of the 2008–2009 school year held promise for those non-reading adolescents who were already classified for special education, by giving them the possibility of more flexible promotion standards. Yet, even this reform for IDEA-eligible students presented numerous logistical uncertainties.

Although this revised provision in the promotion policy represented a positive policy shift for IDEA-eligible students, it remained to be seen if and how it would be followed through properly so that all non-reading adolescents in special education would be exempt from retention due to high-stakes testing. Advocates for Children of New York (2008c) describes the failure of the school system, at times, to meet the needs of special education students. According to Advocates for Children of New York, as a result of insufficient resources, lack of experience, and limited knowledge about special education services and students' rights, teachers and school officials sometimes do not adjust students' academic programs or provide mandated services. Therefore, for example, necessary changes to an IEP may not have occurred or the specifications on the IEP may not have been followed.

Such a circumstance could easily have translated into failing to change a special education identified non-reading adolescent's IEP to indicate modified promotion standards, or, in some cases, alternate testing as well, so that the student's promotion did not depend upon passing the standardized state grade-level exam. Furthermore, inadequacies on the school system's part to provide every special education child the support indicated on the IEP also could have led to the mistaken retention of a child. For example, inefficiencies could have caused a child whose IEP designated modified promotion standards or alternate testing, to, instead, be measured against standard promotion criteria and the standardized grade-level exam. In this latter case, however, the parents/guardians of the child would have been able to appeal or invoke due process rights.

Additionally, the 2008–2009 revised policy for IDEA-eligible students did not negate the psychological damage inflicted on those non-reading adolescents within special education who were subjected to the earlier retention policy. Furthermore, this testing modification for special education students did not account for the large population of non-reading adolescents who were not identified for special education, which included, for example, those who were within bilingual/English as a Second Language programs (to be discussed further) and those with undiagnosed learning differences. Therefore, had the single-test promotion policy continued the NYCDOE still would have subjected these two populations of non-reading adolescents to a promotion policy that penalized them for not having the academic skills mandated for their grade level without providing them a comprehensive intervention program for addressing their literacy needs.

It is still too early to tell, on the whole, the efficacy by which schools incorporated the reform provisions for IDEA-eligible students indicated in the 2008–2009 school year promotion policy. Yet, in light of the most recent policy shift, enacted in June 2009, which has moved away from the single-test promotion policy for all students, we may never know how well the school system accommodated, during the 2008–2009 school year, the specifications for special education students.

Detriments of Recent Single-Test Promotion Policy in New York City for Students

The single-test retention policy in New York City, enacted under Mayor Bloomberg and School Chancellor Klein, presented numerous reasons for alarm, as educational research reveals that retention significantly increases dropout rates and that over time it does not improve student achievement (Advocates for Children of New York, 2004; Haney et al., 2004). Additionally, the more times students are retained, the likelihood increases of their dropping out later in their school career (Roderick, 1995). To adopt a policy, therefore, that automatically determined whether students were retained according to one standardized test—as opposed to leaving such a serious decision to the administrators, teachers, and parents actually involved with the student's education—created a pernicious educational situation. The damaging legacy of the single-test promotion policy will be felt for years to come, particularly by those children who were retained one or more times during the policy's existence.

Rather than help students' achievement, the policy of relying on a single test—instead of using multiple measures to determine retention decisions—affects students detrimentally. Given the ample educational research indicating that retention policies heighten the probability that retained students will drop out, single-test retention policies, no doubt, served as a mechanism for "pushing out" non-reading adolescents, among other student populations. Although the policy change enacted at the beginning of the 2008–2009 school year allowed a larger percentage of non-reading adolescents to have alternative promotion criteria (i.e., those within special education with an IEP indicating modified promotion), even this policy did not go far enough. It continued to exclude those non-reading adolescents who were either not in special education or who were in special education but had not yet had their IEP changed in accordance with the new provision. Furthermore, as the highest retention rates are among economically disadvantaged, "racial"/ethnic minority, and inner-city youth, retention policies in fact heightened "racial"/ethnic and class inequities.

This systematic manufacturing of academic failure takes a major toll on students' well-being, particularly those who, despite grade retention, are still not taught print literacy skills according to their needs. Although curriculum that teaches students how to decode and encode print exists in the early elementary years of school, the mainstream educational system did not (and still does not) provide whole-scale provisions for teenagers who still require such instruction. This lack of support can cause many non-reading adolescents to feel that school does not give them the teachings that pertain to their lives, or circumstances, and, therefore, does not serve their academic, emotional, intellectual, and even, economic and social needs. Such policy clearly illustrates the workings of the push-out/dropout relationship between the school system and non-reading adolescents: rather than feel frustrated, bored, angered, and degraded by educational policy and curriculum that ignore these student's academic requirements and, thus, position them as "academic failures," many choose to drop out, or opt out, of school.

Past Single-Test Promotion Policy in New York City Informs the Present

An overview of New York City's promotional policies since the early 1980s reveals the dangers of the most recent high-stakes testing practices in New York City. Yet, Mayor Bloomberg and School Chancellor Klein ignored the lessons of the past.* From 1981 to 1991, New York City Board of Education followed a retention policy called the Promotional Gates program, which like Mayor Bloomberg and School Chancellor Klein's program retained students according to a high-stakes test. However, research data showed that this program, initially enacted under School Chancellor Frank J. Macchiarola, was ultimately creating higher dropout rates and did not improve the academic achievement of those students held back (Chaifetz & Kravitz, 2005). Learning from the failures of the Promotional Gates program and after great pressure from advocacy groups, in 1999, the then School Chancellor, Rudolph Crew, implemented a policy in which promotion was contingent upon whether a student met two of the following three criteria: if a student (a) scored between 2 and 4 on standardized state and city tests, (b) produced class work that was on grade level, and (c) attended school at least 90% of the time. After Crew's departure as the School Chancellor, his policy continued until Mayor Bloomberg and School Chancellor Klein, attempting to "stop social promotion procedures," implemented their version of a high-stakes single-testing promotion policy in the 2003–2004 school year. They did so despite evidence from the Gates Promotional program of the harmful effects of blanket retention procedures.

Punitive Policy versus Nurturing Initiatives

While the recent single-test grade promotion policy in New York City aimed to prevent social promotion, many policy questions still remained unanswered:

---

* In November 2010, as this book goes to publication New York City School Chancellor Joel Klein has announced his resignation. Mayor Michael Bloomberg has named Cathleen (Cathie) P. Black, the chairwoman of Hearst Magazines, as the new chancellor of New York City's public schools. Like Black's predecessors, Joel Klein and Harold Levy, her appointment requires a waiver from The State Education Commissioner. Mayor Bloomberg's decision is mired in controversy, as critics argue that Black does not have proper education credentials and lacks professional experience in the field of education. The choice of Cathie Black is a continuation of the Bloomberg administration's approach to pedagogy, which favors a business model at the expense of quality education.

- For how many consecutive years, did the NYCDOE intend to retain, in their respective grades, those students who could not pass the state assessment?

- What did the NYCDOE plan to do with the numerous non-reading adolescents who, before the enactment of the recent policy allowing special education students to have modified promotion standards if indicated on their IEP, were often repeatedly retained and were, thus, overage for their grade?

- For those non-reading adolescents who did not pass the ELA exam and were retained, either because they did not have an IEP indicating modified promotion standards or because they were not in special education, would the NYCDOE provide an intensive literacy program? Or, would students merely repeat the same classes and curriculum as the previous year with minimal literacy support throughout their school day?

- What systemic approach did the NYCDOE have in place to serve the print literacy and academic needs of the population of non-reading high school students who were promoted through the school system before the current administration's single-test promotion policy?

- What did the NYCDOE plan to do with students entering the New York City school system for the first time in upper-middle or high school who were classified as non-readers?

- In light of the NYCDOE's revised policy as of the beginning of the 2008–2009 school year enabling special education students to have modified testing indicated on their IEP, to what extent would this policy have been enacted effectively so that all non-reading adolescents in special education would benefit?

Ultimately, time revealed that during the single-test promotion era there was no systemic remediation plan for students who were retained. Students often repeated the same classes they had taken the previous year without a comprehensive approach for addressing the literacy difficulties of students who needed literacy intervention. The June 2009 promotion policy reform provides further clarification to some of the aforementioned questions.

With regard to overage middle school students, or students who were retained one or more times, the June 2009 promotion policy offered a solution to the previous policy, which had led to a large increase of this student population. As of August 2009, in every grade except 8th grade, if a child had been retained previously or was overage and did not meet the new promotion criteria at the end of the summer, then principals and community superintendents decided what was in the best interest of the student with regard to his/her promotion. However, for students in 8th grade, if they had been retained previously in grades 6–8 or they turned 16 years old by December 31, 2008 and, therefore, were overage, then these students automatically advanced to 9th grade, even if they did not meet the required criteria, as long as they attended summer school (New York City Department of Education, 2009a).

Surely, this practice for overage 8th graders is a version of social promotion, which the Bloomberg-Klein administration initially attempted to abolish. Furthermore, even within the June 2009 promotion reform, students who have either been socially promoted or have been retained and also need intensive literacy intervention still do not receive it—as was the case within the former promotion and literacy policies.

In general, for students in grades 3–8 the new promotion policy no longer relies on just the ELA and math standardized state tests as the sole criteria determining promotion for the previously targeted grades. Now, for promotion from grades 3rd, 5th, 7th, and 8th, when students do not achieve at or above Level 2 on the state ELA and math tests, principals may promote students if they, instead, demonstrate Level 2 performance in a promotion portfolio assessment. The promotion portfolios are specified exercises, delineated in a Department of Education manual, that test Level 2 proficiency for each grade.

For 8th grade, students must also pass ELA, math, science, and social studies—the core courses. This added requirement for 8th graders is new since the 2008–2009 school year. Promotion of students from 4th and 6th grade, similar to practices in the prior policy, incorporates multiple criteria for assessing students' ELA and math performance. Principals determine students' promotion in these grades based upon the tests as well as students' schoolwork, teacher observation, course grades, and attendance. However, there has been some discussion among the Bloomberg-Klein administration about changing promotion standards in 4th and 6th grade to reflect the same state test criteria as those currently in place for 3rd, 5th, 7th, and 8th grades (New York City Department of Education, 2009c).

While all students in grades 3, 5, and 7 who score a Level 1 on the state ELA and/or math test may be promoted on the basis of their promotion portfolio, 8th grade students have an added component to their appeal process. Since 8th graders are also expected to pass their core courses, in addition to the state tests or promotion portfolio, there is an option for them if they fail a core course. In this case, students may attend summer school so that they have the opportunity to receive a passing grade. All students who are not promoted in June may attend summer school. They have the possibility of promotion in August, if they score a Level 2 on both ELA and math exams. However, in the case of 8th graders who failed a core course, they may be promoted in August if they receive a passing grade in the core course—provided that they have also passed their state tests.

The June 2009 promotion policy maintained the stipulation for IDEA-eligible students introduced in the reform enacted at the beginning of the 2008–2009 school year. Therefore, this newer policy also enables IDEA-eligible students to have IEPs indicating that the child is held to modified promotion criteria. While the stakes are not as high as they were for these youth when the standardized ELA and math tests served as the sole criteria for promotion in specific grades, it is still essential that this provision for IDEA-eligible students be adequately provided so that promotion standards are in accordance with students' academic needs.

With the June 2009 policy, promotion criteria for English Language Learners depends on the amount of years that students have been enrolled. For ELLs who have been enrolled in the school system for less than 2 years, they are exempt from promotion criteria in grades 3–7. However, in 8th grade they must pass the core courses for promotion. For ELL students who have been enrolled in the school system for 2–3 years, grades 3–7 criteria differ from that of the 8th grade. If this group of ELLs is in grades 3–7, promotion is determined through a comprehensive evaluation of their performance, which includes class work, test results, and attendance. If this group of ELLs is in 8th grade, however, in order to be promoted they must: pass core courses, demonstrate gains in either the state ELA assessment or New York State English as a Second Language Achievement Test (NYSESLAT), and achieve a Level 2 or higher on the state math test (New York City Department of Education, 2009b).

After enrollment in the school system for 4 years, ELLs face severe measures. ELL students in grades 3–7 who have been enrolled for 4 years or more are held to standard promotion criteria—unless they have an approved extension of services. In 8th grade, promotion of these ELL students in the general education population is based on standard promotion criteria only.

While time will reveal the full effects of this most recent promotion policy, it still falls short of addressing non-reading adolescents', and other struggling readers', academic, social, and emotional needs. Furthermore, even with the move away from the single-test promotion criteria for all students and potential for modified promotion standards for students identified for special education, the promotion policy does not ensure that struggling readers will receive the literacy teachings they require. Without a comprehensive literacy intervention throughout the school system at each grade level, struggling readers who are retained under the new plan do not have a structural means for attaining the literacy skills they require for school success. This inadequacy also applies to the contingent of overage 8th graders who were socially promoted in August 2009.

Additionally, within even the new promotion policy, numerous students will still experience grade retention, which can result in school dropout—given the relationship between grade retention and dropping out. Some of these students, most likely, will include a disproportionate number of economically disadvantaged as well as ELL youth. It could possibly include special education classified students whose IEPs were, in error, not changed to indicate modified promotion standards. Lastly, and of great importance, the promotion policy implemented as of June 2009 does not eradicate the harm of the recent single-test promotion policy.

The legacy of New York City's single-test high-stakes testing policy under Mayor Bloomberg and School Chancellor Klein has produced a mass population of students who are overage for their grade. Additionally, the policy engendered a psychologically damaging educative process for students who struggle with reading. To avoid both retention and social promotion policies, which both fail to address the literacy support that striving readers require, educational policymakers, as discussed above, must create literacy programs as an integral part of the school infrastructure within elementary, middle, and high schools to address students' varying print literacy needs.

Since June 2009, while students in the targeted grades are no longer held to the ELA and math assessment as the sole criteria for promotion to the next grade, there is still no comprehensive basic-literacy program for adolescents who read and write in English within an early elementary grade level range. Regardless of the promotion policy that is in use at a given time, non-reading adolescents, and other students who struggle with reading, need literacy intervention programs that are built into the school structure at every grade level. Policymakers, furthermore, must provide separate literacy-centered schools at the middle and high school levels to provide intensive and meaningful literacy development for adolescents whose literacy abilities fall within early elementary grade level equivalents. (An empowering critical literacy curriculum for these youth will be explored in chapters five and six.)

Rather than prioritizing these literacy programs and schools, however, in recent years, policymakers have allocated increasingly more money for building and maintaining detention centers. With students identified for special education representing close to 50% of students in New York City juvenile detention center schools (Correctional Association of New York, 2004b)—many of whom read below a 3rd grade level equivalent—it seems that, tragically, juvenile detention centers have become the contemporary solution for warehousing those students who did not pass high-stakes criteria.

Far from advocating social promotion over a retention policy and barring the necessary endeavor of a complete restructuring of how education is done to our students in this country (a topic on which I will devote extensive focus later in this chapter and in chapter four), the NYCDOE must adopt a well-funded, systemic literacy intervention initiative for students of all ages throughout the school system. Such a literacy program would emphasize early childhood reading readiness; and, it would provide child-centered literacy intervention programs within each school at all grade levels comprised of highly trained print literacy educators. The literacy curriculum employed would address the academic, emotional, and intellectual needs of students of all ages and stages in literacy development who struggle with print. Literacy teachers would provide extra assistance to those students who need more time to develop their decoding, encoding, and comprehension abilities to perform on the print literacy level that the school system has designated for each grade. All content area teachers throughout the school system would also be trained in print literacy instruction to support students within each content area class.

As part of this literacy initiative, non-reading adolescents' parents/guardians would have the choice of sending their child to specialized literacy schools designed specifically for these students. In these literacy intervention schools, educators trained in emergent print literacy teachings for adolescents would provide empowering instruction (a concept that I will detail extensively in future chapters) tailored to each student's particular literacy needs and pace. Furthermore, parents/guardians of adolescents within these literacy intervention schools would have the option of applying for a waiver so that their child, regardless of whether they are in special education or not, would be exempt from taking the grade-level standardized state ELA and math assessment. Instead, these youth would have the possibility of taking alternative assessments that are commensurate with their performance level, rather than grade level.

While there currently is no comprehensive, systemic pedagogical plan within the NYCDOE for adolescents who still require teachings to decode and encode print, some New York City public schools—particularly those that service students who are detained in New York City juvenile detention centers—have tried to support these youth. These schools have taken the initiative through the past years to provide educational programs that have a strong emphasis on remedial print literacy development for non-reading adolescents. Although the efforts of these schools in delivering print literacy instruction tailored to non-reading adolescents' individual literacy levels, by all means, has been laudable, it is unjust that, in general, non-reading adolescents do not have such comprehensive instruction throughout mainstream schools, but rather must be detained in order to receive it.

Furthermore, despite instruction that caters to the academic needs of incarcerated non-reading adolescents at the school-level in some New York City juvenile detention centers, these schools have had to contend with dictates of the larger school structure that obstruct meaningful pedagogy. For example, since teachers must give letter or number grades for students' class assignments, tests, and report cards according to designated performance expectations for each specific grade level, this school policy jeopardizes non-reading adolescents. Within this structure, even though a 7th grader who reads below a 3rd grade level may give a 100% effort, in relation to his/her abilities, on all class work in a content area subject when provided accommodations, very often the teacher cannot award the student with as high a grade as a "90" or an "A," since the student's low literacy level is not consistent with the arbitrarily preset 7th grade standards. Additionally, as mandates at the city, state, and federal level impose a "one-size-fits-all" approach within the U.S. education system—evidenced in the state and city standards for each grade level, mandated "scientifically proven" literacy instructional measures, and designated grade-level standardized exams—it hinders the potential for a truly empowering and affirming literacy pedagogy for these youth (to be detailed in chapters four, five, and six).

Special Education and English Language Learner Policies: Implications for Non-reading Adolescents amidst the High-Stakes Atmosphere

Policy initiatives within the high-stakes testing climate targeting special education and English as a Second Language (ESL)/bilingual programs have presented increasingly grave consequences for non-reading adolescents—the majority of whom are identified for special education and/or linguistic minorities. Focusing on New York City, I will first delve into harmful ramifications of policies that have affected students in special education and then discuss those that have impacted linguistic minority students. However, any discussion of special education encompasses numerous linguistic minority students, since English Language Learners are twice as likely as other children to be identified for special education (Least Restrictive Environment Coalition, 2001), given the biases in special education referral and assessment procedures delineated in chapter two.

Rhetoric of Equality in Special Education Policy Shrouds Structural Inequity

A closer analysis of the Individuals with Disabilities Education Act (IDEA)—the federal policy, touched upon earlier in chapter two, that profoundly impacts curriculum and instruction for all students placed in special education—helps historically situate current federal requirements that subject the majority of IDEA-eligible students to high-stakes testing. Although rooted within a positivistic framework itself, which views variation in students' learning styles from a deficit model, IDEA, known before 1990 as the Education of the Handicapped Act (EHA), aims to meet the special educational needs of students with "disabilities" and provide them with related services—such as speech, counseling, physical therapy, and occupational therapy. The EHA of 1975, also referred to as Public Law 94-142 (P.L. 94-142), was one of the most important laws shaping the present-day IDEA and its accompanying federal funding for special education. P.L. 94-142 mandated: a "free appropriate public education" (FAPE) for all students with disabilities; "Individualized Education Programs" (IEPs); placement within the "Least Restrictive Environment" (LRE); and due process.

Prior to P.L. 94-142, although the Elementary and Secondary Education Act drafted special education legislation beginning in 1965, IDEA figures reveal that more than half the students with disabilities in the U.S. were not receiving appropriate educational services. During this time, the public schools excluded a million children with disabilities from the system (National Institute for Literacy, 2002a). School officials often excluded these children with disabilities claiming that they were different or more difficult to educate due to their disabilities.

The passage of P.L. 94-142 marked the attempt to prevent any forms of exclusion of children with disabilities from a public education. This Act was later amended in 1983, 1986, 1990, 1992, 1997, and, again, in 2004. Each separate amendment expanded and improved services to children with "disabilities." Most notably, however, a crucial component of the 1997 reauthorization of IDEA ensured access to general education curriculum so that special education students retained the possibility of graduating with a regular Regents Diploma. Therefore, in light of the 1997 IDEA provisions, since NCLB's authorization in 2001, it has required IDEA-eligible students—except for 1% identified as severely cognitively impaired—to take the same high-stakes state assessment based on grade-level curriculum that general education students take. Therefore, under the guise of a beneficial initiative to include IDEA-eligible youth by providing them access to the same general curriculum demanded of all other students, students in special education, regardless of their textual literacy level, have been subjected to the same high-stakes grade-level standardized exams as the general education population. Such a blanket directive, however, engenders systemic academic failure for an already vulnerable group of students, some of whom are non-reading adolescents. New York City's recent single-test promotion policy prior to the changes in the 2008–2009 school year provides a direct example of the harm that this initiative has presented for IDEA-eligible students; these students faced increased grade retention amidst the high-stakes use of the ELA and math state exams.

Absolutely, within the draconian structure of the school system, those IDEA-eligible students with even the slightest possibility of passing the grade-level state assessments must have the opportunity to take the tests, since these are a requirement for earning a regular diploma. However, for many IDEA-eligible students, particularly non-reading adolescents, the tests represent just another psychologically harmful educational practice that undermines their self-confidence and manufactures their academic failure. As such, for this latter group of youth, taking the test does not provide any true opportunity; instead, it allows the blame to be placed on the students rather than the actuality of a school system that fails to support them. Furthermore, with the stated goal of treating all students equally, the application of NCLB's directive in fact has translated into: subjecting every student, including the majority of IDEA-eligible students, to a "banking" education maintained through high-stakes culturally and class-biased assessments. As such, federal policy ensures that all students encounter assessment procedures that inhibit instruction tailored to each child's specific academic needs; do not take into account socio-cultural dimensions involved in educating students from diverse cultural, socio-economic, and linguistic backgrounds; and, ultimately, serve as social and ideological control apparatuses.

The Equal Opportunity Argument

In its most positive light, the policy of mandating high-stakes testing for all students can be seen as an attempt to guarantee equal educational rights to all student populations. Many policymakers, educators, and concerned citizens, regardless of whether they view the tests as inherently flawed or not, argue that since these high-stakes assessments grant access to greater educational privileges, then all students must at least have the equal opportunity to participate in them. At its best, this stance aims to prevent ways in which discrimination based upon perceived developmental, cognitive, physical, behavioral, or sensory inability of particular students, at times, translates into self-fulfilling expectations of low achievement for these students. In such cases, a culture of limitation can arise in which administrators, educators, and sometimes the students, themselves doubt the likelihood of academic achievement for these youth thought to be at a disadvantage. It, subsequently, can block them from educational privileges afforded to student populations perceived to be more academically capable.

Even well intentioned, progressive educators can fuel this folly and deny these students, viewed as less academically inclined, access to educational practices in an attempt to protect them from failure. As such, this culture of low expectation can prevent students perceived as disadvantaged from receiving equal distribution of resources and opportunity, as the belief system itself becomes a self-limiting and self-fulfilling hindrance to their academic success. Therefore, presuming good intentions of NCLB's requirement that all IDEA-eligible students take the high-stakes state tests (barring 1% classified as severely cognitively impaired), such a policy can be seen as a mechanism for ensuring that perceptions of academic inadequacy do not prevent this student population from having all the rights and opportunities afforded to students in the general education population.

Avoiding the Tyranny of Systemic Humiliation and Failure

The above stated stance represents a commendable goal of providing all students equal opportunity. However, despite rhetoric of equality, prejudicial ideologies, in fact, underscore policy regarding these testing procedures and their accompanying high stakes. As the dominant class' values inform culturally specific knowledge included in the tests, the very structure of the tests, themselves, systematically exclude a large percentage of IDEA-eligible students across economic and "racial"/ethnic boundaries. Given the disproportionately high representation of low-income, historically discriminated "racial"/ ethnic and linguistic minority students in special education, a policy of high-stakes testing intrinsically translates into unequal outcomes for numerous IDEA-eligible students from these marginalized backgrounds.

Furthermore, for numerous students in special education, particularly non-reading adolescents, high-stakes, grade-level standardized tests are wholly inappropriate for assessing both students' academic progress and their schools' instructional efficacy, even when tests are taken with accommodations (such as extended time and testing in a small group or individually). Nevertheless, the NCLB accountability framework requires, for example, 7th and 8th grade students who read print on a 2nd grade level equivalent to take a grade-level ELA assessment.

Making matters worse, failure to pass in places such as New York City, during the recent single-test promotion policy period, led to retaining students, some times repeatedly, and/or penalizing their school. Prior to the 2008–2009 school year, this New York City school initiative especially impacted special education students and English Language Learners. In the case of adolescent age students whose textual literacy level fell below designated 3rd grade limits, high-stakes testing and their ensuing use in promotion decisions were unrealistic, cruel practices and, as research on retention shows, ineffective in the long run.

Although a non-reading adolescent may not attain the predetermined literacy criteria for grade level performance, s/he may personally learn and grow tremendously throughout each school year. The student may very well progress toward the dominant culture's expectations, reinforced in high-stakes tests, of developmentally appropriate print literacy abilities for his/her specific grade; yet, the child may not reach this textual literacy level by the time s/he is, for instance, 16 years old. During the recent single-test promotion era in New York City, such a student, therefore, all too often, was repeatedly retained and chose to leave school at the age of 16, rather than partake in a humiliating process that produced his/her academic failure.

Such a circumstance reveals that amidst the educational environment's whole-scale embrace of high-stakes standardized testing, many special education identified students, particularly non-reading adolescents, required alternative measures of student progress that assessed individual student achievement according to the child's specific academic needs, level, and interests. Yet, unfortunately, Mayor Bloomberg and School Chancellor Klein's administration did not implement such a humane assessment approach for these youth prior to the 2008–2009 school year. The NYCDOE is only now making amends for their previous detrimental assessment design by enabling IDEA-eligible students to be held to modified promotion criteria, if indicated in their IEP, as well as NYCDOE's recent move away from a single-test promotion policy for all students. However, it does not reverse the harm that has been done to scores of IDEA-eligible students. It cannot erase the damaging educational and emotional affects for the past several years on numerous special education students who were merely penalized through high-stakes testing for their lower performance level without systematically receiving the educational support they required.

As of 2005, statistics on students in New York City's District 75—the centrally operated, all-special education district servicing approximately 22,000 moderate to severely challenged students—indicated that IDEA-eligible students were failing the grade-level state tests at rates of over 60% (Council of the City of New York, 2005). (Statistics are not available on pass/fail rates of IDEA-eligible students in their regular zoned schools, outside of District 75.) Some policymakers and educational analysts have used these statistics to suggest that District 75 schools have failed to instruct students adequately so that they may achieve designated standards. Instead, I would argue that these figures indicate that such tests have been inappropriate measures for evaluating special education identified students (as well as other student populations) and their schools. As such, these tests, therefore, have been symptomatic of the school system's manufacturing failure for these youth and their schools.

Under the previous single-test promotion policy in New York City, only a small percentage of students in District 75, who were identified as having severe cognitive disabilities, could take the New York State Alternate Assessment (NYSAA), which is based on alternate achievement standards. While these students had an IEP specifying participation in alternate state assessments, the majority of non-reading adolescents within their regular-zoned schools and within detention center schools were not afforded this policy alternative. Thus, most non-reading adolescents within zoned schools and alternate school sites, such as detention center schools, as detailed previously in this chapter, had to sit through grade-level, high-stakes tests although they could not even read. Considering the negative impact failing these tests has on non-reading adolescents' morale, self-esteem, and attrition rate, amidst the inhumane, high-stakes testing fervor, these youth needed an alternative. Thus, the possibility, for example, for 7th and 8th graders who read print below a 3rd grade level and attended their regular zoned schools to have had the option of taking alternative state assessments, as well as of having modified promotion standards, would not have represented an instance of coddling them. Nor, would it have minimized equal opportunity granted to other students. On the contrary, it would have signified a more just educational practice for these youth.

In light of the recent policy change in New York City, for instance, which permits special education students to have modified promotion standards designated on their IEPs, it is the responsibility of educators and school officials to inform parents of this option so that all non-reading adolescents in special education may be exempt from standard promotion, if it is wholly unrealistic for the child. Furthermore, even the new promotion policy reform does not address structural inequities of a school system and society that exclude those who do not conform to the ruling elite's cultural and class bound values, norms, and notions with respect to cognitive and physical ability.

Language Policies Obstruct Linguistic Minorities' Academic Achievement

Contemporary language policies in New York City reveal an ideology of exclusion that underscores discourse pertaining to bilingual education, thereby creating "academic failure" for many linguistic minority students—particularly those from subordinated ethnic backgrounds. An overview of contemporary policy measures impacting linguistic minority students in New York City highlights how these inequitable language policies undermine these students' achievement. Such policies play a substantial part in: the creation of a population of linguistic minority adolescents, many of whom are U.S.-born, with print literacy abilities that fall below 3rd grade levels. These initiatives, furthermore, contribute to low graduation rates among linguistic minorities—evidenced, for example, as graduation rates for Latino students in New York City are as low as 38% (Orfield, Losen, Wald, & Swanson, 2004).

Generating Academic Failure for Recently Arrived Linguistic Minority Students

NCLB's requirement of annual assessments of all students who are English Language Learners (ELLs), for the purposes of measuring English language proficiency and school and district accountability, has perniciously impacted ELLs; however, recent changes in this policy have harmed this student population all the more. Focusing on New York City highlights this issue. From 2003 until the 2006–2007 school year, the U.S. Department of Education (USDOE) authorized the New York State Education Department's (NYSED's) use of the New York State English as a Second Language Achievement Test (NYSESLAT) in place of the English Language Arts (ELA) test for evaluating those ELL students who had attended school in the U.S. for less than 3 consecutive years. Such policy, therefore, allowed this population of ELL students to take the NYSESLAT instead of the grades 4 and 8, and beginning in 2005–2006, the 3rd through 8th grade state ELA assessment. After the 3 years, the New York State Education Department allowed ELL students, prior to 2007, to apply for a waiver giving them 2 more years before they had to take the ELA exam.

In August 2006, however, the USDOE reversed their position and declared that to comply with Title I accountability requirements the New York State Education Department could no longer use the NYESLAT as a substitute for the ELA. As a result of this federal directive, the new policy in New York State requires that, as of January 2007, once an ELL student has been in the U.S. school system for as short a time as 1 year, in addition to the NYESLAT, they must take the same 3rd–8th grade ELA assessments as the rest of the student population. Such language policy presents heightened barriers to subordinated linguistic minorities' academic success, given the sociolinguistic component surrounding their pedagogical experience. Subordinated linguistic minorities—many of whom are non-white and/or low-income—occupy social positions outside of the dominant cultural sphere. Enforcing the ELA assessments so early in their U.S. school career ensures their prompt exposure to academic discourse that disregards their culture, knowledge, and experiences and reinforces the culture of the status quo—a dynamic that often engenders "academic failure" (Macedo & Bartolomé, 1999; Villanueva, 1993).

Within a high-stakes educational setting, requiring newly arrived ELL students to take the ELA assessments, has the potential to increase the population of linguistic minorities labeled as academic failures and inappropriately raise the number of schools in need of improvement. Additionally, this policy particularly jeopardizes those linguistic minority students who struggle, even in their first language, with print literacy. By not allowing them the pace they need to acquire textuality, but rather rushing them to achieve levels that are unrealistic for their academic needs and punishing them when they have not performed within parameters of the unjust time line provided, this language policy denies these students meaningful and nurturing pedagogy. Furthermore, it can possibly create an antagonistic relationship between the student and school, wherein the child disengages from his/her institutionalized educational process.

Even within the original policy, allowing ELL students to apply for a waiver in order to continue to take the NYSESLAT in lieu of the ELA generally did not benefit those parents with limited resources, as they were less likely to receive information about this possibility. Additionally, while even the maximum of 5 years for those who were granted a waiver in the previous policy does not necessarily enable an ELL student enough time to reach academic proficiency in English according to his/her grade level, 1 year absolutely does not provide enough time for a student to attain academic proficiency in English to pass the ELA test.

As Cummins's (1991) research informs, it takes an ELL student 1–3 years for conversational proficiency in English but 5–7 years to attain academic English proficiency. Therefore, the federal government's requirement that ELL students take the ELA test after 1 year (or even after 3 years, as required in the previous policy) has hindered academic success for these youth. I contend that this policy violates the landmark 1974 U.S. Supreme Court's *Lau vs. Nichols* decision, which, although it did not prescribe particular remedies or pedagogical strategies, guaranteed the rights of linguistic minorities.

Amidst New York City's recent single-test promotion policy, which centered on the ELA and math assessments, this federal mandate in which ELL students had to take the ELA after 1 year represented a grave educational reality for these students. The city held ELL students to the standard single-test promotion policy, which centered on passing the ELA and math tests, after they had been enrolled in the school system for as short a period of time as 2 years. Tragically, for ELL students the very nature of this promotion policy identified many of them as "academic failures," despite the fact that many may have been able to read and write at or above grade level in their first language.

According to Cummins's research indicating the amount of time it takes for ELLs to reach academic English proficiency, mandating that they pass the ELA assessment for promotion after only 2 years (even though ELLs already took the NYSESLAT every year to measure their English skills) intrinsically resulted in higher numbers of ELL students who did not pass the ELA exam. Subsequently, such an outcome meant higher retention rates because of New York City's high-stakes testing promotion criteria. Specific statistics are not available on the grade retention rates of ELL students after the enactment of the federally mandated ELA policy during the single-test promotion policy period. However, in light of Cummins's research and the correlation between grade retention and dropping out, it is likely that this testing procedure contributed to a higher push-out/drop-out rate among ELL students.

Additionally, the decline in the scores of ELL students, resulting from the new ELA policy, has had the potential of preventing schools that service ELLs from meeting performance standards required through the NCLB accountability system (to be discussed further) and, therefore, more penalties. Recent language policies in New York City, thus, highlight the way in which an ideology of exclusion has continued to inform pedagogical decisions made on the federal, state, and local level pertaining to linguistic minority students. Within this educational environment, a population of non-reading adolescents from subordinated linguistic minority backgrounds has emerged as a by-product of historically and politically rooted structural inequities.

Certainly, the new promotion policy, as of June 2009, which now holds ELL students to standard promotion criteria after 4 years and additionally does not rely solely on the standardized ELA and math tests, is a move in a more positive direction. However, the overall impact it has on linguistic minority students remains to be seen. Unfortunately, the 4 years now allotted to ELL students before encountering standard promotion standards still does not give them the 5–7 years that Cummins suggests is needed for academic English proficiency. Furthermore, the current promotion policy will likely jeopardize scores of 8th grade ELL students as it mandates that they pass all their core courses after being enrolled in the school system for as little as 2 years. This aspect of the promotion policy for 8th graders is all the more problematic in light of the reduction of bilingual programs that provide students instruction in their home language.

Prioritization of ESL over Bilingual Education and 3-Year Exit Goal

Other language policy has also fostered the miseducation of linguistic minorities in New York City, contributing to the production of a population of non-reading adolescents—predominantly from subordinated ethnic backgrounds and some of whom were born in the U.S. Since 2001, the New York City Department of Education has prioritized an "Americanization" bilingual policy, as it has aimed to teach linguistic minority students English without maintaining their first language. Prior to 2001, students who spoke a language other than English at home and who scored at or below the 40th percentile on the Language Assessment Battery-Revised (LAB-R) exam were automatically placed in bilingual programs unless their parents/guardian opted out in preference of an ESL program. These bilingual programs used the students' home language for instruction and many of them, referred to as maintenance bilingual programs, focused on teaching English and preserving the child's home language.

However, on February 27, 2001, the New York City Board of Education enacted a dramatic change in its bilingual education programs, which became effective in June of 2001. Under the then School Chancellor Harold Levy, this new policy resolution, among other measures, prioritized investment in ESL immersion classes over bilingual education and, in compliance with NCLB, set a goal of 3 years for students to exit English immersion and bilingual programs unless parents consented to their child continuing beyond 3 years. This initiative impacted the approximately 160,000 English Language Learners of the 1.1 million students in the New York City public schools at the time (Advocates for Children of New York, 2001b).

This policy persists to this day and is flawed on several levels. Setting a goal for students to exit English immersion and bilingual programs after 3 years produces unnecessary pressure and stress for the child. Since both bilingual special education classified students and those ELL students who enter the New York City school system during their middle school years have the most difficulty in exiting bilingual/ESL programs within 3 years, these groups become even more susceptible to the school system's production of "academic failure" (Advocates for children of New York, 2001b). Although this language initiative has permitted students to stay beyond 3 years in ESL or in the few bilingual programs still in existence with parental consent, those parents/guardians with limited resources, as in the case with the standardized testing waiver, often do not receive information about this option and, therefore, their child does not benefit from it.

By prioritizing ESL programs, which do not maintain students' first language, the contemporary language policy dismisses student's cultural identity. Moreover, such language policies, yet again, ignore vital research on second language acquisition. As originally presented in chapter two, Cummins's (1991) research indicates that the use of linguistic minorities' first language, among other attributes, can assist in transfer of knowledge, bridging the home–school gap, and building on the students' language base to promote fluid literacy development and academic success. Yet, this recent initiative subverts such a process. As in the case of requiring English Language Learners to take state ELA and math assessments after only 1 year and holding them to the previous promotion policy after only 2 years (and now after 4 years), this 3-year exit plan again ignores Cummins's findings, previously mentioned. The 3-year exit plan, therefore, does not take into account that, as Cummins's research shows, it takes English Language Learners 1–3 years to acquire conversational language, yet 5–7 years—and longer for those youth without literacy in their first language—to acquire academic English language proficiency.

Prior to NYCDOE's 2001 mandate that ELLs exit from bilingual or ESL programs to mainstream English classes within 3 years, The Mayor's Task Force on Bilingual Education (2000) reported that half of the ELL population in New York City had not exited from these programs within 3 years. Some policymakers at the time (as in the case with present-day statistics on IDEA-eligible students' testing performance) used this statistic to assert the ineffectiveness of bilingual programs. I maintain, however, that these figures more specifically indicate the absurdity of expecting children to learn academic English required to participate fully in English content classes within 3 years—especially given Cummins's (1991) empirical research, the type of research which NCLB supporters hold so dear. Policy initiatives must incorporate sound research showing that it takes 5–7 years for children to acquire academic proficiency in a second language.

Undoubtedly, the political controversy surrounding bilingual education has sabotaged bilingual education programs since their genesis. As this agenda of politics has historically prevented sufficient funding for bilingual programs (predominantly those that maintained the student's first language), some linguistic minority students in New York City who have spent their entire lives in the U.S. school system reach adolescence with English print literacy levels that fall within early elementary grade limits. Although the educational system has historically miseducated linguistic minorities, at least prior to the initiative of 2001, the public school system in New York City gave these students more opportunities, albeit poorly financed, to receive schooling that maintained their first language, while it taught the English acquisition essential for, among other benefits, economic survival in the U.S. By emphasizing ESL programs, the New York City Department of Education's current policy disregards linguistic minorities first language and, subsequently, their cultural identity; it, furthermore, as Cummins's research highlights, obstructs print literacy development and, ultimately, leads to inequitable outcomes for linguistic minorities.

Negative Consequences of NCLB's Accountability System for Non-reading Adolescents

As NCLB holds schools and districts accountable for all students' performance on standardized tests, non-reading adolescents and other low-achieving students (according to the school system's standards) face additional perils. A closer look at NCLB's accountability system uncovers further detriments of contemporary high-stakes testing policies for these students. Within the current accountability framework, NCLB requires states to use their 3rd–8th grade standardized reading and math assessments to evaluate whether schools and districts receiving Title I funding are making "Adequate Yearly Progress" (AYP) toward NCLB's goal of bringing 100% of students within the U.S. school system to academic proficiency by the end of the 2013–2014 school year. While the reading and math assessments are the main indicator for whether schools and districts are achieving AYP, NCLB also requires graduation rates and one additional indicator for elementary schools, which each state determines, as part of the AYP requisites. If a school (or district) fails to meet their AYP targets of their total student population and, in particular, specified demographic subgroups—which includes economically disadvantaged students, English Language Learners, students with disabilities, and racial and ethnic minorities—for 2 consecutive years, then the school is classified as needing improvement and must offer students the choice of transferring to another public school. As the number of consecutive years that a school does not make AYP continues, the penalties increase in severity—culminating with school restructuring after 5 years of failure to meet AYP goals.

However, as Orfield et al. (2004) report, in trying to meet the federal mandate of showing "Adequate Yearly Progress" and, therefore, avoid test-driven accountability sanctions, many schools "push out" those youth that the school system defines as "low-achieving" students in order to maintain higher test scores and graduation rates. Gotbaum (2002) further reports that schools in New York City discharge numerous "low-achieving" students and do not count them as dropouts. According to Gotbaum, thirty-one high schools discharged more students than they graduated. She furthermore informs that these schools discharged more than triple the number of those students documented as dropouts and misrepresented the schools' dropout rates by counting these students as transfers to GED programs.

While policymakers' purportedly designed NCLB's AYP framework so as to encourage progress among students within the specific subgroups—who disproportionately have underperformed, due to institutionalized historical discrimination—this accountability system, in fact, presents dire ramifications for many youth within these groups. This pattern of pushing out "low-achieving" students to make AYP has grave implications for non-reading adolescents. Among other tragedies, this "push-out" dynamic, to prevent penalties under NCLB, has the potential, given the relationship between leaving school and spending time in prison, to increase the already high representation of non-reading adolescents in juvenile detention centers.

Countering NCLB's Emphasis on High-Stakes Standardized Tests: The Call for Organic Assessments

NCLB's requirement that schools hold non-reading adolescents to grade-level standards and include them in the accountability system for purposes of "Adequate Yearly Progress," thus, exacerbates the inequitable opportunity afforded to this student population. The mandating of particular standards and curricula prevents teachers of non-reading adolescents, and other student populations, from teaching at each student's appropriate pace. Rather than a barrage of inappropriate testing, these youth—many of whom, as previously stated, are in special education programs and/or are English Language Learners—need maximum time devoted to teaching and learning. Daily and weekly teacher-made assessments can be used to monitor students' progress and adapt lesson plans accordingly in ways that promote students' continued academic achievement, rather than failure. High-stakes standardized test do not provide such crucial information to teachers and, even worse, actually jeopardize these youth.

Instead of standardized tests in which teachers rarely, if ever, see their students' performance on the tests, teachers benefit from analyzing students' understanding of strategies and content pertaining to daily teachings. Organic and continual assessment that emerges from daily lessons provides teachers crucial information about each student's development and is thus more useful for delivering instruction that specifically caters to students' strengths and weaknesses. Useful and humane assessments serve as a means for gaining information for improving instruction to address students' specific needs. However, this use of assessments contrasts their current use as both a means for penalizing students, and even educators, as well as a mechanism for keeping information taught to students within preset boundaries.

Testing is a type of evaluation that must be employed in conjunction with other assessment measures such as classroom observations, anecdotal reports, and analysis of course work. Using one single standardized test for decisions that have long-term consequences, jeopardizes a child's well-being, and represents irresponsible educational policy. High-stakes standardized tests do not consider social, economic, political, and emotional factors that impact students' educational lives. For example, living in a shelter or violence at home, in school, or in the streets may impact students' performance on a high-stakes test and school in general. What if, for instance, on the day of taking a high-stakes exam, a child felt sick, tired, hungry, or recently experienced a traumatic event in his/her life? Such circumstances could seriously interfere with the child's desire and capacity to focus on this high-stakes standardized assessment. (I will return to this topic extensively in chapters four, five, and six.)

Humane pedagogy supports students by recognizing the socio-economic, political, historical, cultural, and personal dynamics shaping their pedagogical lives. It, furthermore, incorporates students' strengths and talents, facilitating every child's academic achievement. Within such a paradigm, schools and teachers deliver teachings in a context of high expectations and quality, yet they have the freedom to create realistic standards and requirements based on each student's individual level and specific pace. This approach to rigorous and authentic standards is in stark contrast to some blanket standard that policymakers and educational researchers determine without knowledge of particular socio-educational, academic, and psychological contexts surrounding students. Since pedagogy is a mode of being, teachers must have freedom to modify policy mandates to fit their particular classroom environment. In this way, within a context of high expectations, educators can tailor instruction to the needs of a school's student population and, more specifically, each individual child.

Since non-reading adolescents do not have the textual literacy, as of yet, to reach the designated standards for the grade level in which they are placed, then what is the logic guiding NCLB, which mandates that these youth take grade-level standardized exams? Similarly, what is the logic that has guided local school districts' subsequent use of these assessments for high-stakes testing? I maintain that this protocol can only serve the purpose of creating a hostile educational environment for these non-reading adolescents so that they choose to leave school. In this way, rather than embracing the reality that the school system did not provide nurturing and adequate instruction for these youth, policymakers can erroneously claim that the children did not want to learn. This mechanism of exclusion, which ultimately "pushes out" many of these youth (among other marginalized student populations), hardly fulfills the stated national educational goal in which "no child is left behind."

Here, we profoundly see the way in which high-stakes tests, in line with Foucault's (1980) analysis of power and knowledge, operate as one of the many hegemonic apparatuses that dominant culture uses to regulate and dominate. A more humane approach for measuring how well students are learning the outcomes identified in states' curriculum framework, although still within a positivistic vision that inherently confines boundaries of thought and knowledge, would be (as currently done in the NAEP assessments) to take selective sampling across student populations and content areas on a systematic basis, but not every year. In this way, fewer students take the test and the tests do not have a high-stakes impact. While still assigning particular skill ability to a student's particular age and restricting knowledge to a specific curriculum and skill set, which prevent empowering educational opportunities, such assessment measures would reduce the harm currently inflicted on our youth, given the intrinsic dehumanizing design of the school system.

Furthermore, if federal policy continues to force educators to operate within the positivistic confines of NCLB's standardized evaluation mandates, further amendments must free non-reading adolescents—whether or not they are identified for special education or are in ESL/bilingual programs—from the same testing standards as general education students. At the least, all non-reading adolescents must have the possibility of taking alternate forms of assessment without any imposed time limit that are specifically adapted to each child's individual level. Education policymakers must also implement intensive literacy intervention programs in every grade level within all schools as part of the infrastructure, as well as create specifically designated literacy schools for non-reading adolescents to address their academic requirements.

Policy Recommendations for Supporting Non-reading Adolescents amidst the Restrictive Paradigm Shaping the Current Educational Structure

This section presents various ways in which the school system can improve non-reading adolescents' print literacy development within the confines of the contemporary school structure. The chapters that follow, however, envision a transformation of the existing educational system by describing an empowering paradigm and curriculum that incorporates multifaceted components of education and that facilitates non-reading adolescents' textual as well as contextual literacy development. This latter analysis will furthermore delve deeper into ways in which the flawed assumptions guiding NCLB and the emphasis on high-stakes standardized exams do not capture complex dynamics involved in learning, knowing, and teaching.

As described previously in this chapter, only a few schools in New York City with a population of non-reading adolescents, for example, some schools within detention centers, take it upon themselves to teach non-reading adolescents print literacy at students' required level and speed. Admirably, such schools even offer those non-reading adolescents without special education classification the same support as those who are identified for special education.

These schools often create classes with small groups of non-reading adolescents, regardless of whether or not they qualify for special education services, and provide a daily class schedule specifically designed to enhance their print literacy. As students' literacy development level increases, they are placed in classes commensurate with their level. The supportive measures taken in these basic-literacy programs, as they provide non-reading adolescents instruction tailored to their level of performance, offer a model that necessitates replication throughout the school system. Yet, the instrumentalist framework guiding the larger educational structure's literacy policies and practices still restrains this approach. It, merely, serves a purpose until a paradigm shift occurs in schooling.

Rather than consigning non-reading adolescents to fail standardized tests, thereby paving their way for "academic failure"—or, as is the case for some, incarceration—educational policymakers need to create system-wide literacy programs and schools to address this student population's academic issues, as well as develop alternative testing policies for all of these youth. Furthermore, literacy programs need to be implemented within the school infrastructure at every grade level to support struggling readers and minimize the production of future populations of non-reading adolescents. However, instead of creating comprehensive literacy programs and schools to attend to the specific academic needs of non-reading adolescents and struggling readers, it appears that policymakers' solution has been to build more prisons to house those who are not able to read well enough to pass standardized tests and, thus, become incarcerated. Such a dynamic seems probable in light of, as noted earlier, the proliferation of prisons and also the large percentage of students classified as non-readers and those who read on a 4th grade level represented in the juvenile and adult prison population.

Until a consciousness of student empowerment informs the educational system, policy procedures within the present school system could at least promote more inclusive textual literacy development pedagogy for non-reading adolescents. Improving education for these youth within the current educational system requires that policymakers implement educational policies and practices that, as opposed to current practices, support each child at the specific level at which they are actually performing, regardless of age. Therefore, to move adolescents who read within early elementary grade level equivalents to higher textual literacy stages within a more affirming context, educators must have the liberty to develop curriculum based on students' particular print literacy needs. Within these parameters, although still short of providing a transformatory pedagogy, additional instruction and policy measures that encourage more appropriate teachings within the existing school structure include, but are not limited to

- Creating literacy intervention schools and programs specifically for adolescents who are still in the emergent stages of literacy acquisition

- Early literacy intervention—as early as pre-school, since 3rd grade is already too late to address reading difficulties

- Rigorous curriculum tailored to each child's specific needs with continual and consistent support at the child's required pace

- Teachings that gradually push students beyond their academic comfort zone to engage in more challenging material in a manner that does not produce frustration

- Teacher education courses—must ensure that all teachers are trained in early literacy teachings and are taught strategies for working with English Language Learners

- Highly trained teachers at every grade level who understand literacy development strategies for struggling readers

- On-site teacher training at every school to enhance literacy instruction in every grade

- Professional development for content area teachers that focuses on strategies for supporting non-reading adolescents

- Multi-age groupings according to ability level

- Comprehensive basic-literacy programs—provide all-day programs to all adolescents whose literacy abilities in English fall within early elementary grade level equivalents, regardless of whether or not they are identified for special education services

- First language textual literacy development—support English Language Learners' textual literacy in their first language, while simultaneously developing their speaking, reading, writing, and listening skills in English

- Individualized education for every student—designed according to student's specific strengths and weaknesses

- Reading specialists in every school

- For those adolescents who read and write on early elementary grade level equivalents, provide one-on-one literacy development with a trained reading specialist for at least one hour every day

- Smaller class sizes

  o In general, no more than 20 students in regular classrooms with a minimum of two teachers

  o In literacy intervention classes designed for non-reading adolescents, a maximum of five students (in addition to the daily one-on-one instruction)

- More time with students—longer school day as well as school on Saturday and during the summer

- Self-advocate

  o Teachers can encourage students to self-advocate for the literacy teachings they require

  o Teachers can also help each student understand how the child learns best and encourage them to articulate this learning style to their teachers

- Professional counseling for all students who require emotional support

- Parental supports—parental outreach programs to effectively advise parents/guardians on educational options for their child and enhance parents' comfort with schooling process

- Parental choice—give parents/guardians the opportunity to apply for a waiver on a yearly basis so that their child may have exemption from grade-level standardized state tests, when appropriate, and may, instead, participate in alternate testing that is more suitable for the child's performance level

- Organic assessments

  o Use assessments as supportive, rather than punitive, tools for measuring students' development

  o Base assessments on daily lessons, grounded in each child's level and pace to provide teachers more useful information about students' progress

Conclusion

Rather than confronting the macrostructural forces of poverty in this country underlying the cause of crime and violence, or considering the ways in which these forces impact the daily lives of inner-city youth and their schooling experience, a discourse of high standards and high-stakes standardized testing has been employed as an excuse. These tests allow the blame to be put on, for example, the teenager who, as the excuse goes, cannot learn. It, therefore, diverts attention away from a reality in which a school system cannot adequately care for its students—an educational system that cannot educate its youth meaningfully so that dropout rates can be lower and print literacy rates can be higher.

Policy that (a) addresses the specific academic, emotional, and social needs of students, particularly underachieving youth and (b) recognizes the socio-economic, socio-political, and socio-cultural conditions impacting their pedagogical lives would offer just, rigorous, and humane educational alternatives. Educational policymakers must consider: the social conditions surrounding youth that can lead to their under-achievement; the ways in which the school system itself contributes to and creates this academic failure; and the intricate nature of learning, teaching, and knowledge. Chapters four, five, and six will delve into these and other complexities of the pedagogical process that must be taken into account to provide non-reading adolescents educational excellence rooted in a democratic and empowering purpose.

FOUR

Democratic versus Antidemocratic Pedagogy for Non-reading Adolescents

Paradigm of Complexity Offers a Democratic Educational Experience for Non-reading Adolescents

Instead of viewing education as merely a cognitive, technical, and verbal process and rather than using high-stakes tests to punish students for not reaching grade-level textual literacy, a more democratic pedagogy considers schooling within its social and cultural context. Rooted in the complexity of learning, teaching, and knowing, a critical-democratic framework embraces multiple dimensions involved in education—including but not limited to cognitive, emotional, critical, intuitive, creative, social, economic, and political components—while building on students' strengths and promoting their textual as well as contextual literacy. Beginning with an analysis of social forces influencing inner-city students' academic life, I will explore further this issue of democratic and antidemocratic education for urban non-reading adolescents to accentuate additional inadequacies and domesticating purposes of contemporary educational policies and literacy curriculum.

Social Conditions Surrounding Inner-City Youth: Pedagogy Rooted in Students' Lived Experiences

A critical-democratic pedagogy grounds policy and curriculum on humane structures as it recognizes social (both individual and collective), psychological, cultural, economic, political, and historical contexts of non-reading adolescents' educational lives. Critical-democratic pedagogy seeks to understand historically rooted socio-cultural and socio-political dynamics influencing the pedagogical experiences of marginalized populations, such as under-performing urban students from economically disadvantaged backgrounds. Education centered in this perspective understands that inner-city youth are immersed in oppressive material conditions that, undoubtedly, can have a negative effect on their academic performance. High-stakes policies become all the more inequitable for urban non-reading adolescents when we consider lived experiences of inner-city youth.

Since health-related conditions can lead to poor school performance, a critical-democratic pedagogy recognizes barriers to the health of children from economically disadvantaged communities and the impact that such limitations have on school performance. Poor adolescent health outcomes, including teen pregnancy, predominantly result from limited access to primary and reproductive care. Since low-income minority children have less access to comprehensive health care services than other youth populations, their morbidity rates are higher than youth in the larger population. Democratic education requires an understanding of these health issues and the ways in which a limited access to quality health care for inner-city youth can impede educational success.

Inner-city youth also encounter emotional stresses from familial economic hardship and environmental perils. As a result of social structural constraints and resulting diminished economic opportunities within inner-city communities, inner-city youth, more than urban youth from economically privileged positions, must contend with daily dangers at home, in school, or in the streets spurred by high levels of unemployment, drug and gang activity, and the excessive prevalence of firearms (Snyder & Sickmund, 2006). While many inner-city children resourcefully manage to develop survival mechanisms for surmounting these obstacles to achieve academically, difficult living conditions and limited possibilities created by economic disadvantage interfere with the educational performance and everyday school experiences of numerous inner-city youth.

The increased dangers and violence that inner-city youth experience lead to significant "racial"/ethnic differences across a range of health status measures, in which black and Latino adolescents have poorer health than white adolescents. Black males have a significantly lower life expectancy than their white peers. For both black male and female adolescents, homicide is the leading cause of death. According to Snyder and Sickmund's (2006) Office of Juvenile Justice and Delinquency Prevention Report, the homicide rate for black youth in 2002 was more than four times the rate of their white counterparts. This "racial"/ethnic disparity additionally existed across age groups and increased as youth grew older.

Amidst a violent environment and traumatic experiences brought about from living in poverty, some inner-city youth join gangs as protection and for emotional support. Furthermore, as schools and other social institutions ostracize inner-city youth, gang affiliation often provides a sense of belonging. While recognizing the negative and very often deadly consequences of gang life, when acknowledging its positive attributes in the lives of economically, politically, and socially marginalized youth, the psychological forces motivating youth to join become more understandable.

Common lived experiences for many adolescents in detention centers—who, as delineated in chapters one and two, due to limited opportunity and social discrimination are predominantly inner-city youth—present an additional picture of various challenges that some inner-city youth confront. Since at one point before arrest, these students were enrolled in the school system, commonly the poorest school districts, this profile, therefore, also reflects experiences of some inner-city youth within mainstream schools. Detained youth generally have a history of physical/sexual abuse, parental neglect, substance abuse, and gang affiliations (Acoca, 1999; Beautrais, 2006). The aforementioned experiences, perhaps except for variation in gang affiliation, impact youth across ethnicities and social-economic status; however, given added barriers to societal opportunities due to inequitable power configurations, school outcomes can prove direr for those among this group from historically marginalized minority groups and economically disadvantaged backgrounds.

Numerous inner-city students, whether or not they have familial support and caring, just like youth from economically privileged positions, find creative ways to negotiate such negative experiences to perform well academically and, for some, even exceptionally. However, as a result of dangerous environmental conditions brought about by social dislocation and limited opportunities within economically impoverished neighborhoods, many inner-city youth have serious emotional concerns that interfere with their achievement in school. An educational policy grounded in high-stakes exams and accompanying test-driven curriculum fails to recognize that traumatic lived experiences, like abuse and neglect, can create emotional distress that temporarily or permanently obstructs students' academic performance. Such economically, socially, and emotionally unresponsive policy and curricula can often produce more anxiety for students' living through these high stress experiences—particularly for those who are unable to read print beyond upper 2nd grade levels. It can lead many to feel, rightfully so, as though school does not pertain to their lives and needs.

Instead of creating a nurturing and caring educational environment for these youth, and others—one in which, for example, all students receive textual literacy instruction tailored to their specific level and pace so as to promote, among other attributes, self-sufficiency and productive civic engagement—the current curriculum mandates of No Child Left Behind (NCLB) and high-stakes testing practices prevent such meaningful and relevant pedagogy. Yet, given the importance mainstream society places on print literacy, inner-city non-reading adolescents endure heightened difficulties; without textual literacy, they have even fewer societal options for reversing their circumstances. In subsequent sections of this chapter and also in chapters five and six, I will discuss in detail pedagogy that facilitates non-reading adolescents' print as well as critical literacy, thereby encouraging the enactment of their agency to transform their reality.

Focus on Transfer of "Official Knowledge" through Instrumentalist Literacy Framework Subverts Empowering Literacy Teachings

Within NCLB's standardized test-driven curriculum the purpose of education becomes antidemocratic, as it ensures the reproduction of the dominant culture's values, attitudes, beliefs, and language to maintain and perpetuate the current social class order. Among other detriments, this hyper-standardization of teaching and learning negates the potential for education to (a) promote critically thinking citizens necessary for a thriving democracy and (b) nurture a combination of cognitive, emotional, critical, and spiritual tools necessary for students to attain their fullest human potential. Through standardized assessments and test-driven curriculum, educational evaluation serves as a means for inculcating students with the "official knowledge"—information that the ruling elite presents as universal knowledge but that, in fact, represents their culturally bound narratives and historical decisions.

Within this "banking" educational paradigm, students positioned outside of the dominant culture are viewed as deficits, who lack culture and language, and the imposition of "official knowledge" operates to silence their cultures and knowledges. Standardization, therefore, allows a transfer of the dominant culture's knowledge without any potential for critical analysis, creating an anti-democratic education that excludes particular groups and promotes a monological view of knowledge to ensure the continuation of the status quo. Rather than a pedagogy that enables a profound self-awareness, students and teachers alike are subjected to a schooling process that reifies the social order and attempts to stifle growth in consciousness.

Such a pedagogical focus on social control and an authoritative imposition of standard canon, presented as unquestionable fact, subverts and denies education for a democratic society. However, non-reading adolescents have confronted even greater perils than other students with the enforcement of "official knowledge," furthered through NCLB's test-driven curriculum and the implementation of high-stakes standardized testing policies. In addition to non-reading adolescents' inability to even read the "official knowledge" printed in the state standardized tests in order to pass, and thereby, up until recently in places such as New York City, positioning them for grade retention, the school system has neglected to offer these youth appropriate teachings—even after grade retention.

Barring a failed attempt for a few years, which ended in the 2002–2003 school year, to provide additional teachings to underperforming eighth graders in an under-funded, poorly managed program called "Eight Plus," the New York City school system systematically prevents an appropriate education for non-reading adolescents. By emphasizing the teaching of grade-level standards and curriculum, which promotes the "official knowledge," students who require emergent literacy skills development do not receive it. Even during the single-test promotion policy, the New York City Department of Education (NYCDOE) generally placed retained students in the same content classes that they had previously attended to again learn the "official knowledge" designated for their grade level, albeit with some extra support. Such protocol, however, denies a meaningful, caring, child-centered pedagogy for non-reading adolescents within special programs or schools that focus on their specific literacy needs.

Additionally, the literacy curriculum that non-reading adolescents who are identified as special education receive within their academic support classes or resource class ensures the transfer of "official knowledge," as federal mandates and state and city standards limit critical analysis and keep the focus of literacy curriculum within an instrumentalist framework. Subsequently, these teachings focus primarily on mechanical skills involved in reading and writing and ignore the more compelling facets of literacy such as affective, critical, imagistic, and experiential aspects to name just a few of the multiple components involved in reading and writing (a topic to which I will return in greater detail in chapters five and six). The emphasis within curricula provided to non-reading adolescents is, thus, not comprehensive, empowering literacy teachings, but rather acquisition of the "official knowledge" with some mechanical print literacy support. Through this school practice, which fails to address non-reading adolescents' intricate academic and socio-cultural needs, we see, yet again, ways in which the educational system compels many of these youth to "drop out" of school, or rather pushes them out.

Impact of Curriculum on Students' Behavior and Motivation

Just as retention practices can lead to behavior problems (as described in chapter three) so can the actual curriculum that is taught. Educational policy and the values and content of the curriculum have a great impact on the behavior of students. Within the context of curriculum centered on "official knowledge," very often, students "act out" or become "behavior problems" as the curriculum does not incorporate their specific academic, emotional, socio-cultural and intellectual needs and interests. By "acting out" students assert their opposition to educational practices that they confront and through this resistance students enact a form of agency. An exclusionary curriculum that does not allow student participation in the construction of the syllabus, thereby disregarding knowledge they possess, and that is not relevant to students' lives can ignite such negative emotions as: hostility, resentment, self-doubt, disinterest, disrespect, anger, and fear.

Like most human beings, a student can just be having a bad day due to circumstances beyond the classroom and can, therefore, behave disruptively even when the lesson provides engaging pedagogy. However, students generally perform well, when they are mutually respected. For the most part, students stay on task and are more likely to partake in the flow of the lesson, when they believe in the relevance of the material, feel as though their strengths are recognized, and have contributed to designing the lesson plan. Behavior issues often stem from a student's discomfort with the level and/or content of the material covered in the lesson plan. Many non-reading adolescents would much rather be labeled a "behavior problem" in front of their peers rather than appear, as students often say, "stupid," since they are unable to keep up with the daily lessons because they cannot read. Amidst the frustration of being exposed to teachings that are beyond a student's reading abilities, the student may yell profanities or engage in defiant acts so as to vent anger about the situation and/or to maintain his/her sense of dignity. As mentioned, in front of peers, and perhaps even in one's own self-image, it is more "righteous" to appear to be a "behavior problem" rather than "stupid." All too often, students who read on early elementary grade level equivalents definitively exclaim, "I'm not stupid!"

Then, there are those non-reading adolescents who, despite their confusion about the content material, do not want to disrupt class by assuming the role of the "behavior problem." This non-reading adolescent, instead, puts his/her head down on the desk, either to sleep or merely to escape from the anxieties and frustrations of not understanding the advanced academic literacy required in the daily teachings. In an over-populated class of 35 or so other students (as is the class size in many under-funded public schools), this kind of non-reading adolescent often goes unnoticed. Amidst a classroom filled with 35 students to one teacher, these students who struggle with reading and writing commonly do not have their textual literacy needs met. As such a dynamic persists at every grade level, these youth spend their school career feeling excluded and isolated from the school process.

Compounding the problem for non-reading adolescents, the current test-driven curriculum does not allow for teachings that intensively and directly re-mediate their textual literacy abilities. Within a test-driven curriculum, instruction cannot slow down for particular groups of children who may require teachings at a slower speed. Instead, teachers must cover the designated material in time for students to take and pass the tests, since these tests, according to policy dictates, determine (a) if the teachers taught the material and (b) how well the students "learned" the fragmented bits of information—knowledge that, as previously outlined, is specific to the dominant culture.

The Double-Edged Sword of Special Education Identification for Non-reading Adolescents

While many non-reading adolescents are designated for special education ser-vices and, therefore, receive support services in a resource class that often tailors instruction to each child's academic level, these students still must attend their content subjects without the literacy abilities to do more advanced work desig-nated for their grade level. Additionally, some non-reading adolescents have not even been identified for special education, as of yet, for many reasons which, for example, can entail: parent(s)/guardian(s) lack resources—including, sometimes, a limited grasp of the English language to understand the process; the student has recently entered the school system from another country or state; the school system has not referred the child for a special education evaluation; or the par-ent/guardian does not want their child to have the special education identifica-tion, as some perceive it to be a stigma.

Special education, no doubt, represents another practice within the U.S. school system that can damage a child's self-esteem and serves as a safety net for dealing with the system's creation of students' academic failure. However, special education has a positive aspect within the dehumanizing nature of the U.S. educa-tion system, which disregards students' strengths if they do not match the verbal mode of learning emphasized in school and also maintains a pre-determined pace of instruction regardless of students' particular learning needs. Special education services afford students various accommodations, such as modified curriculum as well as extra support through what is often referred to as a "resource class."

Until a consciousness of empowerment informs the school system, the resource class provided to those non-reading adolescents identified for special education can often minimize, for at least one class period, the psychological anguish that many of these students must endure. Ultimately, a consciousness of empowerment paradigm would render resource classes obsolete as (a) all students would receive, for example, print literacy teachings at their required pace and (b) schools would teach the various disciplines within a critical lens to promote critical self and social awareness. As the school system's current design fails to nurture students' academic, intellectual, and emotional growth and stifles their inquisitive spirit, the Band-Aid, fragmented approach of resource class, while clearly not enough in the pedagogical lives of non-reading adolescents, can offer the children a class during their school day that provides print literacy instruction at a level and speed suitable for each child.

Education Finance Reforms in New York City May Hold Promise of Improvement but Cannot Ensure True Equity

While initiatives in 2007, enacted under New York Governor Eliot Spitzer before his resignation, hold the prospect of improving some educational circumstances for inner-city students in New York City, even these efforts have their limits. Spitzer's education finance reforms complied with the Campaign for Fiscal Equity's mandates in their long-standing lawsuit, since 1993, against the State of New York. The Campaign for Fiscal Equity called for the implementation of a fair state funding formula that accounts for poverty; and, in January 2007, Governor Spitzer announced statewide increases, phased in over 4 years, of $7 billion in annual state education aid, including $5.4 billion for New York City (Access Quality Education, 2007).

However, not even taking into account the current economic crisis (intensified in October 2008 with the stock market crash) that has subsequently impacted every facet of society, the educational finance reform only addresses one aspect of the larger issue. Apart from the economic downturn, the fairer funding formula absolutely, in theory, has promising potential for improving conditions in New York City—particularly for many marginalized student populations. However, economic reforms cannot ameliorate the heinous psychological and social impact of the U.S. school system's legacy of positivism and prejudice. Non-reading adolescents have limited opportunities for success despite a more equitable funding formula. As previously discussed, they are mired in an educational structure in which the original architects created a mechanism for "sorting" children into varying achievement levels predicated on their social position and their ability to attain culturally specific information arbitrarily deemed developmentally appropriate for each grade level. The cause of the educational systems' ills for non-reading adolescents, therefore, rests in this perverse ideological foundation (currently disguised in No Child Left Behind's language of "standards" and "accountability") that has, and continues to (a) inform policies and practices that subordinate particular student populations and (b) confine learning and knowledge to pre-determined, culturally bound bits of information for all students. I now turn to a more in-depth analysis of this latter dynamic and the fallacies of the traditional cognitive psychology mindset that fuels it.

Transforming the School System: No Child Left Behind's Positivistic Approaches Present a Restricted Understanding of Learning, Knowledge, and Evaluation

The inhumanity of the current school system—which manufactures school failure for many students across "racial"/ethnic, class, gender, nationality, linguistic, perceived ability, and other identity categories and, as a by-product of this mechanism, produces a population of non-reading adolescents, many of whom are U.S.-born—testifies to the necessity of redesigning the entire educational system. This restructuring must ensure that all policies, practices, and resources are geared toward successful learning outcomes for every child. Ultimately, no matter what reforms are implemented within the existing school structure, only a system-wide shift in the persisting dehumanizing consciousness informing pedagogy can promote critical awareness and self-actualization for all students and can contribute to the development of a democratic society made up of critically informed, civic minded citizens. Within a school system structured on standardized test-driven curriculum, non-reading adolescents indeed face even more dire consequences amidst this sorting and ranking apparatus.

Before continuing to unravel structural factors under-pinning non-reading adolescents' particular experience, I will first delve into the flawed assumptions about learning, teaching, and knowing that guide NCLB and its emphasis on standardized assessments and test-driven curriculum, which impact all public school students.

The Limited Framework of Knowledge Presented with Quantitative Assessments

The positivistic quest for numeric indications of how students learn and how best to teach them—endemic to the research paradigm underlying NCLB—disregards vital elements involved in pedagogy and knowledge. In addition to the inherent subjectivity of standardized tests, this technical form of educational evaluation ignores facets of education such as intuition, creativity, compassion for self and others, justice, good citizenship, self-awareness, imagination, imagistic thinking, critical thinking, and intellectual curiosity to name just a few. Student progress determined empirically by quantitative test scores fails to capture the complexity of learning, knowing, and teaching.

Attempts to numerically measure knowledge and learning through standardized testing arise from a traditional cognitive psychology perspective. A social cognitive psychology, however, illuminates that knowledge is situated within a particular moment that is tied to culture and history. It is, thus, contingent upon the positionality of the knower. Therefore, the very design of standardized assessments obscure this interpretative nature of knowledge, as they are comprised of multiple-choice and/or open-response questions and essays that are developed and corrected according to the elite class' culturally specific standards. Within this monological structure of standardized evaluation, diverse cultures and forms of knowing are rendered irrelevant.

While traditional cognitive psychology has historically guided research and practices within the school system—culminating in the present-day NCLB initiative—an exploration of social cognitive psychology further unravels the limitations of traditional cognitive psychology's view of knowing, learning, and the mind.

Social Cognitive Psychology: Cognition Viewed within a Social and Historical Context

Situating an understanding of knowledge, intelligence, and consciousness within a social cognitive vision highlights the inaccuracies and injustice of positivistic attempts, promoted through traditional cognitive psychology, to quantify these attributes through psychometric testing measures, such as standardized tests. Social cognition psychology opens the gates for a more complex understanding of cognition and the mind. Framed by a critical multilogical perspective, as opposed to the monological lens inherent to traditional psychology, social cognitive psychology focuses on the process-oriented notion of self and its inter-relation with the world.

While traditional cognitive psychologists disregard the historical and social context of cognition, social cognitive psychologists embrace the inter-connected social, political, and economic dimensions of knowledge production and consciousness. Social cognitive psychologists, thus, consider the way in which these social forces have an impact on cognitive development. Exploring the work of social cognitive psychologists Francisco Varela, Lev Vygotsky, Jean Lave, and Etienne Wenger, reveals the expansive understanding of cognitive functions within this psychology. As they analyze the mind and consciousness via a socially constructed conception of self, their notions inherently refute the legitimacy of psychometric tests.

According to Varela (1999), the mind, due to its complexity, cannot be measured and quantified. He argues that knowledge, and subsequently consciousness, is a process that emerges and expands through interaction and relationship. Within Varela's theory, "interconnections among the sub-networks of the brain" (p. 46) interact with the environment. Varela further explains that knowledge is situated in history and context; it is "embodied, incorporated, lived" (p. 7). There-fore, unlike traditional cognitive psychologists who just focus on neurological impulses, Varela accentuates the social and historical component of cognition.

In line with Varela's paradigm, Vygotsky (1978, 1989) and Lave and Wenger (1991) also contend that the formation of identity and consciousness is the result of distributed processes mediated by social interactions. Knowledge is, therefore, enacted in the present. The concept of the self as socially situated recognizes the ontological and political significance of one's "racial"/ethnic, class, and gender background on shaping one's consciousness. This perspective reveals the errone-ous and useless nature of standardized testing and the concept of quantifying knowledge and consciousness. In emphasizing the impact of social and cultural influences on cognition, social cognition psychology highlights that standardized tests do not simply measure one's cognitive ability, but rather the cultural relation-ship between the learner's social context and the test-makers' social context.

The theories of the aforementioned social cognitive psychologists powerfully expose the social eugenics foundation underlying the research of psychometri-cians, such as Goddard and Terman (discussed in chapter two) who alleged the biological inferiority of marginalized populations. The critical paradigm of the self as socially situated and relational highlights how attempts to measure knowl-edge and consciousness—through psychometric testing—serve as hegemonic mechanisms designed to impede societal achievement and ensure the subjugation of particular groups outside the dominant ideology. Such an analysis supports Morris's (2004) critical assertion that the agenda of the traditional psychological research that has informed the educational system has blatantly produced "a poli-tics of oppression, a politics that is insidiously racist, sexist, and classist" (p. 160).

Amidst the profound implications that social cognition theory has for knowl-edge production, it has crucial implications for the treatment of children with so-called learning disabilities. As such a position accentuates how psychometric assessments are merely instruments that reflect the cultural and class biases of their creators, rather than valid tools for measuring cognitive abilities, it invali-dates persisting special education procedures. Social cognition theories expose the absurdity of current-day practices in which educational psychologists still use IQ tests to determine special education identification. Social cognitive psychol-ogy, thus, provides a vital perspective for analyzing the institutional outcomes of urban, low-income African American and Latino students. As social cogni-tion establishes the inadequacies of special education identification, it serves as another lens for illuminating the underlying structural forces contributing to the over-representation of African American and Latino students in special educa-tion and their ensuing higher push-out/dropout rates and over-representation in juvenile prisons.

Ultimately, viewing cognition within a socio-cultural context, calls attention to the way in which lower standardized test scores, and even academic difficulties, among particular groups, in large part, emerge from students' social and cultural exposure to the knowledge being tested—as opposed to their actual cognitive abilities and mental processes. However, as standardized tests continue to determine important educational decisions for students—causing detrimental affects for non-reading adolescents and others—social cognition psychology powerfully exposes the inefficiencies and oppressive nature of traditional cognitive psychology and its accompanying positivistic research paradigm, which have encouraged these inequitable school practices.

An Expansive Understanding of Knowledge: Whole in the Parts

There is a plethora of knowledge that cannot be reduced to positivistic methods of knowing and measurement. More specifically, various types of knowledge and ways of knowing cannot even be understood using such approaches. For example, powerful healing approaches, which are grounded in a spiritual understanding of the oneness of all and the interconnections of energy, use ways of knowing beyond the positivistic cosmology. Some of these methods harness intuition combined with awareness perceived through the senses to raise the electromagnetic energy field of an ailing person to restore their health. This knowledge of subtle energies and how energy flows has guided Eastern health practices, such as acupuncture, and healing traditions of indigenous peoples throughout the Americas, Asia, and Africa.

Furthermore, indicators of the efficacy of these healing approaches additionally highlight the limits of positivistic modes of mathematical measurement as the sole basis for assessment. In line with positivistic methods, there are ways to numerically measure increased health of a person once a patient has received appropriate treatment. These measurements entail, for example, numeric indicators of change in blood composition and/or vibrational rates of a person's electromagnetic field. However, a more significant manifestation of the impact of these healing modalities goes beyond quantitative expressions. Improvement in the way the ailing person actually feels, not simply mathematical indications, profoundly illustrates the efficacy and power of these healing methods.

As these Eastern/indigenous healing techniques embrace sensory awareness, cognition, intuition, and spirituality—among other means of knowing—they reveal the limited view of positivistic forms of assessment. Unlike Eastern/indigenous healing practices, the positivistic perspective does not consider the multiple dimensions involved in ways of knowing and the interconnected nature of information. Therefore, standardized test-driven curriculum positions knowing and learning as a purely cognitive, mechanical act in which students must uncritically examine and memorize pre-selected, fragmented information for success on high-stakes exams. Yet, knowing and learning is an active process of creation that at different times and in varying degrees involves among other aspects cognitive, affective, sensory, intuitional, and experiential components—employing these traits as each situation requires. Thus, as standardized exams emphasize the rational component of knowledge and learning, such a reductionist view discounts other emotional, reflective, experiential, and spiritual elements involved.

Employing a Holistic Vision to Pedagogy: Education Centered on Standardized Testing Ignores Vital Dimensions of Learning and Knowledge

In addition to a social cognitive perspective, Eastern/indigenous healing techniques, which valorize intuition and knowledge gained through the recognition of the interconnections of all energies, have profound implications as well for expansive approaches to pedagogy with non-reading adolescents—and all other student populations. This consciousness informing Eastern/indigenous healing methods underscores the necessity of appreciating and promoting students' intuitive capacities. Furthermore, it highlights the importance of perceiving interconnections and holistic approaches to gathering information and building knowledge. Eastern/indigenous healing practices furthermore illustrate that, instead of breaking the whole down into its parts for understanding—as the positivistic perspective advises—the parts represent aspects of the whole. Thus, meaningful knowledge entails recognizing patterns and interconnections of dispersed information and seeing the whole in the parts, rather than uncritically memorizing fixed bodies of fragmented knowledge encouraged within the school system's high-stakes test-driven curriculum.

A holistic pedagogical paradigm requires that contemporary literacy teachings with non-reading adolescents be reconceptualized to look at the whole experience, embracing the social and emotional context rather than just the parts involving the mechanical skills necessary for reading and writing. Literacy is a process and as such does not lend itself to technocratic evaluation measures. Standardized evaluation does not capture affective components of learning. For example, standardized testing cannot measure the positive shift in non-reading adolescents attitude toward reading and writing. Standardized tests cannot measure the behavior change in non-reading adolescents who, once they receive literacy teachings on their level, go from being "behavior problems" in class to students who are so interested in literacy that they become well-behaved students who regularly request more books to read and extra literacy teachings from their teachers. Standardized tests cannot measure the new joy and enthusiasm non-reading adolescents experience from engaging in meaningful literacy pedagogy tailored to their particular level, in comparison to the fear, frustration, or anger that literacy used to arouse in them before receiving these meaningful teachings.

Standardized tests cannot measure the passion with which non-reading adolescents write a story with the teacher's assistance. Standardized tests cannot measure the courage with which non-reading adolescents can express in writing their feelings, vulnerabilities, joys, dreams, concerns, desires, intellectual curiosity, personal experiences, reflections, and hopes with a teacher's assistance. Standardized tests cannot indicate the growth in adolescents' self-esteem once they learn the principles of letter/sound coordination to decode and encode words. Standardized tests cannot measure non-reading adolescents' deepening critical consciousness, facilitated in critical literacy pedagogy, as they learn to read and write themselves into the world—a topic to which I will return subsequently in this chapter and extensively in chapters five and six. Standardized tests profoundly obscure these emotional, spiritual, passionate, humane, creative, experiential, critical, cognitive, situated, reflective, and expansive elements of learning among adolescents who are emergent readers of print.

Many non-reading adolescents possess certain cognitive and intuitive capacities, which although they may not be able to verbalize it, make up part of their arsenal of knowledge. As social cognitive psychologists point out, evaluation of this tacit knowledge is best demonstrated in its enactment and does not easily fit into standardized categories of assessment inherent in the positivistic cosmology. For instance, although they may not be able to articulate this awareness, many non-reading adolescents are deeply aware of how to maneuver and survive on the streets in an environment that is characterized by violence. More specifically with regard to literacy, they also know how to move and negotiate within the space of social interactions in order to conceal their inability to read and write from those of their choosing. Standardized tests do not measure such cleverness and savvy.

Many of these youth can read people to know with whom they do and do not feel safe telling that they cannot read and write. Additionally, to maintain their dignity and minimize possible embarrassment in front of others, many non-reading adolescents have learned adept ways of attending their classes for extended periods of time without their teachers or other students realizing their limited textual literacy abilities. Non-reading adolescents exhibit this knowledge of how to negotiate both dangers in the streets and/or their inability to decode and encode text in the enactment of it; standardized tests cannot assess such keen cognitive and intuitive social maneuvering abilities.

Pedagogy centered on high-stakes standardized testing, therefore, delivers a fragmented vision of evaluation as it dismisses vital dimensions of knowing and learning and it denies detailed, authentic, situated assessment based on students' daily, or even minute-to-minute, development. While it also strips teachers of their agency by enforcing top-down "Big Brother" standards that dictate what educators are suppose to teach, the current use of high-stakes standardized tests, as discussed earlier, do not even provide any diagnostic value for teachers. Amidst the current testing procedures, teachers do not even view their students' performance on the standardized exams to determine specifics about each student's strengths and weaknesses for subsequent classroom teaching. As sorting and tracking to maintain the status quo serves as the driving force for standardized testing, it renders their use as a valuable diagnostic for teachers of their individual student's abilities irrelevant. While teachers' daily (sometimes minute-to-minute) evaluation of their emergent readers' progress in class provides an abundance of knowledge for lesson planning, standardized assessments provide no useful measurable outcome for teachers to gauge each student's particular learning process.

Democratic Education Requires New Concepts of High Standards and Forms of Evaluation

To provide democratic education that promotes both intricate ways of thinking and academic achievement for all students, old definitions of standards and forms of testing must be transcended. While always keeping standards high, educational excellence requires that standards be flexible, rather than the fixed and technical nature of current national top-down standards enforced through standardized testing and test-driven curriculum. Adaptable standards take into account the following:

a.   Individual needs and interests of students;

b.   Diverse socio-economic, socio-cultural, and socio-political contexts surrounding different student populations;

c.   Integral components of education, beyond merely the cognitive realm—such as affective, critical, creative, and experiential factors to name a few.

Furthermore, standards and assessments facilitate quality education when they are centered on holistic, process-based thinking approaches—as opposed to the existing positivistic and "banking" frameworks shaping U.S. education. Educational standards, therefore, grounded in a student's ability to: produce meaning through understanding and interpreting complex information; question; infer; apply learned material to new situations; convey thoughts and feelings through various forms of expression; connect newly acquired knowledge to one's self and the world; and perceive interconnections among dispersed information to see the whole in the parts offer a dynamic pedagogy that embraces multiple perspectives. As these complex and process-oriented standards encompass the multidimensional, relational nature of reality, they honor diverse ways of learning and knowing to support the personal growth of all students and, additionally, cultivate the formation of critical democratic citizens.

Empowering pedagogy for non-reading adolescents focuses on high expectations wherein failure is not a possibility. Within such a context, students are provided the support necessary for them to meet realistic goals based on their specific academic needs and print literacy level. Furthermore, rather than using evaluation of students to determine, for instance, whether they can advance to the next grade or must instead repeat the same grade, assessments are used as guides for teachers to create lesson plans according to students' strengths and weaknesses. They are also considered within a framework of situational learning. Assessments thus serve as diagnostics for the teacher and student to assess the student's literacy development as well as "teachable moments" from which the teacher can draw relevant material to be taught immediately or in subsequent lessons.

To provide an example of how an assessment can turn into a "teachable moment," let us say a child has taken a test on a decoding aspect involved in print literacy. Once the teacher has corrected any errors, the teacher and student would go over the mistakes together so that the child would be able to learn the information until reaching mastery. In this holistic approach, the aim for teaching is to ensure learning, maintain a joy and love for it, support the child's inquisitive nature, promote a student's strong self-esteem, and use assessment as an additional opportunity for teaching and learning. Such a goal is in stark contrast to the learning favored in curricula geared toward standardized testing.

Student-centered educational evaluation structures that, in fact, meet students at their performance level and enable students to push themselves to their greatest potential and work at their own pace, in contrast to standardized testing, create affirming and supportive school experiences for students. Criterion-based assessments, students' self-assessments, narrative grading, and portfolio assessments allow for such an evaluation process. With criterion-based assessments—also known as mastery learning—a child masters skills and content specific to his/her academic needs at his/her own speed before moving to the next level of skills and content to be mastered. Students' self-assessments also serve as authentic forms of assessment. They encourage students' development in self-direction and provide valuable input for teachers to shape instruction accordingly. Narrative grading liberates students from the fear of a bad letter grade and offers a more complete picture of each student's accomplishments and challenges. Portfolio assessments, wherein students put together, over time, a collection of their work and teacher observations, provide comprehensive evaluations of students' development. These tools for measuring student achievement facilitate democratic education that encourages success for all students—even non-reading adolescents.

This analysis of process-based democratic standards and forms of assessment naturally leads to the following discussion of process-based democratic teaching and curricula for non-reading adolescents. Such empowering practice centers on students' experiences, language, and interests; involves their participation in curriculum construction; and promotes critical thinking and action. Furthermore, recognizing the complexities of literacy development with non-reading adolescents (as well as all student populations), it takes into account cognitive, affective, critical, experiential components of education as well as historically rooted socio-economic, socio-political, and socio-cultural factors impacting these youth. Ultimately, as opposed to functionalist and instrumentalist literacy goals, this model facilitates non-reading adolescents' critical literacy—"reading and writing the word and world" (Freire, 1974, 1985; Freire & Macedo, 1987). While the democratic pedagogy described in the next section focuses on literacy development with non-reading adolescents, it also provides quality, self-actualizing teachings for all students in all content area subjects that encourage critical thinking and democratic action.

Laying the Foundations for Democratic and Humanizing Pedagogy

Within an education for democracy, knowledge is not viewed as a fixed body of information that authorities determine and transfer to students. While state standards and teaching to the information in the tests enforce "banking" pedagogy and negate the possibility for students to participate in constructing their own curriculum, school in a democratic society requires that students collaborate in creating their curriculum to initiate learning from students' personal experiences and background knowledge as well as to cultivate democratic habits. By collaborating in the development of their own literacy curriculum, non-reading adolescents can create teachings of intrinsically high interest value.

Democratic education with non-reading adolescents (and all students) generates knowledge from students' lived experiences. Emphasizing the value within democratic schooling of grounding a curriculum on students' experiences in order to gradually incorporate knowledge beyond students' immediate experiences, Dewey (1990) describes that the student and the curriculum "are simply two limits which define a single process" (p. 189). With regard to the importance of students participating in the construction of their own course of study, Dewey (1963) also informs:

> There is I think no point in the philosophy of progressive education which
> is sounder than its emphasis upon the importance of the participation of the
> learner in the formation of the purposes which direct his activities in the learn-
> ing process, just as there is no defect in traditional education greater than its
> failure to secure the active cooperation of the pupil in construction of the pur-
> poses involved in his studying. (p. 67)

Through participation and co-development of the curriculum, students learn
how to build on knowledge already familiar to acquire new information; engage
their curiosity; actively pursue intellectual interests; foster self-discipline and self-
direction; and frame their learning around relevant and meaningful knowledge.
Pedagogy, on the other hand, that centers on standards and standardized testing
in which knowledge is viewed as something limited and finite that needs to be
simply "poured" into students, to use Dewey's metaphor, denies education as a
practice of democracy. It stifles inquiry-based learning in which students and
teachers together become critical producers of knowledge and meaning.

In a truly democratic society, as highlighted in previous chapters, education
fosters critical analysis of the social order and democratic social action through
teachings that promote reflection on self and society for every student. Within
this context, all students are educated for critical citizenship. They are encouraged
to actively challenge and question so as to develop the knowledge and values
necessary to participate as agents of social change. Critical literacy roots the purpose of education in these democratic principles, as it fosters students' ways of
thinking, speaking, reading, and writing that delve beneath surface meaning and
question the status quo.

Critical Literacy with Non-reading Adolescents: Countering Instrumentalist and Functionalist Approaches

Throughout this chapter and the previous one, we have predominantly explored
issues related to textual literacy. However, we will now return to the notion of
critical literacy, which represents a vital aspect in providing democratic teachings
and curriculum for students—particularly for non-reading adolescents, who, even
more so than other student populations, are subjected to watered-down, purely
technically oriented instruction. Situating learning within students' social, historical, and political conditions, critical literacy facilitates learners textual as well as
contextual literacy so that they develop a critical consciousness—the awakening
of one's critical awareness in order to act on their reality and transform it.

As such, critical literacy pedagogy, as illuminated throughout this book, goes
beyond merely the mechanical aspects involved in reading and writing; it additionally develops students' ability to critique the status quo, probing deeper to
understand hidden meanings and root causes, in order to envision and create

more just alternatives for self and social change. Freire's problem-posing model, intrinsic to his critical pedagogy initially described in earlier chapters, cultivates this socially situated critical way of thinking, speaking, reading, and writing in students and accentuates the shortcomings of longstanding, instrumentalist literacy teachings within the school system. Expanding on the analyses of Freire's theories from prior chapters, I will elaborate on his problem-posing model, as its insights help inform the critical literacy curriculum for non-reading adolescents presented in the following chapters.

Freire developed his "problem-posing" approach from Dewey's (1991) emphasis on active, inquiry-based pedagogy in which students construct their own knowledge and nurture scientific habits of mind. Within his problem-posing framework, as teachers situate academic courses within the context of historical constructions created within unequal relations of power, they engage students—using learners' lived experiences and speech—in critical dialogue to challenge the status quo. From this starting ground, the problem-posing technique integrates structured, scholarly studies into the curriculum and roots it in students' participation, knowledge, and critical reflection.

Problem-posing education, therefore, offers learners, such as non-reading adolescents, democratic literacy pedagogy as it centers on students' co-development of curriculum and unravels the role power plays in knowledge production through critical analysis of society. It takes students' socio-economic and socio-political conditions as its point of departure. In so doing, the problem-posing strategy leads them to critical literacy using their daily experiences as the springboard for instruction. Rather than memorizing fragmented facts that dominant culture deems essential knowledge, Freire's critical pedagogical method involves the learners as participants, or co-researchers, who actively problematize power relations in school, other social institutions, and society on the whole. While enlightening for all students, critical pedagogy modeled on Freire's concepts has particularly powerful implications for those who are in heightened positions of subjugation, such as non-reading adolescents.

Problem-posing education provides a narrative for agency and an alternative to the dehumanizing nature of the "banking system" and antidemocratic education. Freire (1970) describes:

> Whereas banking education anesthetizes and inhibits creative power, problem-posing education involves a constant unveiling of reality. The former attempts to maintain the *submersion* of consciousness; the latter strives for the *emergence* of consciousness and *critical intervention* in reality. (p. 68)

Central to Freire's problem-posing approach is the concept that humans have an understanding of temporality as well as the capacity to interact and reflect upon their actions. As such, humans possess agency, which enables them to transform their present conditions—creating culture and history—through praxis, a continuing dialectic between action and critical reflection. This praxis is facilitated in problem-posing education within a horizontal teacher-student relationship through critical dialogue, which Freire (1970) describes as "the encounter between men [women], mediated by the world, in order to name the world" (p. 76). Freire warns that in order to avoid domination this dialogue must be rooted in love, humility, faith, and hope and must additionally incorporate critical thinking.

Such critical dialogue leads the way to humanization, what Freire views as the human vocation to become more fully human. According to Freire (1974), this critical dialogue enables the learner to become "consciously aware of his [her] context and his [her] condition as a human being as subject" (p. 48) so as to improve his/her reality. Freire, therefore, describes that this dialogic praxis, inherent to problem-posing education, offers "an education as the practice of freedom" (Freire, 1970, p. 81) and "education for critical consciousness" (Freire, 1974).

In order to communicate productively within a liberating purpose of dialogical education and since social conditions shape consciousness, Freire (1970) urges that educators and politicians understand the "structural conditions in which the thought and language of the people are dialogically framed" (p. 86). As such, "generative themes," themes representing a group's reality, are a crucial element of the "dialogue of education as the practice of freedom" (p. 86). The investigation of generative themes, when explored in conjunction with conscientization, introduces those in subjugated positions to a critical form of thinking about their world. Therefore, as teacher and student explore, as co-investigators, "generative themes," a forum is created in which students can reflect on their reality and, subsequently, act upon it to counter limiting forces and develop more positive alternatives.

A problem-posing approach to critical literacy pedagogy with non-reading adolescents may engage students (and their teachers) in inquiry into the social, economic, and political circumstances of why the majority of teenagers who are unable to read and write in New York City are those youth who come from economically impoverished backgrounds. Questioning, particularly for those born within the U.S., may also examine how these youth have been in the educational system throughout their schooling lives and still have not been taught print literacy. It may explore the impact that these students' limited economic and political resources have had in denying them print literacy. It may also look at ways in which they negotiate their limited textual literacy within a literate society.

Among its far-reaching potentials, since problem-posing education focuses on student culture, student-centered curricula, power, social justice, and democracy, it offers a deeply meaningful and inclusive pedagogy for non-reading adolescents (as well as other marginalized student populations). Literacy pedagogy from this critical perspective recognizes that there are multiple ways of know-ing, including, but not restricted to, through one's intellect, intuition, emotion, spirituality, and self-reflection. Contrary to the positivistic paradigm informing the educational system, such a critical pedagogy understands that learning is a relational and interpretive act.

Problem-posing education, therefore, allows students to make connections between school, their experiences, and the workings of power and privilege in-fluencing their lives. It roots itself, just like the perspective of social cognition psychologists, in the idea that knowledge develops in relationship to the context in which it emerged and cannot be separated from the knower. Subsequently, in a problem-posing method with non-reading adolescents, their experiences serve as themes and texts from which they generate both their own knowledge and cur-riculum. Furthermore, they analyze the imprints of power within these texts to counter oppressive structures and strive toward justice.

Conclusion

A critical literacy for non-reading adolescents, thus, teaches these youth to de-code, encode, and comprehend the printed word, while simultaneously fostering their critical thinking to read the world. Teachings stimulate an understanding of how meaning is produced in society within configurations of power and knowl-edge to ultimately encourage students' intervention in transforming their realities. Going beyond mechanistic and functional concepts of literacy development, this critical pedagogical approach to literacy places reading and writing within a cul-tural and social context and facilitates students' process of critical consciousness. Therefore, contrary to an instrumentalist perspective, and its functionalist coun-terpart, critical literacy enables an empowering, transformative form of reading and writing instruction for non-reading adolescents.

Borrowing from Freire's problem-posing model, a democratic education for adolescents who read below the school system's arbitrary standard of a 3rd grade level equivalent requires the development and implementation of a critical literacy curriculum that involves these students' co-construction; centers on their person-al experiences and their specific academic needs; incorporates their language and knowledge; and engages and enhances their critical thinking abilities. Knowledge generated by students' reflective understanding is more meaningful than knowl-edge consumed through just pure memorization of facts or ideas. Learning that centers on critical reflection in which non-reading adolescents consider their own values and worldview and relate them to conditions in society offers meaning and purpose, as opposed to learning imposed and transmitted from top down. Grounded in Freire's insights, in the two chapters that follow I will expand on the enactment of a critical literacy curriculum with non-reading adolescents.

FIVE

Reconceptualization: Inclusive and Empowering Literacy Education for Non-reading Adolescents

Introduction

The critical literacy curriculum theorized in this chapter and the following chapter, which borrows from many of Freire's pedagogical insights, is designed for one-on-one lessons with non-reading adolescents. It bears clarification that, in large part, I will describe the philosophical frameworks and instructional strategies adopted in this critical literacy curriculum through a description of the critical teachers who implement them. For brevity sake, rather than referring to them as *critical literacy teachers of non-reading adolescents*, I will instead use the terms *critical literacy teachers* and *critical literacy educators* interchangeably.

Target Population of Non-reading Adolescents that This Curriculum Serves

This critical literacy curriculum model is designed for any non-reading adolescent who already has a strong verbal foundation in English. In particular, since verbal language is a precursor to textual literacy, the English phonics component of this curriculum cannot be incorporated until the student has a strong foundation in spoken English. As a learner attempts to segment and blend a word in the beginning stage of learning to decode print, s/he must have previously heard the word in order to identify the actual word that the phonemes represent. Once a child, who has a solid verbal English base, understands the concept of letter/sound coordination and becomes familiar with the sounds that letters represent, then s/he can begin to read words, even those that s/he has not heard previously. As such, English Language Learners who do not have a substantial understanding of spoken English and who do not have print literacy in their first language would need the phonics component in this curriculum taught in their first language.

However, if assessment of an English Language Learner's literacy abilities in his/her first language indicates that the child has limited textual literacy abilities in the first language, then the critical language experience component of this curriculum model (a process, which I will detail later in this chapter, that serves the dual purposes of enabling students to become authors of their own written stories and promoting critical reflection) can provide powerful literacy pedagogy for these students as well. With a bilingual teacher, the child can create the critical language experience stories advocated in this curriculum in his/her first language and then together, with the teacher, the two can translate the final version of the story into English—additionally serving as an English language development activity. Many literacy abilities that English Language Learners gain while learning literacy in their first language will transfer to their English literacy acquisition.

Overview

To offer an empowering pedagogy, which encourages non-reading adolescents to attain their greatest potential and strives for personal and societal change, this critical literacy curriculum positions student and teacher as co-researchers constructing meaning and generating knowledge together. Rooted in questioning and critical dialogue, this curriculum enables non-reading adolescents and their teachers to challenge existing, restrictive social forces by delving beneath surface meaning. As such, it stimulates students' and teachers' critical reflection on the ways in which power and ideology—or the dominant culture's hidden and sometimes overt messages—shape their own lives as well as the teaching and learning process.

Within this perspective, critical literacy teachers critically self-reflect on their actions, preconceived notions, and teaching-world to best support non-reading adolescents intellectually, emotionally, and spiritually. They also research who their students are and listen to their concerns and interests to ground instruction in students' co-construction, language, and lived experiences. So as to facilitate non-reading adolescents' critical reflection on self, society, and the world, critical literacy teachers engage them in critical literacy activities that center on critical dialogue and the creation of language experience narratives—a literacy development strategy in which the teacher writes what the student orally relays.

As this curriculum embraces the transformatory nature of reading and writing, it encompasses intricacies involved in teaching literacy. Striving to deepen non-reading adolescents' understanding of their positionality within the social fabric to promote self and social transformation, critical literacy teachers situate instruction within an historical, socio-cultural, socio-economic, and political framework. They, furthermore, integrate affective, cognitive, intuitional, emotional, rational, creative, spiritual, and experiential aspects of learning. Critical literacy teachers comprehend that contrary to the functionalist belief, literacy pedagogy for non-reading adolescents (or any student for that matter) is not just about preparing them for economic advancement or participation in the global economy. They recognize therefore that literacy development is much more complex than the mere mechanics of reading and writing print, as it can also provide a tool in which non-reading adolescents, if provided the proper educational environment, can learn about themselves and their position within the world for self-actualization.

Critical literacy teachers, thus, facilitate this vital focus of literacy pedagogy within their classes to assist in preparing non-reading adolescents for movement through and beyond limitations faced within the unequal structure of society. As non-reading adolescents increasingly understand themselves and their world through a critical, or political, lens to see historically situated root causes and interconnections of situations that limit them—which Freire refers to as "limit situations" (1970)—and simultaneously develop their print literacy, they gain the tools to analyze, speak, read, and write their realities. Such awareness has the possibility of cultivating students' self-confidence and knowledge of self as subjects who are capable of taking action to overcome, or move through, personal and structural obstacles. With this growing consciousness, as many non-reading adolescents come to understand failures of the school system in providing them adequate literacy instruction thus far, they realize the necessity of self-educating. They, therefore, often assume the responsibility of advocating for themselves to receive literacy teachings, within schools or other educational settings, according to their individual needs and interests. In so doing, through this process of reflection and action, or praxis, students counter ways in which society attempts to silence them.

Rejecting Prefabricated Instruction: The Significance of "Place" in Education

The critical literacy model described in this chapter, in contrast to instrumentalist literacy approaches, is not a prescribed curriculum in which specific lessons must be taught in succession within a pre-determined time frame. On the contrary, this critical literacy curriculum (like all critical pedagogies) offers theoretical frameworks and instructional strategies to shape critical teachings. Daily instruction itself is, therefore, flexible as it relies on teachers' and students' creativity and agency as they co-create the syllabus. As such, instruction is situated in the time and place in which these lessons occur.

While the current standardization of curriculum disregards the importance of "place" in educational experience, this critical literacy curriculum rejects such restricted research assumptions informing the positivistic approach. Instead, this critical curriculum deeply understands that the place in which human activity occurs affects human behavior. By conducting educational research within an artificial setting, such as a laboratory situation, and not considering the varying conditions in which this technique is enacted, positivistic educational researchers present a flawed view. When the context of any human phenomenon under study is not recognized in research, validity claims become questionable.

Research on, for instance, the success of an instructional technique, must consider the different educational settings in which the procedure is implemented, as these differing environments will impact the outcomes of such a strategy. Let us say that a strategy for non-reading adolescents has proven successful in laboratory experiments with non-reading adolescents. However, it is then introduced in a real school setting in which non-reading adolescents are placed in the same classroom with adolescents who read on grade-level. The strategy previously proven successful in the laboratory may now prove to be ineffective in this real life classroom situation.

In contrast, informed by a multilogical research frame this critical literacy curriculum incorporates strategies useful for the various settings in which it is employed. As such, it does not prescribe one set way of conducting a lesson or a step-by-step method, but rather presents a model that can be adapted to account for the place and circumstances in which the teachings happen. In understanding among other factors the importance of "place," this literacy curriculum allows for adaptability based on particulars of each site. These differing "place" considerations of various educational sites—such as detention centers, high schools, and community centers—may include (a) spatial limitations, (b) confidentiality of information requirements, and (c) varying time frames in which students attend these particular settings. Critical literacy educators, thus, have the freedom to alter their instruction to account for such differences within each educational setting.

Integrating Structured Phonics and Whole Language Approaches

The instructional component of this critical literacy curriculum revolves around two specific strategies: systematic phonics instruction and critical language experience, a whole language technique placed within a critical framework. While the phonics teachings provide structured analysis of decoding (reading) and encoding (spelling) print so that students have technical tools for sounding out words to read and write, critical language experience—a process in which a student orally tells a narrative as the teacher serves as scribe, writing the student's exact words—embodies the critical nature of this literacy curriculum. Critical literacy teachers employ both methods as each child's particular literacy needs and interests determine. Yet, critical language experience plays the primary role in this curriculum, given its potential for facilitating textual and contextual literacy development as well as personal and social transformation, stimulated through students' critical reflection on their lived experiences.

While I focus on structured phonics and critical language experience, since they form the basis of this critical literacy curriculum—particularly the latter—it bears illumination here that the types of print literacy activities that critical literacy teachers can additionally include in this curriculum are, in fact, as limitless as the teacher's and student's vast imaginations. Beyond these two approaches, critical literacy teachers also use culturally diverse published and non-published texts to engage students in print literacy development activities such as guided reading, read-alouds (wherein the teacher reads out loud to the students), and independent reading of material written on students' specific levels. Grounded in the teacher's and each student's joint decision-making process, to mention just a few possibilities, textual literacy lessons can involve

- Doing "read-alouds" from short stories, myths, magazines, news articles, lyrics, poems, educational Internet sites, and so on

- Having students listen to a song of their choosing, while reading a printed version of the lyrics at the same time

- Using lyrics of popular songs to study language structure and phonics patterns

- Having students use educational computer programs designed for promoting phonics development, reading fluency, comprehension, and problem-solving

- Listening to books on tape or CD while students' follow along with the print

- Reading picture books and/or comics and students, in turn, create their own

- Having students read children's books written on their literacy level to kindergarten students

A Paradigm of Possibility

The theoretical frameworks of this curriculum and the accompanying conscious-ness and intentionality guiding critical literacy teachers provide the foundation for involving non-reading adolescents in meaningful teachings that cultivate their textual and contextual literacy. I will, therefore, first explore in greater detail these philosophical underpinnings. Situated in this theoretical grounding, in the next chapter I will then highlight the role of direct phonics and critical language ex-perience in promoting this transformatory literacy process for non-reading ado-lescents.

Key Starting Points: Creating an Emotional Space Conducive for Learning

Critical literacy educators understand that for most non-reading adolescents school has been a place of frustration and emotional anguish. Therefore, before even beginning to engage non-reading adolescents in literacy activities, critical literacy teachers, always aware of affective influences in teaching and learning, focus on allaying any anxieties students may have about learning to read and write. Critical literacy teachers create this non-threatening tone from the very first lesson. They recognize that sometimes their role entails assisting their students in healing from damages done to their psyche by demoralizing educational policy inflicted on them during much of their schooling years. Critical literacy teachers realize that non-reading adolescents, for example, need to individually hear that with the teacher's assistance the student can learn to read and write.

Positivistic literacy teachings jeopardize the self-worth and self-esteem of adolescents who read on early elementary grade level equivalents by failing to value students' strengths. In contrast, critical literacy teachers see the brilliance in their students. Equally important, they support their students in recognizing this intelligence for themselves throughout their literacy development work together. To dissipate any fear, shame, and defensiveness that a child may exhibit, critical literacy teachers, thus, employ humor, patience, and understanding to build stu-dents' confidence in their capacity to excel in their literacy endeavors.

As the teacher covers new material with students, according to the required pace that a student processes these literacy skills, the critical literacy instructor provides ongoing positive reinforcement to maintain each child's enthusiasm and perseverance as well as to enhance his/her self-esteem. Critical literacy teach-ers, furthermore, support their students' academically and emotionally by making each student feel good about the literacy knowledge that s/he already possesses, no matter how basic these skills may be. For example, if the child is beginning to learn the sounds represented by letters, critical literacy teachers, in such cases, may commend the student on the consonant and/or vowel sounds that the child already knows; or, critical literacy teachers may praise the child's knowledge of reading from left to right.

Critical literacy teachers understand the developmental nature of learning and variations among students' learning styles. As such, they give their students the time each child requires to complete his/her work. These teachers realize that every person learns at his/her own pace. As opposed to positivistic psychologists and policymakers who, far from educational settings, create a predetermined time frame. Critical literacy educators take into account human difference in learning diverse realms of knowledge. Therefore, critical literacy teachers root teachings within the child's performance level, and more importantly, according to what constitutes a rigorous pace specific to each child. Critical literacy teachers subsequently keep print literacy lessons within each child's comfort zone and gradually push students to more challenging literacy work as the child's particular literacy development process dictates.

Beyond literacy, the critical literacy teacher understands that every child has a deep knowledge about something that is of interest to him/her. The critical literacy teacher, therefore, encourages non-reading adolescents to discuss such knowledge so that each child may feel proud and capable in his/her domain of expertise. This process also offers the teacher useful information about the student's interests and passions to ultimately be included in the literacy lessons as part of the curriculum. Recognizing each youth as the deeply thinking, creative, competent soul that s/he is, fills a child with the fuel and motivation needed to eagerly partake in the rigorous and challenging endeavor of literacy development. Within this emotional and psychological context, adolescents quickly realize that if given the proper instruction, they have the capacity to learn to read and write—a skill that mainstream society has conditioned many to believe is beyond their ability.

The Power of Sharing Power

Critical literacy teachers know that many non-reading adolescents have spent much of their lives hiding the fact that they cannot read and write. With an awareness of the embarrassment and humiliation that some of these students may have felt, critical literacy teachers understand that some of these youth may have adopted a withdrawn demeanor, while others may have developed a more aggressive approach to negotiating their obstructed literacy development. Critical literacy teachers, therefore, create a safe learning environment within, as Freire advocates, a horizontal teacher–student relationship—in which the teacher, as a guide and mentor, shares power with the student, enabling the two to operate from a space of mutual respect.

Within this equitable dynamic, students in turn participate in developing curriculum as their concerns shape the thematic material of the lessons. In this context, in which teacher and student share power and teachings are student-centered, students are not doing the work "for the teacher" nor are they memorizing and regurgitating fragmented information deemed worthy according to the dominant class. By centering curriculum on relevant teachings connected to non-reading adolescents' lives, critical literacy teachers, furthermore, aim to inspire non-reading adolescents to assume responsibility for their own learning with the teacher's support. An important component of facilitating such an empowering literacy curriculum for non-reading adolescents entails leading each student to the awareness that s/he must take charge of educating her/himself and providing each child with the tools to do so. A horizontal teacher–student relationship, therefore, strives to provide a learning experience wherein non-reading adolescents feel validated and affirmed as they generate their own knowledge for personal development and intellectual growth according to their specific interests and needs.

This aspect in which students have ownership of knowledge construction and acquisition creates a whole different environment in the classroom—one in which harsh disciplinary and control measures are rendered unnecessary and students' resistance, a manifestation of their agency, decreases as their voice and critical agency are prioritized. In most cases, although not always, "acting out" and behavior issues, therefore, diminish as non-reading adolescents have more authority, participate in curriculum construction, and are provided meaningful curriculum tailored to their specific print literacy level.

Reflecting on the Significance of Literacy

Critical literacy educators understand that older students learn to read and write with greater enthusiasm when they grasp its relevance in their lives. Having students reflect on the personal and social significance of literacy in their lives creates motivating pedagogy for non-reading adolescents and separates it from the subordinating nature of teachings generally provided to these youth within the "banking" structure of the larger school system. Critical literacy teachers therefore begin the first lesson, which is the only one that follows a pre-determined course of action, with dialogue centered on students' attitudes about literacy and their own personal interests. They build students' interest in literacy development through discussion of the importance of knowing to read and write the printed word. Critical literacy teachers therefore pose the following questions to students:

- Do you think knowing how to read and write is important? If so, why? If not, why?

- Has not being able to read ever prevented, or stopped, you from doing something that you wanted to do?

- Do you think your life would be different in any way if you knew how to read and write well?

As most students regard the ability to read and write as a crucial skill, their reflection on its importance often stimulates their high interest and sense of responsibility and dedication to their literacy development process.

Opening the Space for Literacy to Flow

The critical literacy teacher has laid the groundwork for a rigorous, supportive critical literacy curriculum once:

a. Fears that the student may have of learning to read and write have been addressed and minimized;

b. The teacher and student have established a relationship with one another based on mutual respect and compassion;

c. The student recognizes that s/he shares power with the teacher so that the students, opinions, interests, and suggestions are valued;

d. The student has set her/his intention by expressing the desire to learn to read and write.

Such a positive educational context naturally motivates students to push themselves to their greatest potential with a joy for learning.

Students' Socio-cultural and Political Conditions Affect Their Perceptions of Schooling

Critical literacy teachers of non-reading adolescents understand that students' circumstances shaped by their socio-cultural, socio-economic, and socio-political conditions impact their behavior in and toward school. Critical literacy teachers consider ways in which students' limited access to mainstream economic mobility and the surrounding violent environment that such social dislocation can engender may produce anxiety, fear, despair, and/or anger for many students. Critical literacy teachers, in turn, take note of ways in which students' behavior in class reflects these feelings and emotions. Given the prevalence of, for example, violence in many of these adolescents' lives, critical literacy educators are sensitive to and aware that home and/or community realities, even life and death situations, may take precedence over some students' prioritization of schoolwork. There are a multitude of lived experiences that are rooted in poverty—and thus often racism, due to the integral relationship of "race" and class in the U.S.—as well as violence that can interfere with homework. Just a few possible scenarios can include being hungry regularly, the recent homicide of a relative or loved one, or encountering violent, and even deadly, incidents on the street.

With this understanding that socio-economic conditions affect students' educational process, critical literacy teachers foster a learning environment that balances high expectations for students and intellectual rigor with caring parameters. Therefore, critical literacy teachers do not penalize students for not finishing an assignment "on time." Rather, when necessary, they allow their students the time required for completing any task. They, therefore, provide their students with both emotional and academic support so as to create a space in which learning can happen, despite societal and/or familial intrusions and distractions.

Love as Part of the Curriculum

Critical literacy educators in essence teach from a place of love, as Freire advocates. A health-producing educational paradigm, such as the one presented here, which nurtures students' positive self-esteem and acknowledges challenges outside the classroom, engages the emotional capacity of the student and teacher. A positivistic educational context institutionally negates this affective element of teaching and learning—producing a soulless, technocratic educational system in which loving bonds are rendered insignificant. Contrary to such approaches, this curriculum flourishes through love between critical literacy teachers and their students. This love centers on mutual respect, caring, healthy boundaries, compassion for self and one another, shared responsibility, and understanding.

Critical Literacy Teachers and Students as Researchers

Grounded in a recognition of the complexity of knowledge and consciousness, this critical literacy curriculum encourages both students and teachers to become researchers. To create meaningful, high-interest literacy curriculum, problem-posing—which takes the form of critical questioning—serves as a crucial component of critical literacy teachers' role as researcher and educator. I will first highlight the manner in which critical literacy teachers employ problem-posing to reflect on themselves as educators and to better understand their students lived experiences so as to provide more meaningful and empowering literacy curriculum. I will subsequently discuss the way in which critical literacy teachers position students as co-researchers by integrating this type of critical inquiry with language experience—the core instructional strategy in this critical literacy curriculum—to develop students textual and contextual literacy.

Critical Literacy Teachers Question the Role of Power Operating in the Pedagogical Lives of Both Student and Teacher to Facilitate Agency

Questioning for critical literacy teachers centers on their self-awareness and critical reflection on their teaching practices; their preconceptions that may have influenced their teachings; their attitudes and behaviors toward students; and the imprints of power in their professional lives. This problem-posing also focuses on who students are, as critical literacy teachers research their students. They seek to understand what their students experience, know, verbalize, feel, envision, and hope. Such insights provide the material from which to develop a meaningful and empowering curriculum. Critical literacy teachers, therefore, continually ask themselves questions, for instance, about

a. Their preconceived notions and its impact on their teachings;

b. The ways in which power and politics influence both pedagogy and conditions in which they teach, as well as the degree of agency they possess to counter these forces;

c. Their students' lived experiences, interests, concerns, motivations, academic and emotional needs, personal and collective histories, self-perceptions, dreams and goals, and engagement in each literacy lesson provided.

Viewing parts in their multiplicity in relation to the whole, critical literacy teachers maintain a professional self-awareness as they examine issues of power impacting them, their students, and even their interactions with students. Therefore, when working with non-reading adolescents and/or non-reading adolescents who are also incarcerated, critical literacy teachers consider such emancipatory questions as

• Where are these youth located within the hierarchical socio-economic and socio-political web?

- What are the social positions of those who engage in formal teaching and research with this population?

- In what ways do these social positions influence pedagogy and research?

- What are the structural and personal power relationships embedded within the literacy process?

- Who in the social matrix is granted access to literacy and who is denied?

- What is literacy in a sociolinguistic and socio-political sense?

In considering the influences of power informing their lived professional experiences, development of curriculum, knowledge production, instruction, and their students' lived educational experiences, critical literacy teachers are aware that in the positivist world of technical standards, teachers and students are fed knowledge that so-called school experts have produced far from the schools in which this knowledge is actually implemented. Critical literacy teachers, therefore, reject claims of neutrality and objectivity in research, as they understand that a researcher's preconceptions and specific position within the social matrix affects the research act.

In contrast to reductionist views characteristic of positivism, critical literacy educators are cognizant of the complexity of the lived world. As such, they understand the importance of the interaction of social, cultural, economic, political, psychological, and pedagogical forces within the educational research process. Since these dynamics are not considered in the positivistic research shaping the school system's standards movement, curriculum mandates, construction of educational purpose, and assessment of student performance, critical literacy teachers recognize the fallacy in such school policies and practices.

Critical literacy teachers recognize the political dimensions underpinning the school system's instrumentalist, "banking" approach to literacy instruction—currently buttressed through the National Reading Panel (NRP) and No Child Left Behind Act (NCLB). Critical literacy educators reject the educational system's limiting emphasis on non-critical and purely technical literacy pedagogy. They, therefore, incorporate, in addition to mechanical and cognitive aspects of reading and writing instruction, the social, cultural, critical, affective, creative, experiential, imagistic, intellectual, intuitional, and transformational components involved.

These aspects are often ignored within mandated top-down, so-called evidenced-based programs.

As critical literacy teachers are profoundly cognizant of the political footprints motivating decisions impacting contemporary literacy policy and curriculum, they understand that NRP's mechanistic view of literacy instruction—which restricts literacy discourse to solely technical boundaries—functions to keep literacy pedagogy within the confines of Western cultural and scientific frameworks. Critical literacy teachers, furthermore, comprehend that ongoing standardized assessments, also promoted in NRP to allegedly ensure accountability, in fact, serve as a technology of power for the transmission of the dominant culture's discourse, values, and ultimately ideology.

Critical literacy educators do not blindly embrace "research-based" literacy programs assuming that the top-down imposition of these techniques signifies their efficacy. Rather, they analyze their relevance for their students, taking into account students' socio-cultural backgrounds as well as requirements specific to the place (such as time restraints) in which such a program is taught. For example, if an "evidence-based" program is designed for use during a 2-year period and the students are only at the given site for 3 months, the efficacy of the program definitely comes into question.

When pressured to use top-down mandated literacy programs, instead of implementing them without critical reflection, critical literacy teachers adapt the imposed programs to accommodate both students' needs and interests and the particular learning environment, whether it be within a detention center or mainstream high school. As critical literacy teachers stay mindful of the imprints of power operating within educational policy and research in the ruling class' attempt to control what is taught and how it is taught, critical literacy teachers retain their ability to make pedagogical choices within their own classrooms, regardless of external pressures.

Critical Literacy Teachers Seek to Uncover Societal and Personal Influences on Students' Literacy Development Process

Although critical literacy teachers understand that they will not arrive at neat, simplistic resolutions to their inquiries, they attempt to unravel various general and particular socio-historical, socio-educational, sociolinguistic, and socio-cultural forces—played out across identity boundaries—which have obstructed each student's literacy process. These teachers, furthermore, research the ways in which possible physiological difficulties with reading and writing print for some students were previously exacerbated and/or improperly addressed within the school system, due to inequities affecting students across economic, "racial"/ ethnic, gender, nationality, and linguistic boundaries. With this understanding of students and the contexts from which they emerge, critical literacy teachers can provide students affirming and relevant literacy curriculum that meets their diverse needs so that students may reach their greatest potential.

Critical literacy teachers, therefore, consider numerous questions (some of which I have already discussed) that include, but are not limited to:

1. GENERAL. What have been factors involved in creating a reality in which adolescents within an industrialized, developed country are unable to read and write? What are various societal, familial, and organic reasons children can become adolescents who cannot read and write print? What are measures that can be done to remediate and reverse this trend?

2. PHYSIOLOGICAL AND/OR ENVIRONMENTAL. Why might it be that adolescents whose literacy abilities fall below 3rd grade levels are disproportionately boys? Is such a pattern based in physiological cognitive gender differences, socio-environmental factors, or a combination of the two? For each individual student, what are issues at the root of his/her low print level in English? Are factors involved physiologically and/or environmentally based or, in the case of English Language Learners, second language related? What instruction, if any, was previously given to these students to address their literacy needs? What has their health care been through the years? For those children who are identified for special education services, what have clinical diagnoses determined?

3. STRUCTURAL FORCES IMPACTING INCARCERATED NON-READING ADOLESCENTS. What is the relationship between being classified as a non-reader and imprisonment? What is the correlation between special education classification and incarceration? What were the conditions in students' previous schools? What were the statistics on student achievement and push-out/dropout rates within these schools? What is the significance of the reality in which 95% of youth in New York City detention centers come from the city's poorest community districts (Correctional Association of New York, 2004b)? What is the meaning of the fact that close to 50% of the students in New York City juvenile detention centers are those who have been classified for special education?

4. IDENTITY MARKERS. What are students' self-perceptions? What are their home languages? What are their family structures? What are their cultural/"racial" and linguistic backgrounds? In what country were they born? Are they U.S. citizens? Were there gaps in their schooling? If so, why? How do they view their school experience? What would each child identify as contributing factors to their not being able to read?

5. SOCIO-ECONOMIC. Do students qualify for the lunch program in school? Do they live with parent(s) or guardian(s) or are they within foster care? What is the literacy level of parent(s) or care-giver(s)? What is the educational background of parent(s)? Are students from an "involuntary minority" background? "Involuntary minority" is a term that Ogbu (1978) coined to refer to ethnic groups that were forcibly brought into the U.S. through slavery or conquest and, therefore, he argued, more likely to see the school culture as an imposition of the ruling class', or oppressor's, language and culture. Or, are students from a "voluntary minority" background? Ogbu's term for ethnic groups that voluntarily migrated to the U.S. and, thus, he proposed, tend to assimilate faster, since they often do not see school culture as hostile but rather believe that schooling presents an opportunity for their societal advancement. For those students who are imprisoned, what neighborhood did the students live in before incarceration? In which school district, or school, were they enrolled?

Recognizing Home-Life Issues within the Curriculum

In order to serve non-reading adolescents more meaningful and emotionally sensitive pedagogy, critical literacy teachers seek to learn about each youth's diverse home life. These educators understand that non-reading adolescents come from a myriad of home-life situations. Critical literacy teachers respectfully ask their students about their living situations so as to provide them with literacy pedagogy that recognizes their potential concerns, relates to their lives, and engages them. Some non-reading adolescents come from homes with loving parents, or a parent, who work(s) hard to provide them with the best conditions possible within the parents'/parent's monetary means. Yet, other non-reading adolescents come from challenging home-life situations. Those more emotionally charged home-life issues that are similar to youth from economically privileged backgrounds can involve the following:

a.   Experiencing physical and/or sexual abuse;

b.   Having a parent(s) who is (are) ill;

c.   Having a parent(s) who has (have) a substance abuse issue [although the choice of substance(s) may vary according to the family's socio-economic position];

d.   Having a parent(s) who suffers (suffer) from a chemical imbalance or other psychological illness.

There are also other challenging family life situations, which although such circumstances exist among wealthier children are more prevalent among inner-city youth, due to historic socio-economic and socio-political forces that limit opportunities and create more precarious conditions for survival. These home-life scenarios may, for example, entail:

a.   Living with a relative and/or guardian;

b.   Living in a shelter;

c.   Being an orphan who lives in a foster home or with a foster family;

d.   Having a parent(s) who is (are) in jail;

e.   Living under the custody of the state away from the home due to parental abuse and/or neglect—generally, children from more privileged backgrounds do not become custody of the state in parental abuse and/or neglect cases.

Critical literacy teachers, in essence, research who their students are on an individual and collective level. From an understanding of their students' interests, dreams, joys, concerns, challenges, and experiences critical literacy teachers ask what type of curriculum could engage them in empowering literacy development? Critical literacy educators thus strive to understand their students' experiences, the nature of their being as related to the forces that impact them, the larger communal and societal structures in which they are rooted, and the circumstances and conditions in which they maneuver. This framework embodies the critical ontological mindset with which critical literacy teachers operate as they consider the ways dominant power impacts these students' consciousness, experiences, perspectives, and, ultimately, their being.

By sensitively asking each child questions about their lives and families, critical literacy teachers garner an awareness of both the struggles students may confront in their daily lives—at school, at home, and in their community—as well as hidden emotions that can interfere with their academic process and initially block learning. With knowledge of these personal and collective issues, critical literacy teachers provide an emotionally responsive curriculum that promotes learning by addressing students' lived experiences.

Critical Literacy Teachers Research Possible Organic and Environmental Obstructions to Students' Print Literacy Development

Among non-reading adolescents, both those who are U.S.-born and those born outside of the U.S., many have dyslexia—difficulties with reading and spelling rooted at the letter–sound correspondence level. The various physiological causes of dyslexia are beyond the scope of this book. Yet, academic support measures generally differ among students across social class boundaries. Students from more economically privileged backgrounds who have dyslexia usually receive interventions and remediation starting at an early age, which often enables them to learn to decode and encode print before reaching adolescence—although they may need continued support to learn more advanced skills involved in reading and writing. However, students from economically impoverished backgrounds do not generally receive such intensive, consistent intervention.

As critical literacy teachers understand the intricate relation of language and literacy development, they seek to unravel the source(s) of a child's literacy challenges. Critical literacy teachers therefore delve deeper to determine if a child with whom they are working has

- A physiological issue—such as auditory processing difficulties—that makes reading and writing more difficult for him/her, which in most cases can be remediated with intensive intervention;

- A natural second language learning issue that has interfered with their literacy process;

- A history of inadequate reading instruction due to negligent schooling or long absences from school;

- Any combination of the aforementioned factors.

Through sensitive questioning, critical literacy teachers explore the complexity within each child's life of the particular elements involved in their hindered print literacy development. For those with physiological cognitive delays, some poisons that may impede the print literacy process, which impact students of all socio-economic and cultural backgrounds, can include the following:

- Exposure to toxic substances from the environment, such as lead and mercury, or other environmental toxins;

- Drug and/or alcohol use while in the mother's womb.

Other physiological influences, which are more prevalent among low-income students, due to limited resources and opportunities, include, but are not limited to poor nutrition while in the mother's womb and poor nutrition during childhood. Some external factors, also resulting from restricted economic opportunities, that may disrupt print literacy development can entail

- Gaps in schooling;

- Limited print literacy of parent(s)/guardian(s);

- Lack of literacy intervention during the child's pre-elementary and early elementary years;

- Inadequate academic support throughout the child's schooling;

- Movement from another country, state, or school district.

Critical literacy teachers are also cognizant that for adolescents who have immigrated—primarily those from economically impoverished backgrounds—some may not have gone to school regularly in their parent country or may not have been taught adequately in school. As such, they cannot read and write print, as of yet, in any language.

Inquiry Centered on Linguistic Minority Students' Language and Geographic Histories

Critical literacy educators realize that while some non-reading adolescents from language minority backgrounds may have dyslexia and, due to lack of economic resources, may not have received adequate intervention, many others do not have dyslexia. This latter group of students, instead, in addition to those with dyslexia, has experienced other language-related and socio-political interferences. For example, as discussed in prior chapters, because of political rather than pedagogical motivations, language policy forced many linguistic minorities within this group to use academic English too soon. Such policy, therefore, obstructed students' natural print literacy acquisition, as well as devalued their home language and cultural identity, creating an exclusionary environment.

Critical educators understand that their linguistic minority students represent a diverse group that entails, among other possible combinations, those who:

- Are U.S.-born from bilingual backgrounds and have lived their entire lives in the U.S.;

- Are U.S.-born from bilingual backgrounds and have lived back and forth between the U.S. and a non-English speaking country (or countries);

- Were born outside of the U.S., in a non-English speaking country, and speak English as a second language.

In recognizing the diversity and complexity of literacy issues among this population of students, critical literacy teachers ask their linguistic minority students questions about their language and geographic histories in order to better understand each child's specific language and literacy needs. This inquiry involves questions such as:

- In what country were you born?

- What language(s) do you speak?

- What was the first language you began to speak?

- At what age did you start learning to speak English?

- What language do you use to speak at home?

- Does your choice of language change depending with whom you are speaking at home?

- Which language do you feel more comfortable using to express emotions?

- Which language do you feel more comfortable using for academic work?

- At what age did you enter the U.S. school system?

- At what age did you start using English in school?

- What language did teachers use for instruction in school, starting in kindergarten up until the present, to teach?

- What language did you feel helped you understand best what was taught in school?

- Did you go to school regularly throughout your life or were there periods when you did not attend school?

- Can you read and write in your first language?

Critical literacy teachers also inquire about linguistics-related topics pertaining to students' parents (if they are present in the child's life). Some questions include where were your parents born? What languages do they speak? And, can they read and write in these languages?

Critical literacy teachers also understand that for those adolescents who have recently immigrated, particularly those who have grade-level print literacy abilities within their first language (if it is other than English), the limited English print literacy of many of these youth stems from having just started to learn English as a second language. Therefore, when beginning to work with non-reading adolescents who speak English as a second language, critical literacy educators assess these students' print literacy abilities in their first language to gain a better understanding of students' literacy knowledge in their first language. Understanding that literacy skills can transfer from the first language to the second language, for those students who can read and write in their first language, critical literacy educators use students' print literacy knowledge in their first language to build on literacy skills in English.

In light of recent policy initiatives, critical literacy teachers grasp the tragic implications of New York City's NCLB-driven language policies, which prioritize ESL over bilingual education; set a 3-year goal for ELL students to exit out of language programs; and require ELL students to take state standardized tests if they have resided in the U.S. for as short a time as 1 year. Grounded in language research that indicates that it takes English Language Learners 5–7 years—and longer for those without literacy in their first language—to acquire academic language proficiency, critical literacy educators understand that the recent language policies in New York City have the harmful potential for (a) increasing the population of linguistic minority students who will become non-reading adolescents and (b) raising push-out/dropout rates among linguistic minority students who struggle with textual literacy.

Critical literacy teachers thus consider the various forces potentially operating in linguistic minority non-reading adolescents' print literacy difficulties. They understand that elements may include physiological influences causing dyslexia; disruptions resulting from language policy that enforced premature transition to academic English and alienation of students' cultural identity; lack of schooling in the student's home country and/or lapse in schooling within the U.S.; and natural second language development issues. Critical teachers carefully and respectfully attempt to unravel these intricate possibilities that may have played into the obstruction of non-reading adolescents' textual literacy abilities to better address each student's unique needs.

The following chapter will now focus on the instructional aspects of this critical literacy curriculum for non-reading adolescents.

Six

Critical Literacy Instruction: Joining Phonics and Critical Language Experience

The Role of Direct Phonics and Critical Language Experience

Although systematic phonics plays an important role in this curriculum, the following discussion of direct phonics and critical language experience places greater emphasis on the latter, given its potential for facilitating students' critical reflection and transformative action in addition to print literacy. Furthermore, since the phonics teachings are rooted in already published Orton-Gillingham-based approaches, such as the Barbara Wilson Reading System (Wilson, 1988), the phonics section in this chapter provides only a brief overview of the skills, or rather word structure analysis, taught in this curriculum.

While I will describe the phonics and critical language experience strategies one after the other in this chapter, I emphasize that determining which of these two approaches to implement each day does not follow a linear, set course for every student. Rather, as discussed in chapter five, teacher and student together decide (or sometimes the teacher does so with the student's democratic input) which technique to use based on the individual child's literacy needs and interests at the given moment. Critical literacy teachers thus rely on continual, ongoing evaluation of students' needs and progress to shape daily teachings.

A lesson can even include the use of both strategies. Rather than adhering to a fixed pattern, instructional use of each approach is flexible in that when using either strategy critical literacy teachers can suddenly implement the other one if the moment calls for it. For example, within the day's lesson, a critical literacy teacher may spontaneously teach a phonics point when coming across a particular word that the child just used in his/her language experience story. In this way, beyond the systematic phonics teachings provided in this curriculum, students also receive phonics instruction that is embedded within the context of stories that they have written with the teacher as scribe. As such, the critical language experience stories themselves infuse students' emerging understanding of phonics with meaning.

Critical literacy teachers strive to involve students in the joys of learning to read and write, regardless of any challenges they may have. For the first lesson, therefore, to draw students into the literacy activities quickly, the critical literacy teacher intuitively determines for each student, based on the initial discussion phase with him/her, whether it is best to start with phonics instruction or to begin with a critical language experience story centered on the child's life. All the while the critical literacy teacher displays a non-authoritative, easy-going manner so as to enable the child to feel comfortable about what s/he does not know as of yet, with regard to print literacy. This non-threatening attitude also encourages the student to open up to learning, despite possible feelings of vulnerability. The critical literacy teacher additionally maintains all textual literacy teachings within each child's "comfort zone"—which, in this sense, refers to covering textual literacy material that the student can manage with ease while gradually introducing more challenging print literacy work.

An Overview of the Direct Phonics Instruction Employed

This critical literacy curriculum repositions Freire's (1970, 1974) method of phoneme analysis and syllabication to best serve non-reading adolescents. As a result of their prior experiences of neglect and failure within the educational system, they may not always bring with them to beginning literacy lessons the same intrinsic motivation to learn to read and write that the non-reading adults with whom Freire worked possessed. Therefore, the critical literacy curriculum described here veers from Freire's approach in which phonemic and syllabic structural analysis centers on generative words—multi-syllabic words that learners produce to describe prominent themes of their lived experiences, which are used both for learners to critically examine their realities and for teaching print literacy.

To support students as they learn to decode (reading) and encode (spelling) print, this critical literacy curriculum employs an Orton-Gillingham-based approach for phonics teachings, such as the Barbara Wilson Reading System (Wilson, 1988). This method offers a multisensory, individualized, structured, and sequential process. In Orton-Gillingham-based programs, the structured, sequential phonics instruction stresses language and word structure by focusing on sound-symbol correspondence and structural elements of language (such as syllable types) within a multisensory, cumulative approach. To provide students practice decoding and encoding words based on phonics rules that the teacher has taught, these programs use controlled texts (pre-selected words that follow phonics patterns already covered in lessons) in worksheet exercises, wordlists, sentences, and/or stories. These programs also employ various modalities, such as kinesthetic sound (or phoneme) cards (one card for each phoneme) and syllable cards.

Phonics teachings are systematic in that they proceed according to a sequence of progressively complex phonics patterns. Phonics instruction starts with an understanding of the alphabetic principle (i.e., that letters represent sounds or phonemes). Lessons thus proceed by teaching students the connections between letters and letter patterns (groups of letters) and the specific sounds they represent. With this understanding, students sound out these sounds in each word from left to right to read (or decode) the word.

To teach the phonemes represented by consonant, short vowel, and digraph sounds, critical literacy teachers have students make consonant, short vowel, and digraph charts (see Appendix for "Clue Word Chart" process). These charts consist of "clue words" to help students remember each phoneme sound. Each phoneme has a "clue word" whose initial sound is made by the given phoneme. For example, for the phoneme /b/ a clue word could be "bat" or "baby." In the case of the consonant "x" and the digraph "ck," however, a clue word is used in which the phoneme is represented in the final sound of the clue word (e.g., "fox" and "rock," respectively).

While teaching each phoneme, the critical literacy teacher says the name of the letter (or letters in the case of digraphs), its corresponding sound, and then asks the student if they can think of a word that starts with that sound (or ends with that sound, in the case of "x" and "ck"). Once the student (or teacher, when the student cannot) generates a word, the child writes the letter with the clue word after it and draws a picture of the clue word next to the word. Creating a picture of the word helps the student know what the clue word is when s/he looks at it, although s/he cannot read it.

Critical literacy teachers encourage students to participate in developing each clue word for their charts, but the teacher provides a clue word when a student cannot think of one. However, if time constraints are an issue (i.e., the student will only be attending the educational site for a few months), instead of having students create their own vowel, consonant, and digraph charts with pictures representing each clue word to learn the phoneme sounds, the teacher can provide a copy of already made charts with pictures included.

Once the student has learned many of the consonant sounds, critical literacy teachers introduce one short vowel sound at a time, starting with "a." They provide instruction on each subsequent short vowel sound once the student has developed a solid understanding of the preceding one taught. Critical literacy teachers teach the remaining consonant sounds, while reinforcing the consonant sounds already learned and continuing to teach the short vowel sounds. Often a student can begin to learn diagraph sounds once s/he knows all the consonant sounds and most of the short vowel sounds. However, critical literacy teachers use their judgment to determine when the student is ready to gradually learn these sounds. As students work with the short vowel sounds, they learn to decode mono-syllabic and then multi-syllabic words with the closed syllable. (Students learn the long vowel sounds when lessons focus on the vowel-consonant-e syllable.)

To decode (read) words, critical literacy educators teach students to identify the sound-symbol correspondence by first segmenting, or separating, each sound in a written word from left to right and then blending these sounds together in their sequential order (see Appendix for example of segmenting and blending instruction using phoneme/sound cards). As promoted in the Barbara Wilson Reading System (Wilson, 1988), to aid in the segmenting process in the early stages of decoding and encoding, critical literacy teachers teach students to tap each sound with their fingers to distinguish speech sounds in each word. To tap, for instance, consonant-vowel-consonant (cvc) words (e.g., *cat, sit, set,* etc.), the critical literacy teacher instructs the student to count the three sounds in the *cvc* word using the index finger and middle finger to touch the thumb for the first letter (consonant sound), the middle finger to touch the thumb for the second letter (vowel sound), and the ring finger to touch the thumb for the third letter (consonant sound) to demonstrate that there are three sounds and three letters in the word. The student then slides his/her thumb across the three fingers as s/he says the word.

For writing (or encoding) a word, students follow a similar technique as described above (see Appendix for example of spelling instruction using phoneme/sound cards). By sounding out and tapping each sound in the spoken word, one phoneme at a time, students spell the word using their knowledge of sound-symbol correspondence. When having a student read and write a word on paper, critical literacy teachers separate each phoneme into its own box so that students may visually differentiate each phoneme. In particular, however, during the emergent stages of print literacy development, the manipulation of sound/phoneme cards to read and spell provides a kinesthetic approach, helps students visually see the separation of each phoneme, and creates a more playful learning experience.

With an understanding of the sound-symbol relationship, students ultimately learn the elements of language (e.g., consonants, short and long vowel sounds, digraphs, blends, etc.) and the rules of the six syllable types (see Appendix for description of six syllable types). Thus, while emergent readers begin by learning sounds in isolation and focus on the short vowel sounds to read and write *cvc* (consonant-vowel-consonant) words, they often quickly advance to a level in which they can read and write, for example, multi-syllabic words involving the closed and the vowel-consonant-e syllables. Furthermore, through on-going, criterion-referenced assessments, critical literacy teachers can highlight students' success and tailor instruction to each child's specific academic needs and pace.

While direct phonics instruction covers language and word structure principles and controlled texts reinforce these concepts, critical language experience (to be discussed) enables students to employ these rules in the creation of meaningful texts related to their lives. A structured phonics program that relies on controlled words is not inherently tied to critical literacy principles—in part because these words do not emerge from students' experiences. However, since the critical literacy curriculum described here integrates these structured phonics lessons with critical language experience, the phonics instruction employed does not stifle non-reading adolescents' or critical literacy teachers' creativity and agency—as is often the case within "banking" education when educators use only structured phonics programs. Additionally, as opposed to a "banking" approach, in this critical literacy curriculum students and teachers have the power of choosing what lessons are most appropriate for the day's lesson. Therefore, the direct phonics instruction employed in this critical literacy curriculum offers students immediate tools for "breaking the code" of the printed word—an essential skill for adolescents who were not taught to decode and encode adequately in their early elementary years. At the same time, this critical literacy curriculum uses direct phonics teachings in a manner that respects and honors the teachers' and students' ability to control the learning process.

Adapting Synthetic Phonics Programs

Within this critical literacy curriculum, teachers have the freedom to use the systematic phonics program in ways that they see fit, according to an individual child's needs and allowing for possible time constraints particular to each educational site. These adaptations may entail utilizing only parts of the already-published systematic phonics program at any given time, in order to meet students' individual academic needs and to keep instruction engaging and relevant. For example, after teaching a phonics lesson, instead of having the student complete all the workbook pages on this given skill, the critical teacher may have the child do just a few of these pages. Such flexibility also enables critical literacy teachers to adjust a systematic phonics program, designed for use over a two-year or three-year period, for a student with whom the teacher will only be working, for instance, for a few months.

Rather than serving as a means for "banking" education or deskilling teachers by relegating them to the role of mechanical functionaries carrying out top-down mandates (as is usually the case with pre-packaged educational programs), critical literacy teachers adapt the systematic phonics program that they are using in a manner that fits students' particular needs, thus keeping these teachings interesting and pertinent. As critical literacy teachers pick and choose the parts of a synthetic phonics program that best suits each individual student's print literacy purposes, this selective use of the program simultaneously: (a) honors critical literacy teachers' professionalism and creativity and (b) motivates students to push through possible challenges involved in literacy development by exposing them to direct instruction of rules that unlock the door to print literacy at the level and pace they require.

Initial Phonics Assessment

In the beginning stage of phonics instruction, critical literacy teachers informally assess student's memory, decoding, and phonemic awareness. The first phonics lesson entails a low-key assessment using either a printed wordlist, which many published phonics programs provide or that the critical literacy teacher can create, or sound/phoneme cards to spell words for the student to read. Since students have been so damaged psychologically by a borage of testing given in school of material that is out of their range of understanding, the critical teacher allays students' fears by explaining the idea that the wordlist is not a test but is a way for the teacher to find out what "tricks" the student may already know about reading words and what "tricks" the teacher needs to start teaching the student.

The words on the list represent progressively more complicated word structures—starting with *cvc* words (consonant-vowel-consonant words, such as *cat, sit, let,* etc.). The wordlist assesses a student's understanding of: reading from left to right; segmenting and blending phonemes; consonant, short vowel, long vowel, and letter pattern sounds; blends and digraphs; and syllable types. The words on the wordlist thus include mono-syllabic and multi-syllabic words using all six syllable types, as well as, for example, digraphs (such as *sh, ch, ck,* etc.) and two and three letter blends (such as *st, br, nd, str, spr,* etc.). The critical literacy teacher stops the assessment when the student miscues (is unable to read) five consecutive words on the list. Both the words read correctly and the miscues give the critical literacy teacher helpful information in determining both the student's phonics knowledge and which phonics rules to begin teaching.

To assess the decoding knowledge of students who appear particularly anxious about learning to read and write and/or intimidated by the printed wordlist, critical literacy teachers use sound/phoneme cards instead. Using the cards, critical literacy teachers initially create *cvc* words (such as *cat, sit, let,* etc.). If the student seems to have a solid understanding of *cvc* words, then the critical literacy teacher can commend the child on his/her knowledge of the fundamentals of print literacy and ask him/her if s/he feels comfortable reading some words from a list of words that get increasingly more difficult. If the student wants to read from the wordlist, then the critical literacy educator uses the wordlist to continue the assessment; and, if the child does not want to use the wordlist, then the critical educator uses the cards to spell the words written on the wordlist, in their given order. In either case, the critical literacy teacher stops the assessment once the child cannot read five consecutive words.

Motivating Phonics Pedagogy

Within the phonics lessons, critical literacy teachers make sure that lessons allow the student to feel successful, despite possible difficulties. Critical literacy educators, therefore, continually monitor the student's attitude toward the teachings and carefully avoid pushing the student into an area of discomfort. By teaching within each child's "comfort zone," critical literacy educators maintain a balance between activities that are within a student's ability and those that challenge. If the activity appears too difficult, and is therefore causing frustration, then critical literacy teachers return to the previous phonics activities—which are within the student's "comfort zone"—and gradually teach the new material.

For non-readers, whose motivation has often been submerged through negative schooling experiences, the initial success that they have in reading and writing print with a synthetic phonics approach often engenders instant "buy-in" to the literacy teachings, enhances their self-esteem, and encourages them to push through challenges as they learn progressively advanced literacy skills. While the controlled words do not pertain to students' lived experiences, these phonics teachings serve as yet another means, and perhaps a more direct and explicit means, for students to understand the technical rules of decoding and encoding. The critical language aspect of this curriculum, which I will subsequently highlight, serves the purpose, however, of situating literacy teachings within students' background knowledge and engaging them in the social, critical, and creative elements of literacy.

Learning to read requires the proper guidance and teachings and is not a skill that is automatically acquired, such as learning to speak one's first language. Hope emerges for these students when they realize that they are capable of learning to read, when presented with instruction at their level and pace. Once non-reading adolescents receive teachings that unlock the door to the world of textual literacy, they become overjoyed and motivated when they see that they too can be a part of this world of the printed word—a world from which they had previously been excluded. Such a realization and reality does wonders for these students' self-esteem. Their excitement and interest in literacy activities soars. Many of these students become self-motivated in their pursuit of more advanced literacy skills and even advocate for themselves.

Critical Language Experience Enables
Critical Pedagogical Goals

Critical literacy teachers embrace the complexity and diversity of their students' experiences. They are aware that many of their non-reading adolescent students, in most cases, did not have classes tailored to their literacy needs throughout their school years, but rather generally have been placed in the same content area classes with students who read on or close to grade level, or even those who read beyond grade level equivalents. Critical literacy teachers respect their students' language, knowledge, insights, and experiences. They recognize that these youth are already writers, or authors, filled with complex, creative stories, even though they do not as of yet have the mechanics to write these stories on their own. Critical literacy teachers do not view these students as cultural deficits. They recognize that these youth were caught amidst socio-economic and socio-political circumstances and did not have the economic resources needed for access to effective remediation in their younger years, as children from economically wealthier backgrounds generally receive.

Critical literacy educators, therefore, understand that while these youth may not have acquired textual literacy, as of yet, they are rich with ideas, stories, perspectives, and opinions about themselves, their community, and the world. Critical literacy teachers understand that these students can be knowledge producers by tapping these sources of their personal knowledge and using these insights as catalysts for generating new critical knowledge and academic capacities. Through critical language experience, the critical literacy curriculum described here facilitates this student generated knowledge production, and it enables students to become authors of their own texts.

Language experience emerges from students' linguistic and socio-cultural backgrounds, lived experiences, and imagination. As this curriculum further situates language experience within a critical context, producing what I refer to as critical language experience, it simultaneously serves, as a vehicle, in the Freirean sense, for students to read and write not just the word but the world as well. In a language experience approach, students dictate non-fictional and fictional stories, rooted in students' personal experiences and language, while the teacher scribes exactly what the student says. Once the student and teacher have written the first draft, this written piece serves as the text from which critical literacy teachers engage students in textual and contextual literacy development. I now turn to the way in which critical literacy teachers employ critical language experience to both teach textual literacy and to promote students' praxis, reflection and action on the world so as to transform it. I will begin with a description of the former.

Critical Language Experience and Print Literacy Development

To develop students' print literacy, after the student and teacher have created the first written draft of a language experience text, the student reads it aloud, with the teacher's assistance if needed. After the student has read the story aloud enough times so that s/he knows how to read the majority of the words in the story, s/he types it on the computer to produce a second draft. Some students may need some initial instruction on various aspects of typing, such as the functions of the *tab, delete, enter*, and *shift* keys. Once typed on the computer, the teacher edits a printed out version of this second draft. The student then implements the corrections using a computer to produce the final draft. This third draft does not have to be the final draft, if both the student and/or teacher would like to continue working on the piece. Together, the critical literacy teacher and the student determine the pace of these lessons according to each child's specific needs.

When reading a language experience story, a student often can decode unknown words since s/he knows the content meaning, or rather has background knowledge, of his/her own text. Students' knowledge of content meaning also aids in their learning to use semantic cues—wherein readers identify unknown words through their understanding of the meaning of what they read and determining what word would make sense in the given context. Writing the language experience stories on the computer provides students further exposure to the correct spellings for words, while teaching them computer skills. Through language experience, critical literacy teachers also model the thinking aloud and rereading strategies involved in writing, which respectively help writers put down their thoughts into words and allow them to remember what they have written previously in the text in order to sequence subsequent ideas in a way that conveys meaning.

Activating Students' Imagination and Nurturing Critical Consciousness through Critical Language Experience

The above process teaches the mechanics of writing (such as decoding, encoding, and punctuation). However, critical language experience also allows students to engage their imagination as authors of their own text. As students create fictional, in addition to non-fictional, critical language experience stories, this literacy curriculum encourages them to play with text. Critical language experience therefore offers a pedagogical means for tapping into non-reading adolescents' vivid imagination and facilitating their expression of it in writing.

Since language experience furthermore naturally integrates students' personal experiences, critical literacy teachers, in large part, use it to elicit critical reflection on such experiences, ultimately promoting students' agency. As the creation of critical language experience stories relies on critical dialogue between teacher and student it enables students to become co-researchers, generating their own knowledge by engaging in speaking, reading, writing, and critical reflection on their lived experiences. In keeping with critical pedagogical tenets, such a method positions students at the center of their literacy development lessons. It additionally places knowledge within a dynamic and holistic context that aims to unravel interconnections of information and expose the ways in which power operates in students' experiences so that they may visualize and actualize positive alternatives to institutional and personal obstacles.

Critical literacy teachers dialogue with students about their hobbies, interests, passions, lived experiences, and relationships with important people in their lives to serve as material from which students can develop critical language experience stories of high interest. Critical literacy teachers employ these issues—or rather in Freire's terms, generative themes—in critical literacy activities. They expose students to textual readings and/or an analysis of a photograph or picture that are based on the same themes as those that they expressed, to involve students in critical dialogue and reflection on these issues for the ensuing creation of their critical language experience stories (to be discussed further). Through the combination of these critical literacy activities and the development of critical language experience stories, critical literacy teachers place students' realities within their historical, socio-economic, socio-cultural, and socio-political contexts and encourage students to envision positive alternatives. Critical literacy teachers, furthermore, read aloud various genres of text from diverse cultures—such as short stories, myths, autobiographies, songs, personal essays, and/or letters—to stimulate students' ideas and to enhance their knowledge of different print material to aid in the production of their own written work, their language experience texts.

Critical literacy teachers do not censor students' story lines, whether based on fiction or non-fiction. For example, some students may want to create a piece that is heavy on violence, either a story based on fiction or a real life scenario. Critical literacy teachers recognize that writing can often provide healthy outlets for aggressive feelings—especially in light of violent environments from which some non-reading adolescents come. Along the same vein, through critical language experience, writing can be therapeutic and help work through emotionally difficult experiences, such as, death or illness of a loved one, murder of a loved one, history of physical or sexual abuse, familial drug addiction, personal drug addiction, violence at home and/or in the streets, or other traumatic experiences. Since the act of writing can provide a way for the writer to work out problems and release negative feelings, like anxiety, anger, emotional pain, and frustration, in a productive manner, creating critical language experience texts can often serve as a cathartic process. Similarly, but from a different perspective, critical language experience offers a means for students to express positive feelings, for instance, celebrating their triumphs and joys.

Critical language experience enables critical reflection and processing of information, as the critical literacy teacher asks a student open-ended questions about the experience that the child describes. Critical literacy teachers engage students in this questioning during the writing process and even after the texts have been written. Self-reflection can be uncomfortable at times, as it can bring to light difficult recollections and/or insights. With care and compassion, a skilled teacher can guide a student through this critical reflection in a positive and constructive manner that bolsters the child's inner strength, resilience, and critical self-awareness. The critical literacy teacher does not push students to discuss any information that the student does not feel comfortable talking about, but the teacher also knows how to offer emotional support to students when they do talk about difficult or disturbing life experiences. With critical literacy teachers, the student knows and feels that the teacher is not judging him/her when revealing difficult episodes in his/her life, but rather facilitating the child's self-expression and critical reflection. The writing of traumatic experiences can often help the student release negativity surrounding it and gain new understandings. However, the teacher maintains sensitivity to the child, recognizing when s/he may need an affirming remark.

Some non-reading adolescents, particularly those youth in detention centers, could be implicated by some stories if written in the first person. Therefore, for those non-reading adolescents whose critical language experience story plotlines come from life experiences that involve illegal activities, for example drug dealing or prostitution, the critical literacy teacher takes precaution by explaining to the student that together they will write such stories in the third person, rather than the first person, using fictitious names for all the characters. Again, here the critical literacy teacher treads lightly; without censoring, critical literacy teachers balance a child's motivation and desire to write his/her lived experience with safety measures that will not put anyone, especially the child, in jeopardy.

Exploring Issues of Power and Language

As critical language experience stories emerge from students' verbal language, these texts provide an excellent means for engaging students in critical dialogue about power dynamics involved in language. In addition to students' language experience stories, critical literacy teachers can also use magazine and news articles, popular songs, excerpts from novels, movies and documentaries, etc., to compare Standard English and non-Standard English forms, as well as slang usages of language. Since language is intrinsically tied to culture, helping to form individual and group identity, the use of slang among many of these youth can be very valuable. It is a part of self-definition and represents group affiliation. Language, such as slang, can be used as a site of resistance. However, prejudicial perceptions among some people in positions of social privilege exist with regard to which type of language (which register) a person uses. These elite visions promulgate faulty theories such as Bereiter and Engelmann's (1966) "verbal and cultural deprivation" (see chapter two).

Given the abundance of such flawed theories, critical literacy teachers can focus critical dialogue on sociolinguistic issues, such as the way language can present barriers that obstruct access to mainstream success and the ways in which it can also mark group membership. For example, critical literacy teachers can discuss with their students a social dynamic in which a person's limited knowledge of Standard English can prevent access to mechanisms of power within society, in other words exclude and dominate. Critical literacy teachers can ask their students how they feel about this unjust reality in which some people believe that individuals who speak grammatically "correct" forms of Standard English have higher mental abilities; or, how students feel about those who believe the opposite assumption as well, that those who do not speak Standard English have lower mental capacities.

Amidst this critical dialogue on linguistic discrimination, critical literacy teachers involve students in reflection on the power of slang within certain social atmospheres and how it can also inhibit upward mobility in other social arenas. By comparing Standard English and slang in speech and in writing, students become familiar with codes of speech. With this consciousness, they learn to code-switch (choose between codes of speech), when necessary, with greater facility so as to transcend potential oppressive structures. The ability to change speech patterns according to a particular social context, ultimately, provides survival tools within different socio-economic social settings.

Once the critical literacy teacher and the student have examined the issue of language and codes of speech, students can incorporate this understanding in the creation of subsequent critical language experience stories, as well as during the editing stage of writing. For example, critical literacy teachers and students can discuss if a certain sentence or line in a poem would sound better with a Standard English or non-Standard English form of language. As these teachings expose students to language dynamics and enable them to deepen their awareness of different codes of speech, students develop an empowering tool—the conscious choice and use of language.

Using Critical Language Experience to Create Literacy History Narratives: Facilitating Textual and Contextual Literacy Development

While critical language experience serves as a tool for critical literacy teachers to engage in critical dialogue with their students, it also enables critical literacy teachers to listen to students' themes, opinions, and insights. With this knowledge, teachers can understand their students better—a continual aim for critical literacy educators, as previously highlighted, so that they may construct curriculum that is more relevant to students' lives. Non-fictional critical language experience stories, thus, have the added benefit of offering critical literacy educators rich material for understanding the inter-relations and particularities of each child's experience. As students' non-fictional critical language experience texts focus on, for instance, autobiographic accounts of their lived experiences, these written pieces also create an avenue for students' personal exploration of self, family, and society. I will now describe the creation of students' literacy history narratives as an example to illustrate the way in which the literacy curriculum detailed in this chapter positions critical language experience as a method for facilitating students' critical reflection on their lives and circumstances.

Literacy history narratives, produced through critical language experience, provide a means in which non-reading adolescents can discursively reflect on their literacy experiences and illuminate issues for both themselves and their educators. These anecdotal narratives, which Van Manen (1990) refers to as "poetic narrative" (p. 119), penetrate the multifaceted reality of lived experiences and, thus, enable "an immanent account" (p. 119) of the nature of the phenomenon described. Non-reading adolescents' personal narratives of their literacy histories, therefore, enable a rich, textual reflection on the fundamental meaning of being a teenager who is unable to read and write. Van Manen points out that anecdotal narrative depicts the particular, while at the same time representing the general, or universal. Through this ontological description, students deepen their own transformatory, critical self-awareness. Simultaneously, critical literacy teachers increase their understanding of their individual students, as well as see the commonalities of their students' experiences.

Literacy history narratives can delve into numerous questions, which have profound pedagogical, psychological, and social implications:

- What are the various ontological aspects of life as an adolescent who is unable to read and write?

- What is it like to be a teenager who is unable to read and write?

- How do non-reading adolescents describe their relationship with literacy and school?

- What factors do non-reading adolescents believe have contributed to a reality in which they are teenagers with early elementary literacy levels?

- What have been various societal, familial, and/or organic factors involved in the obstruction of their literacy process?

- What suggestions do these youth have for preventing and reversing the creation of a population of adolescents who are unable to read and write?

Centering critical dialogue on problem-posing, the critical literacy teacher asks open-ended questions about a student's lived literacy experiences to: (a) lead the student to a deeper understanding of the causes of their obstructed literacy process; (b) develop alternative possibilities; and (c) transform these literacy experiences into a written account through critical language experience. By reflecting on the role of literacy in their lives, as well as other autobiographic experiences, students gain a heightened sense of the historical and cultural environment, the place and time, in which these events occurred. Critical literacy teachers further situate this understanding of "place" in a "racial"/ethnic, class, gender, nationality, and linguistic context to encourage students' development of a deeper sense of self and the complex ways in which "place" has contributed to their identity formation.

In the collaboration process of constructing a literacy history narrative, the teacher facilitates a student's awareness of the imprints of power in his/her literacy experiences. To generate discussion and foster critical reflection, critical literacy teachers use, for instance, popular songs, books or excerpts from the books, news or magazine articles, Internet sites, historical texts, and/or pictures relevant to students' literacy experiences (e.g., their daily struggles, classroom challenges, the interplay of educational access and social position, structural impediments to literacy development, etc.). Critical literacy teachers employ these materials to stimulate students' awareness of the larger socio-historical, socio-economic, and socio-cultural influences impacting their own experiences. As non-reading adolescents dialogue about their literacy circumstances and read and write it, critical literacy teachers assist each student in understanding that their limited literacy is a part of a social phenomenon. As such, it is thus not just specific to him/her—thereby minimizing possible feelings of alienation and isolation. Within this perspective, students furthermore come to realize that since their limited literacy skills have been socially created they can, in fact, change this circumstance in their lives.

To initially prepare students for the creation of their personal literacy history narratives, critical literacy teachers situate reading and writing within a context that calls attention to the relationship of literacy and power. For example, critical literacy teachers can use historical texts, such as slave narratives or legal documents that illustrate the existence of literacy laws in the U.S. in southern states during the period of institutionalized slavery. These laws outlawed teaching slaves to read and write and additionally made it illegal for slaves to know how to read. The literacy laws served as an attempt, according to the slaveholders' ideology at the time, to prevent slaves from reading materials that would lead them to question their conditions and, subsequently, revolt. Along the same vein, lessons can include readings and discussion about how most southern states in the U.S. after the Civil War imposed literacy tests—among other discriminatory measures, including terror—to bar African Americans from voting. As teacher and student explore these historical incidents, which highlight the interplay of literacy and power, critical literacy teachers encourage students to see connections in their present-day experiences. Questions that the critical teacher may ask to illicit deeper reflection can include:

- Did you ever hear about these literacy laws before? What do you think about these laws? Are they fair? Why or why not?

- Who has the power because of these laws? Who does not have the power, or is denied power, because of these laws?

- Do you think being able to read or write gives a person more opportunities, or power? Why or why not?

- Did you ever feel that you were prevented from learning how to read and write?

- Did you ever miss out on an opportunity because you could not read or write?

As students provide their verbal responses to this critical inquiry, critical literacy teachers write down the students' words so that each student can read his/her written remarks several times for both print literacy development and further critical reflection and discussion.

Often, before critical analysis, students blame themselves for their limited understanding of print literacy. They do not recognize the structural forces, operating across "racial"/ethnic, class, gender, and linguistic boundaries that have played a part in their hindered literacy development. Upon initial discussion about students' obstructed literacy process, students may explain that they cannot read because they "didn't try" or they "behaved badly." However, when asked, for example, if teachers worked with them one-on-one and taught them to read and write at the level and pace the student required, the student often, upon reflection, responds, "No." Teachers, then, reconsider students' initial premise; and, particularly for those who had acted disruptively in class or did not attend school regularly, they recognize that maybe had they been given teachings tailored to their specific literacy needs, they would have behaved better or would have stayed in school.

In relation to the connection between understanding causality and critical awareness, Freire (1974) explains: "The more accurately men [people] grasp true causality, the more critical their understanding of reality will be" (p. 39). As these youth—who have been branded with such labels as "academic failures," "special education," "illiterate," and "prisoners"—speak, read, write and critically reflect on (a) their experiences in relation to literacy both in and out of school and (b) personal and societal experiences that may have thus far impeded their literacy acquisition, students gain a critical awareness of their positionality within the social web. This critical understanding, coupled with textual literacy instruction provided in this curriculum, encourages these youth to move beyond previous barriers and through continuing obstacles more effectively. Furthermore, with heightened critical consciousness on the issue, these youth may be more inclined to advocate for themselves as well as garner support of parent(s)/guardian(s) in the advocacy process, so that they may actually receive meaningful and empowering literacy instruction as they travel through subsequent educational settings.

Questions for Creating Literacy Histories Narratives

Questions for creating a student's literacy history narrative can explore how not being able to read and write has influenced, or shaped, his/her lived experiences and what each student believes are the reasons that have contributed to his/her remedial literacy abilities. Such focus can unravel the ontological meaning of being an adolescent who is a non-reader in addition to students' relationship with schooling and learning to read. Critical reflection on these issues serves to offer a forum in which students can gain critical awareness of their literacy experiences with the intent of identifying and even overcoming personal and institutional blocks that may impede their present and future literacy development. While institutional impediments to these adolescents' literacy development may, in fact, be too entrenched to remove, the act of identifying them can assist in enabling students to negotiate around them. Possible questions for stimulating critical dialogue and the creation of literacy history narratives through critical language experience may include:

- Do you think it is important to know how to read and write and, if so, why?

- What is your earliest memory of reading/writing?

- How has not being able to read and write affected, or impacted, you on a daily basis?

- How has not being able to read and write affected, or impacted, your school experience?

- What is it like in your community or in the streets not being able to read and write?

- How would you describe your neighborhood or community?

- What do you think have been some factors that have prevented you from reading and writing on grade level?

- What has school been like for you?

- Can you talk about any teachers who you liked or did not like? And, explain why you liked or did not like them?

- How would you describe your overall school experience and feelings about school?

- Can you talk about any good experiences that you have had with reading/writing?

- Can you talk about any bad experiences that you have had with reading/writing?

- During times when you were not actually in a school building, did anyone ever read to you? If so, who?

- Did a parent(s) (or guardian) ever talk to you about reading/writing? If so, what would your parent(s) (or guardian) say about reading/writing?

- Can your parent(s) (or guardian) read and write? Did they ever read to you? If so, what would they read to you?

- How would you describe the literacy instruction/teaching that you have had in schools?

- What type of reading/writing teaching has been the most useful and/or enjoyable for you? And, why do you feel this way?

- When you do read (or someone reads to you), what do you like to read the most (e.g., books with pictures, books with no pictures, magazines, comics, etc.)? And, why?

- If you have to read a book that you are interested in, would you rather read it from a computer or read the book holding the actual book itself? Why?

- Do you prefer reading books with pictures or without pictures? And, why?

- If, right now, you were able to read and write on grade level, what would you do differently in your life?

- Do you speak another language(s) in addition to English? If so, which language(s)?

- For bilingual students:

    o What was the first language that you learned to speak?

    o At what age did you start learning English?

    o At what age did you start learning Spanish (or other)?

    o Is one language easier for you to speak than the other?

    o If so, which language is easier?

    o Are there certain times that one language is easier than the other?

    o When speaking with other family members or friends who are bilingual, do you have a preference of which language you use?

- o Do you use both languages in the same conversation with someone else who is bilingual, or do you just use one language in the conversation?

- o How do you feel about being bilingual?

- o Have both of the languages that you speak been used to teach you in school?

- o If yes, how do you feel about that?

- o If no, how do you feel about that?

- For incarcerated adolescents: Do you think being incarcerated has anything to do with your reading/writing abilities?

- Did you live outside of the U.S., have lapses in your schooling for some reason, and/or change schools often?

- Are you identified as special education; or, were you recently referred?

- If special education classified: At what age were you referred for special education and what was your classification? How did you feel about being put into special education?

- Who did you live with when you were younger?

- What is your relationship with parent(s) or guardian?

- Did people in your life influence, either positively or negatively, your school experience?

- What could have been done differently so that you would have been able to read and write at an earlier age?

- Now that you have had time to develop your reading/writing skills what do you think you can do differently in the present and will be able to do in the future in terms of your reading and writing?

- If you had a 6-year-old brother or sister and they were not taking school seriously—cutting school, getting into trouble—what would you tell them?

- Pretend you were at a job interview and the person who was interviewing you asked you to describe who you are. What two or three things would you say about yourself? If the person interviewing you for the job asked if you read/write well, what would you tell them?

- What would you tell teachers so that they can give you better reading/ writing instruction?

- Do you have anything specific to tell other people about reading and writing?

After Writing the First Draft of the Literacy History Narrative

After a student has finished the first draft of the literacy history narrative, using questions such as those listed above to serve as a guide and stimulus for remembering past experiences, the student reads aloud his/her co-generated narrative with the critical literacy teacher's assistance, when needed. After reading it aloud one time, the student reads the narrative again, sometimes several times, so that the teacher and student can discuss recollections of experiences provided in the first draft to make changes, if the student sees fit. During this editing stage, to further expand the student's critical understanding of dimensions of power involved in his/her literacy experiences, as well as to, perhaps, provide a deeper structure to his/her text, the teacher may again need to bring in a picture or print material that focuses on a similar theme to one, or several, that a student has written about in his/her literacy history narrative.

Once the student and teacher have made any possible content changes to the literacy history narrative, the student uses the computer to type his/her story. The teacher then edits a printed out copy, correcting spelling and/or punctuation errors. After the student implements these corrections to produce the final copy of his/her literacy history text, s/he reads the story aloud again. Within this process of writing and reading several drafts of the narrative, students enhance both their textual and contextual literacies.

While promoting students' critical literacy, the production of students' literacy history narratives, and all other non-fictional pieces, additionally develops critical literacy teachers' critical awareness. In keeping with Foucault's (1980) emphasis on historicity, the critical literacy teacher searches for the interconnected, multiple historical and cultural contexts in which students' experiences are embedded to uncover various dimensions of power that operate in these youths' lives and that led to their becoming teenagers without being able to read and write. With this understanding, critical literacy teachers can shape teachings to address students' literacy development needs more effectively.

As critical language experience enables a curriculum that honors alternative ways of being in the world and seeing the world, it provides an empowering peda- gogical strategy for a critical literacy curriculum. While offering a content rich op- portunity for print literacy development, it also serves as a means, when creating non-fictional language experience texts, for non-reading adolescents to reflect on and act upon their situation. As these youth tell their story, they read their world and can critically reflect on ways in which (a) structural forces of domination and their own particular circumstances influence their lives; (b) their personal expe- riences are part of larger economic, political, and social dynamics; and (c) they possess the ability to transform negative aspects of their conditions. Therefore, in addition to enabling students to advance their print literacy knowledge and engage their imagination in student-centered, meaningful ways, the creation of their critical language experience stories based on their lives, serve as the contex- tual content from which teacher and student can engage in dialogical praxis and, ultimately, *conscientization*.

Evaluation

Since students' themes and interests drive this curriculum and its syllabus, eval- uation of students' progress requires a different type of assessment than the measurement of fixed, or preset, criteria and objectives. This critical literacy cur- riculum therefore employs continual, process-based evaluation that takes into ac- count anticipated as well as unanticipated developments, which, among numer- ous other possibilities, can include changes such as a student's:

a.   Increased understanding of the mechanics of textual literacy;

b.   Newfound joy and love of reading and writing;

c.   Deepening awareness of his/her personal challenges within their larger structural context;

d.   Reconsideration of a past action or event in a new light to grasp more complex dynamics involved;

e.   Ability to consider positive alternatives to challenging life situations;

  f.   Overall creativity in writing and reading the word and the world.

Within this process-based evaluation approach, ongoing assessment is embedded in the lessons so as to provide subsequent teachings according to specific needs of each child. Critical literacy teachers, therefore, evaluate their students' development daily, even minute to minute at times. However, critical literacy educators implement evaluation in a way that promotes learning, which means that assessments are not used to punish students but, instead, help both teacher and student gauge students' progress. As such, they serve as a means for creating further teachings based on print literacy skills the student may still need to work on or textual skills and critical concepts that the student may be ready to start exploring. Students are, therefore, not given letter grades, but rather narrative reports that highlight students' strengths as well as challenges. Such a report gives a broader picture of the students' progress and presents areas of instruction for future teachings that will benefit the child. This manner of assessment, unlike positivistic measures, allows teachers to evaluate students' progress in relation to the level on which they are actually performing, rather than requiring them to attain arbitrarily predetermined skills deemed developmentally appropriate according to their grade level.

Students can also learn to evaluate their own progression. These self-evaluations can focus on, for example, the effects of the literacy teachings on students' attitude toward reading and writing, students' perception of their print literacy development, and students' thoughts about new understandings of themselves within society. Critical literacy teachers can furthermore encourage students to create their own categories of progress for self-assessment.

Critical Language Experience Situated within Learning and Literacy Theories

In addition to providing a tool for textual literacy development and critical analysis, promoting conscientization, critical language experience accords with key social cognition theories on learning (highlighted in chapter four). Critical language experience embraces the socially situated nature of learning—which Lave and Wenger (1991) describe as "a view according to which social practice is the primary, generative phenomenon, and learning is one of the characteristics" (p. 34)—a notion that is echoed in the work of fellow social cognitive psychologists Vygotsky (1978, 1989) and Varela (1999).

Critical language experience enables what Lave and Wenger (1991) refer to as learning as participation in a "community of practice." A critical language experience approach is positioned within a community of literacy practice that is, as Lave and Wenger also advocate, organized in an apprenticeship arrangement.

In the socially situated, apprenticeship learning construction of critical language experience, the teacher—as the more knowledgeable participant—facilitates the student's textual and contextual literacy development through critical discussion and the teacher's "expert" modeling of the literacy task. As critical language experience, furthermore, centers on student's own experiences, language, interests, and knowledge, it embraces the concept of self as socially situated by integrating students' lived social context into the learning process.

Critical language experience also intrinsically employs social cognitive psychologist Vygotsky's (1978, 1989) concept of "zone of proximal development" (ZPD) and its accompanying scaffolding instruction strategy. Influential in Lave and Wenger's "community of practice," Vygotsky's zone of proximal development represents the distance between a learner's independent performance level and the level at which s/he performs with the assistance of someone who is more knowledgeable about the task at hand. In other words, it is the difference between what the learner can do on his/her own and what s/he can do with assistance. As a more knowledgeable other provides the learner individualized support, known as scaffolding, it promotes the learner's development through their ZPD. This assistance allows the learner to increase their knowledge within a social context that builds on prior knowledge, while exposing them in a non-threatening manner to new information. Critical language experience naturally scaffolds print literacy learning as the teacher's assistance (a) provides an essential support for engaging students in reading and writing activities beyond their independent performance level and (b) augments students' previously acquired knowledge while they learn new information.

Conclusion

This critical literacy curriculum therefore goes beyond just teaching the mechanics of literacy, provided in synthetic phonics instruction. It achieves such a goal as critical language experience intrinsically incorporates students' cognitive and aesthetic capacities within a critical perspective that builds on their prior knowledge in meaningful ways. In keeping with critical pedagogy and social cognitive psychology, critical language experience situates literacy in a critical and social framework, while simultaneously tapping into student's imagination and relating text to student's personal experiences to enhance comprehension of print. Ultimately, while critical language experience occurs within a dynamic social relationship and emerges from students' language and experience—and thus background knowledge—it:

a.   In line with a critical pedagogical vision, positions literacy development within its socio-political and socio-cultural contexts;

b.   Accords with the learning theories of social cognitive psychologists, such as Lave and Wenger (1991), Varela (1999), and Vygotsky (1978, 1989).

Therefore, combining direct phonics instruction with critical language experience offers non-reading adolescents a counter-instrumentalist literacy development approach that enables the delivery of a more holistic, creative literacy curriculum. Such a dynamic literacy curriculum is situated within a critical, social, cultural, cognitive, and affective framework that aims, in the spirit of Paulo Freire, to promote textual literacy as well as critical awareness and transformation.

SEVEN

Conclusion

Curriculum as Political Text: Understanding Structures that Have Created a Population of Non-reading Adolescents and an Unjust School System

As conversation among contemporary educational policymakers omits direct discussion regarding adolescents who read below a 3rd grade level equivalent, school policies, practices, and curricula have disregarded non-reading adolescents' literacy and overall educational needs. These students—who, in urban areas, are predominantly comprised of low-income African American and Latino youth, given discriminatory patterns throughout societal institutions—experience heighten marginalization within an already subjugated population of inner-city youth. They, thus, confront an increased level of dehumanization amidst the antidemocratic nature of the school system. Therefore, as this book called attention to forces that have obstructed opportunities and resources for urban, low-income African American and Latino students, culminating in their unequal educational outcomes, it highlighted specific inequities within the school system perpetrated against non-reading adolescents, many of whom are also incarcerated. By placing an understanding of curriculum within a critical and political context, this book revealed social influences impacting non-reading adolescents. It highlighted that since non-reading adolescents in New York City are predominantly from economically disadvantaged backgrounds and from historically discriminated minority groups, they have not attained print literacy due to unequal social relations. These unbalanced social relations have limited these youths' economic opportunities and have denied them equitable and meaningful educational experiences.

The analytical lens presented in this study, thus, contextualized paradigmatic influences and institutionalized dynamics that have contributed to the creation of a contingent of inner-city youth who read below a 3rd grade level equivalent. It, furthermore, exposed the impact of these forces on their socio-educational lives. From such a perspective, it presented a backdrop for designing a critical literacy curriculum. Positioning this political analysis of antidemocratic educational structures and the ideology involved in their formation within a critical, place-based discourse, additionally, highlighted the harmful ramifications of these practices for non-reading adolescents in New York City. Such a perspective offered insight into the particular, in addition to the general. Understanding causal connections underlying inequitable educational policies and practices and uncovering their effect on non-reading adolescents' pedagogical lives, laid out the context for envisioning alternatives that create humanizing school experiences for non-reading adolescents.

Chapter two revealed educational policies and practices that have historically functioned to maintain the social order and suppress critical social inquiry. In so doing, it critiqued existing exclusionary, positivistic measures that have habitually informed U.S. educational policies, practices, research, and ultimately literacy pedagogy. It, furthermore, emphasized the way in which this restricted consciousness has, in turn, excluded particular student populations, including non-reading adolescents, and has also denied critical literacy teachings for all students. This analysis essentially illustrated the need for envisioning and creating more just and democratic schooling for all students, especially non-reading adolescents in New York City.

In particular, chapter two highlighted the way in which social efficiency ideology and its accompanying move toward scientific management have fueled injustices—enacted across class, "race"/ethnicity, gender, language, and other identity categories—that have been entrenched within the educational system for over a century. At the turn of the 19th century, driven by positivism's claim to scientific neutrality and objectivity and, also, rooted in social eugenics theories, educational policymakers created a system that reflected societal disparities and ensured maintenance of the status quo. They achieved this goal by placing the purpose of education in social control, rather than intellectual growth.

Among these measures, educational policymakers, whom Tyack (1974) refers to as administrative progressives, implemented differentiated curricula and special education programs and used psychometric testing to further their social efficiency goals. Amidst this differentiated curricula, children in higher socio-economic strata engaged in "academic studies," which prepared them for college, while students from lower socio-economic classes received vocational education, which led them to a predetermined lower position within the job market. As increasingly effective compulsory education laws made it mandatory that all students attend schools, all students were subjected to this social engineering process, which relegated students to their prescribed position within the social hierarchy contingent upon their socio-economic status.

Special education, representing the lowest track in the differentiated curricula, additionally emerged as a way for the school system to separate particular students that administrative progressives perceived as especially problematic for society—a practice which Lazerson (1983) points out continues to this day through special education classification. He, furthermore, maintains that while special education, since its genesis, has targeted different ethnicities throughout the decades, as the socio-political climate changes, special education has had especially pernicious consequences for low-income students, immigrant children—particularly from working class families and with darker phenotypes—and African American youth.

Within the differentiated curricula design, psychometric testing also arose as the "scientific" method for determining track placement and special education identification. Steeped in scientific racism and, thus, disregarding the class and cultural biases of IQ tests—which center on the dominant culture's knowledge—administrative progressives used these flawed evaluation tools to speciously justify the over-representation of low income, immigrant, and African American children in the lower tracks and special education.

This book emphasized that even though differentiated curricula based on students' socio-economic backgrounds no longer blatantly exist, they persist to this day in a more concealed form. Despite the *Brown vs. Board of Education* decision in 1954, which sought to equalize schooling for historically discriminated groups, the school system continues to produce inequitable educational outcomes across class, "race"/ethnicity, gender, and other identity categories. First, IQ tests are still part of the procedure for determining special education identification, which, as the elite class' values and culture inform these tests, disproportionately classify economically and socially marginalized student populations for special education. Second, since schools in poorer neighborhoods receive less funding than those within more affluent communities, the quality of education for those youth from lower socio-economic backgrounds still remains unequal in comparison to those within higher social classes.

Third, a profound manifestation that social efficiency ideology has endured lies in the reality that, in addition to the IQ testing still used in special education identification, educational policymakers—espousing rhetoric of standards, as defined by the dominant culture —have whole-heartedly embraced standardized assessments as an integral part of the school system. Currently, as a technocratic, instrumentalist vision informs No Child Left Behind (NCLB)—the contemporary national educational reform policy—this national initiative prioritizes "rigorous" standards and standardized testing procedures. As such, it requires the administration of standardized State ELA and Math exams to all students in grades 3rd–8th. As educational policymakers erroneously contend that standardized tests provide "objective" data on students' academic performance, they continue to ignore the way in which these forms of assessment privilege the dominant culture's history and language and deny knowledge of marginalized groups.

More alarmingly, educational policymakers increasingly have set standardized tests within a high-stakes context. Therefore, regardless of the class and culturally bound nature of these psychometric measures, in the current educational landscape students' results on single standardized assessments determine important educational decisions pertaining to them, their teachers, and their schools. Ultimately, rather than the explicit differentiated curricula of the early 20th century, the present-day focus on standards and standardized testing promoted within NCLB serves as the contemporary mechanism for excluding low-income students, particularly those from historically discriminated "racial"/ethnic groups.

While placing those students whose histories do not coincide with the cultural stance reflected in these standardized exams at a disadvantage, scientific management and standard knowledge create an undemocratic school system for all students. Such pedagogy eradicates multiple ideologies in order to promote a mono-cultural interest and maintain the status quo. Although illuminated throughout the book, chapter two situated the larger domestication effort promoted through this educational paradigm of "objectivity" and standardization. hooks (2003) encapsulates the workings of this domestication dynamic in her assertion that claims to objectivity function as an apparatus "to bring others into conformity with objective 'truth'" (p. 128).

Freire (1970), furthermore, refers to pedagogy grounded on the standardization of information and knowledge as a "banking system." Within this "banking" education educators deposit knowledge into learners, thereby inhibiting learners' critical consciousness in an effort to stifle social critique. Thus, "banking" within the U.S. school system, currently achieved through educational policymakers' emphasis on standards, standardized testing, and test-driven curriculum, aims to inhibit critical inquiry for all students, regardless of their position within the social hierarchy. This "banking" pedagogy preserves the dominant culture's ideology and reinforces the social order—a dynamic that has even more dire consequences for those within marginalized positions.

The prevailing social efficiency theory and scientific management methods that have informed the educational system since the beginning of the 20th century have greatly impacted literacy curriculum. Like all other content areas, literacy instructions and policies have centered on the standardization of information and knowledge—an ideology and practice that is endemic to social efficiency and scientific management. This instrumentalist framework has diminished literacy pedagogy to the acquisition of quantifiable basic mechanical skills. In doing so, it ignores the affective and creative aspects of literacy, discounts its social and cultural elements, and prevents critical literacy.

By negating the social, emotional, creative, and power inscribed contexts of literacy and limiting literacy discourse to solely technical boundaries, the instrumentalist perspective produces a "banking" education and, thus, inhibits self-actualizing pedagogy that facilitates reading and writing the word and the world. As NCLB and the National Reading Panel (NRP) report (the meta-analysis literacy study, released in 2000, that has informed policy set forth within NCLB) embrace a technical, functionalist literacy framework and prioritize standardized testing, they serve as the contemporary apparatus on the national level for creating literacy curriculum that thwarts critical awareness and social critique, ensures social control, and perpetuates dominant ideology. As all other academic subjects, in addition to literacy, continue to be directed toward the dominant cultural framework, which is, in turn, reinforced and tested through class and culturally bound standardized assessment practices, an educational system based on these teachings and testing measures provides the power elite's overall purpose of (a) inhibiting critical thinking, (b) keeping the production of knowledge within fixed parameters, and (c) maintaining the current social order.

Social Cognition Psychology Exposes Shortcomings of an Educational System Informed by Traditional Cognitive Psychology

The analysis in this book accentuated the limited and culturally biased perspective of traditional cognitive psychology, which has historically informed positivistic educational research and, thus, subsequent practices and policies enacted in the school system. It highlighted the way in which understanding knowledge, intelligence, and consciousness within social cognitive psychology allows for a more complex conception of cognition and the mind itself. The social cognitive psychology perspective, ultimately, exposes the injustice of such practices as positivistic psychometric testing measures, which traditional cognitive psychology has promoted. In contrast to the constricted vision of traditional cognitive psychologists, which focuses on only neurological impulses, social cognitive psychologists view the mind and consciousness within a concept of the self as socially situated. Social cognitive psychologists—such as Lev Vygotsky (1978, 1989), Francisco Varela (1999), and Jean Lave and Etienne Wenger (1991)—recognize the importance of social and historical aspects of cognition. They, therefore, understand the ontological and political importance of identity markers, for example, "race"/ ethnicity, class, and gender, in forming one's consciousness.

Given the absence of social and historical contexts within psychometric testing, social cognition underscores the fallacies of standardized testing and its attempts to quantify knowledge, intelligence, and consciousness. Comprehending the self as socially situated and relational, calls attention to the hegemonic interests furthered through psychometric measures. By ignoring social influences on cognition, psychometric testing serves as a tool for justifying the subjugation of those positioned outside of the upper-middle class, Eurocentric historical lens represented within these tests. A social cognitive vision, therefore, reveals the inequity, for instance, of continuing to use IQ tests, which are culturally specific instruments, for determining special education placement.

As social cognition emphasizes social influence on cognition, it, in essence, illuminates inherent inequalities within efforts to "objectively" measure ability or intelligence using psychometric testing, in light of the mono-cultural (i.e., the dominant class') perspective reflected in these forms of assessment. Social cognition, therefore, offers an essential framework for understanding the institutional outcomes of marginalized student populations. As such, it accentuates the structural forces involved in urban, low-income African American and Latino youths' disproportionate representation in special education, lower standardized test scores, and subsequent higher push-out/dropout as well as incarceration patterns.

Situated within the Complexity of the Lived World

While the analysis presented in this book rejected claims to scientific neutrality and "objective" truth and, instead, employed a framework that values historical and cultural contexts for understanding the surrounding world, it furthered a multilogical framework that understands the complexities of the lived world and social inquiry. Foucault (1980) informs, power is always enmeshed with knowledge and, therefore, there is no neutral research. In keeping with Foucault and recognizing the "limits of 'objective science' and its 'universal knowledge'" (Kincheloe, 2004a, p. 25), this book provided a self-aware methodology and expansive research frame. It did so by employing a research lens that acknowledged that the knower and known cannot be separated, as well as that social and historical influences are central to both the production of knowledge and pedagogy. This focus, thus, contrasted the restrictive, positivistic research that has historically guided the U.S. educational system. Therefore, with full disclosure of *The Ghosts of No Child Left Behind's* intrinsic biases informed by my, the researcher's, perceptions, which have been shaped by the interplay of my lived experiences and social positioning, this book offered an analysis that challenged the status quo and positioned education within a social and historical context.

My inquiry additionally implemented a part-whole perspective to understand the larger picture of socio-political, socio-economic, socio-cultural forces operating within non-reading adolescents' pedagogical lives and to reconceptualize literacy curriculum for these youth within a critical framework. This part to whole process revealed the deeper meanings rooted within particular social phenomena, related to non-reading adolescents' educational process, by connecting these realities to their numerous inter-related contexts. Such an emphasis, subsequently, fostered a more textured analysis, as it strove to uncover interconnected social situations affecting these youth. A political understanding of curriculum within a critical framework, ultimately, allowed me to highlight and expand on the interplay of power and knowledge within schooling to understand ways in which this relationship has impacted the socio-educational experience of non-reading adolescents in New York City in particular. My research lens, thus, continually shifted focus throughout the book between part and whole as I explored the workings of power pertinent to the education of non-reading adolescents.

Reviewing the Literature Highlighted Systematic Prejudices and Imprints of Power within Education

The literature review facilitated a critical political understanding of curriculum in the effort to foster empowering literacy pedagogy for non-reading adolescents in New York City. As the literature review discussed educational inequities that target inner-city youth, emphasizing prejudicial practices in New York City, it underscored structures that have contributed to the production of a non-reading adolescent population. Such an analysis highlighted paradigmatic influences and pedagogical policies and practices that have led to disproportionately high push-out/dropout patterns among inner-city youth and their over-representation in special education programs and juvenile detention centers.

In the literature review, education analysts and historians within the critical theoretical tradition exposed the systematic miseducation of, in particular, low-income African American and Latino youth. In addition to Tyack's (1974) analysis of the intentional exclusion of African Americans, specific immigrant groups, and economically disadvantaged students within the initial design of the school system, previously discussed, numerous critical pedagogues delineated the persistence of social engineering within the schooling process and its impact on inner-city African American and Latino students.

Numerous critical pedagogues accentuated the way in which curricula and overall school structure emerge from a Eurocentric perspective and, thus, devalue students from other cultures. In dismissing cultures and perspectives outside the

Western, Eurocentric historical lens, the educational system subsequently excludes students across "racial"/ethnic, class, and gender lines, especially economically disadvantaged African Americans and Latinos. Critical theorists, therefore, called for critical multicultural and multilogical perspectives, which intrinsically validate students from diverse backgrounds and social positions—including youth from historically marginalized populations.

hooks (1994), Kincheloe (2001a, 2004a), and Kincheloe and Steinberg (1997) described the tacit, or sometimes explicit, subordinating "cultural messages," which Illich (1971) refers to as the "hidden curriculum," that are embedded within the school structure and manifested in discriminatory ideology and policies. These practices—such as culturally and class biased standardized tests and Eurocentric curricula—preserve the social order, as they marginalize particular groups while privileging others across identity categories. Foucault's (1980) analysis of power and control within the assessment process additionally situated standardized testing as a "technology of power" for furthering the elite class' domination effort.

Amidst the "cultural messages," "hidden curriculum," and "technologies of power," critical pedagogues highlighted that the power structure deflects responsibility in limiting educational opportunities of historically subjugated groups as dominant discourse blames the "academic failure" of these students on the students, themselves, as opposed to the prejudicial structures creating these inequitable outcomes across "racial"/ethnic, class, gender, and other identity markers.

Although numerous inner-city children have resisted forces of oppression to overcome structural impediments, the critical theories underscored in the literature review—which emphasized the systematic miseducation of low-income African American and Latino youth—contextualized a reality in which literacy levels of many inner-city youth fall below grade level. This group of students includes a population of adolescents, both within mainstream schools and detention center schools, who read below a 3rd grade level equivalent. The National Assessment of Educational Progress' (NAEP) statistics further revealed that economic poverty negatively affects a students' academic performance, producing lower literacy scores. These findings, thus, informed further on societal forces that have created a population of non-reading adolescents among inner-city youth.

Various academics, several of whom are part of the critical theoretical tradition, described other structural socio-economic influences impacting inner-city students' academic performance and, thus, their literacy levels. These scholars pointed out the severe funding disparities between inner-city schools and those in economically privileged neighborhoods. They also noted the lower quality of instruction and content material in inner-city schools in relation to those within wealthy neighborhoods. As such, students in these schools are often ill prepared to compete within the mainstream job-market.

In addition to the aforementioned inequities perpetrated against inner-city youth, the literature review informed on educational injustices specifically targeting historically marginalized linguistic minorities. This analysis focused on prejudicial language policies and their pernicious impact on Latino youth—which includes those who are Spanish dominant, English dominant, or bilingual. It, furthermore, emphasized that despite the Bilingual Education Act of 1968, Title VII, which aimed to create more equal educational opportunities for linguistic minorities, policymakers have employed policies that have reproduced the dominant ideology. In following an agenda of politics, as opposed to pedagogy, policymakers have sabotaged bilingual programs.

Crawford (1991), Trueba (1989), Zentella, (1997), and others asserted that as the power structure has viewed languages other than English and multiculturalism as an ideological threat to the notion of being American, educational policymakers have focused pedagogy for linguistic minorities on Anglo-conformity. Demonstrating the workings of the close interplay between language, culture, and power, as a result of this political controversy over the nature of language, policymakers called for English-only programs—such as English as a Second Language (ESL). The literature review revealed that this prejudicial language policy, therefore, inhibited maintenance bilingual teachings, which had the potential to teach students the English necessary for survival within the U.S., while simultaneously maintaining their home language. Maintenance of students' home language would have the benefit of (a) preserving and affirming their cultural identity and (b) enabling natural progression of literacy development by using students' strong oral first language base for developing literacy skills in their first language, which ultimately transfer to their second language.

Several scholars of education for English Language Learners (ELLs) also pointed out that policymakers employed faulty positivistic research measures to discount bilingual programs and instead promote ESL programs. Macedo and Bartolomé (1999) maintained that, amidst the political controversy surrounding bilingual education, policymakers disregarded sound research (Cummins, 1991; Hakuta, 1986; Troike, 1978) that affirmed the effectiveness of bilingual programs using native-language instruction; additionally, when evaluating the success of bilingual education, policymakers failed to account for social inequalities that inform bilingual programs. Crawford (1991) added that if a political agenda had not formed the basis of the issue, rather than the limited focus of comparing different program models, research could have, instead, addressed the linguistic, psychological, and social components of educating linguistic minority students to improve classroom instruction.

These insights with regard to bilingual education illustrated that even since the Bilingual Act of 1968, political motives through the decades have interfered with the implementation of effective bilingual programs, such as a maintenance bilingual model. This analysis demonstrated the systemic forces underlying high push-out/dropout rates among Latino students and engendering their dispropor-tionate "academic failure." Therefore, politics framed educational decisions about linguistic minorities creating a reality in which many Latinos have not received adequate teachings. As such, this analysis contextualized a phenomenon in which to this day some Latino students, particularly those from economically disadvan-taged backgrounds, reach adolescence without being able to read and write print in English or, for those students who entered the school system as bilingual or Spanish-dominant, in Spanish.

Research Focusing on Inequitable Push-Out/Dropout Patterns, Special Education Placement, and Incarceration

The literature review also presented statistics pertaining to disproportionate push-out/dropout patterns across "race"/ethnicity, class, gender, and ability categories. Orfield et al. (2004) provided national statistics based on the actual enrollment data that each district annually gives to the nation's Common Core of Data. These figures indicated that black, Native American, and Latino students graduate from high school at significantly lower rates than whites and Asian/Pacific Islanders. Orfield et al.'s calculations for graduation rates among male and female students within "racial"/ethnic groups, furthermore, illuminated lower graduation rates among males than females within ethnicities. Fine (1991) reported that 40% to 60% of low-income, urban African American and Latino students drop out of high school—a trend that Orfield et al.'s research indicated has continued at com-parable rates throughout the years. According to Orfield et al., across the nation low graduation rates are more common within high poverty districts in central urban areas with high percentages of students classified as having disabilities, or with high percentages of English Language Learners. Lastly, Orfield et al. re-ported that graduation rates among students identified for special education are as low as 32%.

Various scholars noted the institutionalized biases in special education refer-ral and assessment that disproportionately identify low-income black and Latino youth for special education services. These scholars discussed that the education system's solution for denying curriculum that accommodates students' cultural and linguistic diversity has been to warehouse historically discriminated "racial"/ethnic and linguistic minorities, particularly black and Latino students, in special education programs—a dynamic which impacts economically disadvantaged stu-dents more profoundly. The literature review, therefore, illuminated that despite federal legislation to improve special education (beginning in 1975 with the pas-sage of Public Law 94-142) discriminatory practices persist. It, furthermore, de-scribed that these prejudicial procedures stem from culturally unresponsive curriculum; a deficit ideology that has maintained narrow definitions of "normalcy," which the dominant culture's belief system has shaped; and culturally, class, and linguistically biased classification procedures.

In light of the high percentage of dropouts, thereby diminishing the power of special education programs' role in both social control and providing a lasting safety valve for the miseducation of particular groups of students, Foucault's (1977, 1980) analysis of penal institutions as a central component of the dominant class' technology of power helped situate the proliferation of juvenile detention centers. The disproportionate percentage of inner-city youth within detention centers who are special education classified, including a population of adolescents who read below a 3rd grade level equivalent, displays Foucault's theory in action. Although educational disadvantage in no way inevitably signifies incarceration, reviewing the literature brought to light the way in which the disproportionate representation of low-income black and Latino youth in juvenile detention centers emerges from systematic forces that have produced their over-representation in special education programs and related disproportionate push-out/dropout patterns. The literature review, thus, highlighted the correlation between inner-city students' higher special education identification, higher push-out/dropout rates and their over-representation in detention centers—a manifestation of, as well as result of, the miseducation of this student population.

The Correctional Association of New York (2004a) reported that approximately half of the population of youth referred to the Office of Child and Family Services (the agency that places juveniles in the juvenile justice system) were identified in 2000 for special education programs. Several scholars further outlined the relation between the miseducation of inner-city youth, their special education classification, dropping out, and imprisonment. Amidst exclusionary school practices and ideology, as numerous inner-city youth choose to leave high school before finishing—a large percentage of whom are special education classified (Orfield et al., 2004)—Leone et al. (2003) explained that they have problems finding meaningful work. This predicament presents a higher risk for possible involvement with juvenile courts and detention centers. Researchers who focus on juvenile justice emphasized the relationship between the miseducation of socio-economically disadvantaged black and Latino youth, their limited employment opportunities, and incarceration.

In addition to limited education and poor quality schooling, Wilson (1987, 1996), among others, also emphasized "racial"/ethnic discrimination in the mainstream job market that interferes with gainful employment. Difficulties in attaining work within mainstream institutions compounded with racial-economic biases in arrest and incarceration patterns have created a situation in which youth from substandard inner-city schools make up the majority of the population within New York City juvenile facilities. Various studies additionally pointed out the connection between low reading levels and incarceration. The Coalition for Juvenile Justice reported that in 2001 the average reading level for ninth graders in detention facilities was 4th grade. In a New York City Detention Center, in which the majority of the students' ages range from 13 to 16 years old, statistics indicated that 25% of the students read below a 2.5 grade level equivalent.

The literature review powerfully illustrated that policymakers have institutionally subverted the civil right of equal opportunity by the guarantee of inequitable outcomes across identity categories. As such, this reality contextualized the resulting production of a contingent of inner-city adolescents who read within pre-primer and upper second grade limits.

Literacy as a Means for Self and Social Transformation

As the literature review placed literacy within a cultural, social, historical, and political context, it aligned this book with the critical theoretical tradition of utilizing literacy pedagogy as a means for fostering self and social change to advance an agenda for social justice. Freire's (1985), Giroux's (1988), and Macedo's (2006) analysis of critical literacy embodied Gramsci's (1971) description of literacy as a social practice that is historically connected to knowledge and power and, thus, can serve as a tool for self and social empowerment to counter the dominant class' efforts to employ literacy as a means for domination. Within such a context Freire asserted that illiteracy is a political creation. Their theories, furthermore, situated the type of literacy instruction historically employed within the school system, which aims to inhibit students' critical social critique to preserve the social order. Freire described this pedagogical method as "banking" education, and he proposed a critical literacy, or political literacy, approach to counter the domesticating goals of "banking."

Giroux and Macedo suggested that within the instrumentalist, functionalist literacy paradigm informing the school system, "banking" education denies students from all socio-economic backgrounds empowering pedagogy in which students can critically reflect on causal forces and their interconnections within society. Although grounded in these precepts as well, Freire focused on the dangers of "banking" for marginalized populations. He advocated for a critical literacy approach with learners in subjugated positions to facilitate a liberatory pedagogical experience that promotes critical reflection and action—a process he refers to as "reading and writing the word and the world"—in order to transform limiting conditions.

Positioning literacy pedagogy as a means for self-actualization provided the ideological structure of this book's emphasis on understanding curriculum as political text and creating empowering literacy pedagogy for non-reading adolescents. It, thus, offered a theoretical lens for (a) examining literacy teachings and other structures enacted within the school system since its genesis and (b) informing a critical literacy curriculum for non-reading adolescents in New York City.

The Effects of Contemporary Education Policy on Non-reading Adolescents' Pedagogical Experience

Chapter three focused on recent policy initiatives in New York City, in large part enacted due to NCLB mandates, to understand their impact on non-reading adolescents—many of whom are special education identified and/or linguistic minorities. The analysis presented further exposed the heightened marginalization of this student population. This socio-political analysis of unjust educational practices and policies within the pedagogical life of these youth revealed systemic forces of social engineering that create and perpetuate academic failure at basically every level of their school experience. Within current New York City policy, non-reading adolescents cannot possibly attain the predetermined standards—albeit culturally and class biased standards—tested within standardized tests for each grade level, as they do not have the textuality to even decode the print in these standardized exams. Nevertheless, this student population has had to endure the humiliation of showing up for these grade-level standardized tests.

Even more damaging, however, from 2003–2008 the New York City Department of Education (NYCDOE), informed by a traditional cognitive psychology lens, employed, with increasing severity, high-stakes testing, as they embraced a single-test promotion policy. In a supposed effort to prevent social promotion, beginning in the 2003–2004 school year, NYCDOE based the decision of 3rd grade promotion on the sole criteria of whether a student passed a standardized ELA and Mathematics exam. By the 2005–2006 school year this testing policy had become all the more pernicious as 3rd, 5th, and 7th grade promotion now rested on whether a child passed the standardized exams in each of these grades—a policy that continued through 2008. The 2005–2006 school year also marked, in compliance with a NCLB directive, the administration of the standardized ELA and Math State tests to students in grades 3rd–8th, as opposed to the prior practice of administering them to only 4th and 8th graders.

These high-stakes policies have been psychologically and academically damaging for non-reading adolescents, as well as other student populations. In addition to the negative impact on students' self-esteem, extensive research illustrated that retaining students can cause heightened anxiety and behavior problems (Roderick, 1995; Xia & Glennie, 2005). These studies also showed that students often become withdrawn and disinterested from school as a result of retention, especially multiple retentions. Educational research additionally illuminated that retention increases dropout rates and that over time it does not enhance student achievement (Advocates for Children of New York, 2004; Haney et al., 2004). Roderick's (1995) research added that the more times a student is retained, it increases the chances that s/he will drop out later during his/her schooling years. Such a policy, therefore, had the potential of inflating the population of non-reading adolescents, as well as other student groups, in detention centers, given the correlation between push-out/dropout patterns and incarceration.

New York City's recent single-test retention policy, additionally, inhibited meaningful and empowering pedagogy. It rendered irrelevant students' attitude toward learning, progress throughout the school year, and/or classroom test performance. It also compelled educators to shape curriculum to the standardized state test, rather than content that the child required according to his/her interest, academic needs, and social context. Such a dynamic continues. Although the NYCDOE no longer relies solely on the standardized State test for promotion, they still focus heavily on it as a considerable part of the promotion criteria. Therefore, even now the tests dictate curriculum. Additionally, since educators do not see their students' responses to questions on the standardized exams, these assessments have not provided instructional value for helping students improve their print literacy abilities.

While grave for all students, the previous high-stakes single-test promotion policy had a profoundly negative consequence for students in 3rd, 5th, and 7th grade who struggled with literacy. Many of these students' had literacy difficulties because, for example, they (a) required more time for processing verbal information, (b) had not had opportunities for developing their literacy abilities due to socio-economic challenges, and/or (c) received inadequate instruction. Yet, the single-test promotion policy disregarded these, and other, factors at play. This policy, furthermore, raised many questions as to how the NYCDOE planned to comprehensively address the literacy needs of older students who were classified as non-readers, as well as how many times a child could be retained in a given grade.

During the single-test promotion policy, there was no systemic plan developed to provide remediation and support for the literacy needs of non-reading adolescents, and other student populations, both before and after grade retention. Yet, the new promotion policy beginning in June 2009 answered the question of how many times a student would be retained due to failure to pass the State tests. Within this new promotion policy, for students in all grades except 8th who had been previously retained or were overage: if they failed to meet the new promotion criteria at the end of the 2009 summer, then principals and Community Superintendents determined promotion based on what was in the best interest of the student. For students in 8th grade who had been retained in grades 6–8 or turned 16 by December 31, 2008: they were promoted, even if they did not meet promotion criteria, provided that they attended summer school. In the case of these 8th grade students, the Bloomberg-Klein administration, thus, ultimately embraced social promotion without implementing a systemic literacy intervention plan for struggling students.

Fortunately, the 2009 promotion policy has moved away from the sole reliance on the State exams for promotion in targeted grades. The addition of the promotion portfolio assessment for those students in 3rd, 5th, 7th, and 8th grade who do not score at or above Level 2 on the standardized ELA and Math exams is an improvement from the previous single-test promotion policy. However, grade retention is not the proper solution for students whose performance even on the promotion portfolio assessment bars them from promotion to the next grade. Rather than a whole-scale grade retention policy, a more just and ecumenical promotion policy would be to provide these youth intensive intervention programs as they advance to the next grade.

In contrast to the prior promotion policy under the Bloomberg-Klein administration, their 2008–2009 school year reform for IDEA-eligible students presents a more supportive process. The newer policy allows students identified for special education to be held to modified promotion criteria, if indicated on their IEP. As such, their promotion does need to be contingent upon their passing the standardized ELA and Math tests or promotion portfolio in the targeted grades, if inappropriate for their performance level. However, it is essential that school personnel make the necessary changes to these students' IEPs so that their academic programs can be modified accordingly. It is too soon to say if these provisions have been provided adequately throughout the school system. While this recent reform for IDEA-eligible students offers an important and necessary adjustment in their school process, for many, such as non-reading adolescents, the fact that they still must take the standardized grade-level tests, nevertheless, persists in representing a humiliating school experience for them.

For English Language Learners, while the new promotion policy is less severe than the previous one, it continues to fall short of what sound research (Cummins, 1991) advocates. In holding ELL students to standard promotion after four years (rather than the previous policy's two year period), it still does not provide the necessary 5–7 years ELL students need to attain academic proficiency in English. Furthermore, policy for ELL 8th graders who have been enrolled in the school system for 2–3 years also has negative ramifications. Allowing these ELL students to achieve gains in ELA, rather than score at or above Level 2 (which is required on the State Math test), recognizes the research indicating the time needed for ELL students to acquire academic English. However, on the other hand, requiring this group of ELL 8th graders to pass all core courses, like their English-speaking peers, disregards the language needs of numerous ELL students. Since the majority of these youth must learn their core courses in English, as the maintenance bilingual programs have been phased out in favor of ESL programs, passing these courses becomes all the more problematic.

It remains to be seen how the 2009 promotion policy has played out. However, until the school system incorporates a systemic approach at every grade level for addressing the needs of struggling readers, non-reading adolescents, in particular, will seldom have a chance within the current school structure for a meaningful education that addresses their literacy needs.

Testing and Retention Policy Inherently Inequitable

In light of studies that revealed that retention policies increase the possibility that retained students will drop out, this book asserted that New York City's prior single-test retention policy served as an apparatus for "pushing out" non-reading adolescents. Furthermore, this book stressed that given the cultural and class-biases of standardized tests, the New York City Department of Education's large-scale single-test retention policy disproportionately targeted economically disadvantaged as well as subordinated ethnic and linguistic minority students. Therefore, the inherent inequalities of this policy surface as the highest retention rates were found among poor, minority, and inner-city youth.

Grounded in an ideology of domination, rather than improving "racial"/ethnic and class differences within the school system, such a high-stakes policy, in general, only intensifies the differential quality of education delivered to students on the basis of their economic and cultural backgrounds. There has been a major factor excluded in policy discourse at the federal, state, and city levels pertaining to academic achievement of special education, linguistic minority, economically disadvantaged, and other socially marginalized student populations. Absent from this conversation at the three levels aforementioned has been the way in which prejudicial ideologies inform decisions about practices—such as testing procedures, retention measures, languages used for instruction, and content included in test-driven curriculum, which in themselves often produce academic failure.

Furthermore, this book asserted that if a child's poor performance on the 3rd grade test stems from reading difficulties, then it is irresponsible of the school system to wait until 3rd grade to begin a concerted remediation effort. Intervention for reading difficulties must begin as early as pre-school. For all children, and particularly for those who may not have textual literacy support as part of their experience outside of school, schools must continually provide rich and engaging experiences with print literacy throughout a child's schooling, beginning in the pre-school stages.

For those students who struggle with reading, student performance improves in a supportive academic environment characterized by rigorous coursework, high expectations, and intensive intervention directed at each child's specific needs and level. Student performance in reading does not increase when subjected to single-test retention measures that produce anxiety, lower self-esteem, and detect print literacy difficulties too late in a child's academic development. Nor does achievement improve with the policy, referred to as "social promotion." This policy was pursued before the current New York City Department of Education administration, which promoted students without their having the literacy skills and strategies required for higher grade-level work, and essentially was reinstated under the current administration for overage 8th graders after attending Summer School.

My analysis showed that, in essence, neither social promotion nor single-test retention policies benefit students. Social promotion advances students to higher grades without teaching them adequate skills and basics necessary for completing more advanced work in subsequent higher grades. Single-test retention policies have proven to increase push-out/dropout rates, diminish students' self-esteem, and do not improve academic performance in the long-run. All too often, and as history has proven in New York City alone, both retention and social promotion policies have merely led to the creation of a group of adolescents who read on early elementary grade levels. Thus, such a reality calls for a new educational paradigm in which, among other changes, punitive, top-down standardized assessments are abolished and a literacy intervention program is built into the school infrastructure within each grade, pre-kindergarten–12th grade. With these measures, those students who require extra literacy support may receive it throughout their school careers.

Recent Special Education and Language Policy that Has Negatively Impacted Numerous Non-reading Adolescents

Chapter three described other recent policy initiatives that have targeted special education and English as a Second Language (ESL)/Bilingual programs and, in so doing, have negatively impacted non-reading adolescents in New York City—most of whom are identified for special education and/or linguistic minorities. Since NCLB was voted into law in 2001, it has required that all IDEA-eligible students—barring 1% of IDEA-eligible students (those receiving special education services) who are identified as severely cognitively delayed—must take the same high-stakes, grade-level state tests as general education students. The book argued that rather than the school system's proclamations of providing all students democratic and equal opportunity, this blanket mandate produces academic failure, for many special education students, including non-reading adolescents. Additionally, my analysis contended that for numerous youth in special education, especially non-reading adolescents, high-stakes, grade-level standardized exams are useless measures of both students' academic progress and the effectiveness of their schools in teaching them.

Instead of mandating that all IDEA-eligible students take the high-stakes, grade-level assessment, this book called for a more just policy. Short of a complete transformation of the way schooling is done to our students (detailed later in this chapter), amidst the school system's positivistic drive for quantifying achievement, my analysis proposed a more humane policy. Within this more just policy, all IDEA-eligible youth would have flexibility in taking an alternative exam appropriate to their specific academic performance—determined by various indicators, such as the student's IEP and classroom teacher evaluations. The final decision as to whether the student would take an alternative assessment, rather than the grade-level exam, would rest with the IEP team and the child's parent(s)/guardian(s). These bodies would decide on a yearly basis whether the child would take the alternative assessment or the grade-level exam.

Chapter three also exposed contemporary language policies in New York City that have perniciously affected linguistic minorities, especially those from marginalized groups, and, thus, contribute as well to the creation of a population of non-reading adolescents. Effective in June 2001, the then Chancellor Harold Levy adopted a new language policy that prioritized investment in ESL immersion programs, rather than bilingual programs that maintain students' first language while simultaneously teaching English. In accordance with NCLB, this language policy also set a goal of 3 years for linguistic minority students to exit from English immersion and the few bilingual programs left in existence. While this policy continues to this day, it:

- Produces unnecessary pressure and anxiety for students

- Devalues students' cultural identity as it prioritizes ESL programs—as opposed to maintenance bilingual programs

- Denies the impact of economic disadvantage on a child's school performance

- Ignores crucial second language development research (Cummins, 1991), which shows that, among other assets, the use of the learner's first language can promote transfer of knowledge, bridge the home-school gap, and build on the students language base to foster fluid literacy development and academic success

- Dismisses research (Cummins, 1991) that indicates that it takes 1–3 years for an ELL to develop conversational proficiency in English and 5–7 years to acquire academic English proficiency—and longer for those youth without literacy in their first language

Additional language policies, initiated at the federal level, have fostered damaging consequences for linguistic minorities, adding to the production of a population of non-reading adolescents. Throughout its existence, NCLB's requirement that all states implement annual assessments of English Language Learners (ELLs), in order to measure school and district accountability, has damagingly impacted ELL students. However, changes in 2006 have hurt this student population even more. In this year, the United States Department of Education (USDOE) reversed their position in allowing the New York State Education Department's (SED's) to use the New York State English as a Second Language Achievement Test (NYSESLAT) in place of the English Language Arts (ELA) test for evaluating those ELL students who had attended school in the U.S. for less than three consecutive years. As a result of this reversal, the new policy in New York City, beginning in 2007, has mandated that after an ELL student has been in the U.S. school system for as little as 1 year, in addition to the NYESLAT, they too, just like the other students, must take the ELA assessments in grade 3rd–8th.

As this policy increases linguistic minorities' structural barriers to academic success, it presents numerous reasons for concern:

- Since linguistic minorities generally occupy marginalized social positions, the enforcement of the ELA assessment, so soon in their school career, subjects them to an academic discourse that disregards their knowledge and culture—a dynamic that often produces academic problems.

- It harms those students who struggle with print literacy in their first language.

- It denies students the pace and time they may require for developing literacy in their second language.

- It sets up a hostile relationship between the school and the child.

- It negates Cummins's (1991) research, discussed above in this section, pertaining to the time in which it takes second language learners to develop conversational and academic language and literacy.

- It gave rise to a higher percentage of linguistic minorities who did not pass the ELAs and were therefore retained during the single-test promotion policy—which also had the potential of leading to higher push-out/ dropout rates.

- It can prevent schools who service ELLs from meeting "Adequate Yearly Progress" performance standards, as required in NCLB's accountability system, and thus, subject these schools to greater penalties.

Harming Non-reading Adolescents through the "Adequate Yearly Progress" Policy's Emphasis on Standardized Testing

Chapter three also highlighted the dangerous ramifications of the "Adequate Yearly Progress" (AYP) policy for non-reading adolescents. As NCLB makes schools and districts accountable for all students' performance on standardized tests, non-reading adolescents (and other student populations) confront added systemic threats. Orfield et al. (2004) documented that as schools aim to meet the federal AYP mandate, and, thus, avoid test-driven accountability sanctions, numerous schools "push out" students considered "low achieving," according to the school system's standards, so that the schools can achieve higher test scores and graduation rates. In light of the connection between dropping out and incarceration, this particular "push-out" dynamic, yet again, has the potential of creating an even higher representation of non-reading adolescents in juvenile detention centers.

This book presented additional flaws with the AYP process. Under NCLB's accountability framework, the application of the same "Adequate Yearly Progress" rules to all students in special education and general education poses yet another error in the "one size fits all" approach of the legislation. NCLB requirements of high-stakes exam and its accompanying test-driven curriculum, which enforce curricula comprised of culturally-bound information arbitrarily deemed developmentally appropriate for each grade level, do not suit non-reading adolescents' academic needs. Many non-reading adolescents may process information, particularly verbal information, more slowly than others. They require teachings at a slower pace than afforded under NCLB with its mandated standards-based, high-stakes test-driven curriculum. Mandating that non-reading adolescents receive grade-level instruction when they still require teachings on decoding and encoding print generally devastates their motivation and intrinsic passion for learning.

Additionally, as the AYP component of NCLB requires non-reading adolescents, the majority of whom are from low-income and/or "racial"/ethnic minority backgrounds, to learn the general curriculum, which emphasizes Eurocentric and upper-middle-class values, it subjects these youth to both an alienating academic discourse that preserves the status quo and, equally pernicious, fails to enable high quality instruction that addresses their specific literacy needs. NCLB, therefore, ensures that literacy curriculum for non-reading adolescents (and all students) allows the transfer of "official knowledge"; the focus on standards justifies an instrumentalist framework, which predominantly centers on mechanical skills involved in reading and writing and denies the affective, critical, creative, and experiential aspects of literacy.

My analysis in chapter four further emphasized that the "one size fits all" approach of an education based on standardized testing fails to recognize the interconnected nature of information and the intricacies of learning, knowing, and teaching. For instance, it does not account for historically rooted socio-economic, socio-political, and socio-cultural contexts that can negatively impact students' pedagogical lives. For example, structural inequities that cause restricted opportunities and dangerous living conditions—such as limited access to quality health care, heightened unemployment, and deadly gang and drug activity—can impede academic performance for numerous inner-city youth, although many manage to negotiate such circumstances. Yet, an education driven by high-stakes exams and accompanying test-driven curriculum ignores the reality in which oppressive material conditions and traumatic lived experiences can interfere with student performance. Consequently, as economically and socially unresponsive policy and curricula engender negative emotions, such as anxiety, anger, and indifference, this dynamic can frequently lead to behavior problems among students, as some "act out" to express their opposition and enact their agency.

Focusing on purely cognitive aspects of education and requiring this knowledge to be expressed primarily through written modes of production, NCLB and its emphasis on high-stakes standardized exams fail to capture other complexities involved in learning, knowing, and teaching. NCLB negates the way in which knowledge is situated, enacted within the moment. It also dismisses, for example, intuition, imagistic modes of thinking and expressing knowledge, spiritual ways of relating to the world, compassion, criticality, creativity, self-awareness, experiential knowledge, emotional understanding, among numerous other facets of education. As such, among the many tragedies inflicted on non-reading adolescents, the school process systematically disregards their diverse strengths, knowledge, and talents.

Clearly, NCLB's present accountability framework, which expects children to obtain certain arbitrary, fixed standards for each grade level regardless of their social and economic circumstances and/or their required pace for processing information, does not accurately or fairly assess the performance of either non-reading adolescents or their schools. Even more detrimental, such procedures often engender anger, frustration, and low self-esteem for non-reading adolescents, as well as other marginalized student populations. Despite good intentioned educators and administrators who attempt to provide non-reading adolescents print literacy instruction according to their interests and abilities, the macro school structure demands that non-reading adolescents take and pass high-stakes standardized tests, which is an unattainable goal for these youth. In the current draconian educational environment, this possibility of not demonstrating grade-level academic achievement can result in punishment for these students and/or their teachers, instead of caring, supportive, and relevant intervention methods.

While this book ultimately envisioned pedagogy beyond the confines of the existing school structure and embraced critical literacy, it offered suggestions for improving the print literacy development of non-reading adolescents within the present system. Some of these recommendations included:

- The implementation of system-wide literacy intervention programs in each grade level, pre-kindergarten–12th grade, as well as designated literacy schools to support struggling readers, particularly those students, regardless of their age, who experience difficulties with early stages of print literacy development

- An individualized education plan for all students to meet each child's particular academic needs, interests, and pace

- Professional development for all content area teachers at all grade levels that teaches strategies for supporting struggling readers

- Use of English Language Learners' knowledge of literacy in their home language to develop their speaking, reading, writing, and listening abilities in English

- Non-reading adolescents need to receive one-on-one literacy development with a reading specialist every day for at least one hour

- Smaller class size: in literacy intervention classes designed for non-reading adolescents, no more than five students in each class; in regular classes for all students, a maximum of 20 students with a minimum of two teachers

- Teachers can teach students to self-advocate to receive the literacy instruction they require

- All non-reading adolescents must have the option of being exempt from grade-level standardized assessments

- Parental outreach programs to inform parents of educational options that benefit their child

- Assessments that emerge from daily teachings, rooted in each child's specific level and pace, rather than punitive, standardized assessments

High-Stakes Testing Serves as a Control Mechanism

This book illustrated that practices such as high-stakes standardized assessments represent another social control apparatus. This understanding reveals that the goal of educating critical democratic citizens who critique the social order has not been part of the school system's mission. From a critical theoretical standpoint, high-stakes testing serves as a way for controlling instruction and what and whose knowledge is taught, rather than policymakers' stated claim of gathering information to help students become better readers and promoting academic achievement. A social cognitive perspective further accentuated the fallacies and injustices of quantitatively measuring knowledge, intelligence, and consciousness. It highlighted that knowledge is situated within a specific instant in time that is related to culture and history. As such, social cognition emphasized that standardized tests disregard: the interpretive nature of knowledge, diverse cultures and forms of knowing, and the influence of social forces on cognitive development.

Current types of assessments and the fixed performance levels they aim to measure negatively impact teaching, depth of knowledge explored, student motivation, and the overall quality of education provided to students. They, furthermore, eliminate local decision-making and transfer it to central authorities distanced from students' actual social, economic, and political circumstances. Immersed in positivism, policymakers have created a punitive education structure informed by the inhumane ideology that students' and schools' performance will improve when given standardized tests in conjunction with a reward and penalty system to monitor whether students have attained the rigid, culturally specific standards. These tests, therefore, set out to regulate students and the educators who teach them.

Certainly, assessment is necessary for gathering information about students' strengths and weaknesses in order to adjust instruction accordingly. However, a quality education offers authentic assessment and standards grounded in the child's specific level and designed according to daily instruction. It furthermore roots instruction in a child's ability to apply skills to real-life situations, ability to solve problems, interpret meaning, and understand complex inter-connections of information. The norm-referenced and criterion-referenced standardized tests currently employed purportedly serve policymakers' need to determine how adequately school districts and the state are educating students. Yet, these tests prove alarmingly problematic since they (a) have been used as the sole source for making important educational decisions that have profound psychological, economic, and social ramifications for students and harmful consequences for schools and (b) enforce fixed, culturally restrictive standards to impose the dominant culture's knowledge.

Democratic Education for Non-reading Adolescents

My analysis asserted that a critical-democratic pedagogy, in contrast to the positivistic paradigm that has historically informed U.S. schooling, recognizes social and cultural influences on students' pedagogical lives and, thus, shapes policy and curriculum within this context. Additionally, it promotes multiple dimensions, beyond simply cognitive components, involved in education—such as critical, intuitive, creative, affective, social, economic, and political components—while building on students' strengths and developing their textual and contextual literacy. As such, critical-democratic pedagogy embraces the complexity of learning, teaching, and knowing.

A critical-democratic education fosters complex ways of thinking and achievement for all students, as it incorporates rigorous, yet adaptable, standards and curriculum and grounds them in realistic goals. Such a humane pedagogy, thus, understands that students possess a rich variety of needs and abilities, such as preferred ways of learning and required paces. Critical-democratic education, therefore, allows for a flexible, child-centered approach that takes into account:

a. Each student's particular academic level, developmental pace, and specific interests—as opposed to subjecting students to predetermined curricula that are reinforced and tested through standardized exams;

b. Diverse socio-economic, socio-cultural, and socio-political circumstances for different student populations;

c. Crucial aspects of learning, teaching, and knowing beyond simply cognition—such as affective, critical, creative, and experiential to name a few.

A critical-democratic pedagogy also grounds standards and assessments on holistic, process-based thinking approaches that recognize the multidimensional, relational nature of reality. They, therefore, prioritize, for example, a students' ability to question, infer, create meaning by interpreting intricate information, relate newly learned information to one's self and the world, and understand connections among inter-related information to see the whole in the parts. While enabling students' intellectual, emotional, spiritual, and overall individual growth, such process-oriented standards additionally engender critical democratic citizens.

Informed by Dewey's emphasis on active, inquiry-based education and embracing Freire's related "problem-posing" approach, this book envisioned a framework for process-based, democratic teaching and curriculum for non-reading adolescents. From Dewey's and Freire's perspectives, democratic education fosters learning in which students and teachers assume the role of critical producers of knowledge to prepare students for critical citizenship and participation as social change agents. Rooting the purpose of education in these principles, problem-posing centers on students' co-construction of curriculum as teachers and students, positioned within a horizontal teacher-student relationship, problematize power relations to critically analyze society. Using students' socio-economic and socio-political circumstances as a starting ground for instruction, teachers facilitate students' critical reflection and action through critical dialogue. This critical dialogue aims to develop learners' textual and contextual literacy, or critical literacy, to cultivate critical consciousness—critical awareness of power relations to promote self and social transformation.

Freire's critical literacy goes deeper than simply the mechanical elements of reading and writing, as it nurtures learners' ability to think, speak, read, and write in critical ways that reach beyond surface meaning to question the status quo. Critical literacy situates learning within students' social, historical, and political circumstances. It achieves this focus as students' experiences serve as themes and texts, or what Freire refers to as "generative themes," from which they generate both their own knowledge and curriculum. A critical literacy framework additionally enables multiple ways of knowing, such as, but not limited to, intellect, intuition, emotion, self-reflection, and spirituality. In light of its powerful implications for literacy development with those in positions of heightened marginalization, Freire's critical pedagogical approach served as the inspiration for the critical literacy curriculum model for non-reading adolescents that I developed in this book.

Chapter six presented a critical literacy curriculum model for non-reading adolescents, designed for one-on-one lessons within the context of New York City, to provide a critical-democratic pedagogy for these youth. In contrast to the instrumentalist education historically delivered in the educational system and currently advanced through NCLB, my critical literacy curriculum framework for non-reading adolescents: tailors instruction to each student's level and pace; centers curriculum on their experiences, language, and interests; involves their co-construction of the curriculum; encourages critical reflection and action; and promotes both textual and contextual literacy. In recognizing the socio-historical and political dimensions of education, the literacy curriculum advocated in chapters five and six embraces critical literacy, as it places encoding, decoding, and comprehending print within a critical perspective to promote textual and contextual literacy—thereby offering a liberatory pedagogy. As such, non-reading adolescents develop the skills to read both the printed word and themselves in society.

Employing questioning and critical dialogue, student and teacher—positioned in a horizontal student-teacher relationship in which both assume the role of co-researchers—challenge limiting forces as they critically reflect on the workings of power and ideology in their lives as well as in teaching and learning in school. Within this framework, critical literacy teachers of non-reading adolescents, whom I also refer to as critical literacy educators, encourage their students to problematize their circumstances, both personal and collective, in order to affect positive change. Therefore, in advancing an agenda for transforming literacy pedagogy within the school system, chapters five and six ultimately envisioned a critical literacy curriculum that, in addition to teaching mechanics of literacy, facilitates non-reading adolescents self-actualization, or transformation, through reflection on their experience and subsequent action—their *conscientization*.

Critical literacy educators, as Freire urges, teach from a space of love. Among other characteristics, this love stems from mutual respect, shared sense of responsibility, recognizing healthy boundaries, and understanding. They create a safe learning environment with high expectations and a rigorous pace specific for each child, accompanied by a consciousness that students' socio-economic, socio-political, and socio-cultural circumstances impact their pedagogical lives. Critical literacy teachers employ problem-posing to analyze imprints of power affecting them, their students, and their interactions with students. They, therefore, critically self-reflect on their own actions, preconceived perceptions, and teaching process to better support their students academically and emotionally. Through such critical questioning, critical literacy teachers, furthermore, research who their students are on an individual and collective level. From this understanding of students' interests, dreams, challenges, lived experiences, concerns, critical literacy teachers shape curriculum accordingly to engage students in emotionally sensitive and meaningful literacy pedagogy.

As this curriculum incorporates the transformatory component of reading and writing, it positions literacy instruction within an historical and social context. Within this context, critical literacy educators, create meaningful opportunities—stimulated through speaking, reading, and writing—for non-reading adolescents to reflect on their lived experiences, including those related to literacy. In so doing, the curriculum thus encourages non-reading adolescents to establish a more in-depth understanding of their realities to forge positive alternatives to limiting forces, or what Freire terms "limit situations." For example, the curriculum promotes students' understanding of multiple factors that have contributed to a reality in which they are unable to read and write. With this awareness, students may, in turn, be more inclined to (a) move beyond previous barriers to literacy more effectively and (b) self-advocate to receive on-going literacy instruction tailored to their specific needs.

This critical literacy curriculum offered theoretical frameworks and instructional strategies to shape instruction, which centers on two strategies in particular, systematic phonics and critical language experience—a whole language literacy development approach in which the teacher scribes what the child orally relays. The systematic phonics offers students a direct and explicit means for learning the principles of decoding and encoding, while the critical language component encompasses the critical literacy aspect of this curriculum. Critical language experience involves complexities of teaching, knowing, and learning, as it roots literacy development in students' language, background knowledge, and social contexts. It, furthermore, integrates, among other aspects, affective, experiential, creative, critical, political, situated, and self-reflective elements of learning.

Critical language experience, additionally, encompasses social cognition theories. For example, it embraces Lave and Wenger's (1991) "community of practice," Vygotsky's (1978, 1989) "zone of proximal development" (ZPD) and scaffolding, and Varela's (1999) related concepts of knowing and consciousness—which view learning as a social practice in which knowledge is enacted in the moment. Critical language experience also embodies key features of literacy, beyond simply verbal processes, that are rooted in experience, emotion, and creativity—such as imagination and visualization. Above all, however, it provides meaning to print and enables students' critical reflection on self, society, and the world—as their experiences, issues of power, and societal problems serve as integral components of the literacy lessons.

Situating teachings in their time and place, the curriculum allows for flexibility in instruction to meet the needs and interests of children at the given moment that lessons occur. The critical language experience and structured phonics strategies employed, thus, are not taught in the same uniform, linear fashion for each child, but rather are taught according to what will serve the student best in the specific moment and time, determined with the child's mutual input as a partner in their literacy instruction. As such, this critical literacy curriculum engages non reading adolescents in teachings, in rigorous and meaningful ways, that honor their knowledge and lets them co-create the syllabus to intrinsically integrate their academic needs and interests. It nurtures students' as well as teachers' critical consciousness as they, together, synthesize meaning about texts that emerge from the students' experiences and language.

To ensure democratic assessment that promotes success for all students, this critical literacy curriculum employs process-based assessment to gauge students' understanding of content material and monitor their developments on an on-going basis. Critical literacy teachers rely on these daily assessments to shape subsequent instruction according to each student's particular needs and required pace. Process-based assessment, therefore, enables critical literacy teachers to assess students at the level at which they are performing—rather than imposing predetermined criteria that the dominant culture has arbitrarily deemed appropriate for students according to their age or grade level. Such process-based assessment, tailored to each child's academic level and needs, inherently incorporates the social, economic, political, "race"/ethnicity, class, gender, and historical dimensions of education as it supports all students, regardless of their positionality within the social web. In keeping with a holistic vision for assessment, rather than letter grades or other quantitative measures, the curriculum entails narrative reports, which present a deeper analysis of students' progress through detailed description of their strengths and challenges.

Utilizing an Orton-Gillingham-based method, such as the Barbara Wilson Reading System (Wilson, 1988), the systematic phonics aspect of this curriculum focuses on language and word structure within a multisensory, individualized, and sequential approach. To ensure students' feelings of success within each phonics lesson, critical literacy teachers maintain instruction within each child's comfort zone as they gradually move students to more challenging word structure analysis—always maintaining the balance between ease and challenge so as to avoid producing frustration. Critical literacy teachers, among other qualities, provide students with continual positive reinforcement to enhance their self-confidence about their expanding literacy knowledge and to encourage students to push through any difficulties in acquiring print literacy.

Both non-fictional and fictional critical language experience stories provide texts for print literacy development—as students re-read, type, and edit several drafts. However, non-fictional critical language experience narratives, additionally, foster students' contextual literacy development. Critical language experience promotes students' understanding of their existential situations and the historical and social forces that shape these experiences. To facilitate non-reading adolescents' critical reflection, critical literacy teachers again use problem-posing to generate critical dialogue, which centers on students' generative themes. The generative themes that emerge from this critical dialogue serve as the material from which students create their language experience stories.

To stimulate students' deeper critical reflection and situate these experiences in their historical and social contexts, critical literacy teachers use culturally diverse published and non-published texts and/or a picture, based on similar themes as the lived experiences that students have described. This instructional focus aims to expand students' understanding of societal forces and the way in which power impacts both their lived experiences and consciousness so that they may actualize positive solutions to personal and institutional "limit situations." As critical language experience positions students as authors generating knowledge from critical reflection on their lived experiences, it engages them in what Freire (1970) refers to as the emancipatory act of praxis—the dialogue between action and reflection, practice and theory, and experience and knowledge—to encourage *conscientization*.

My discussion of a critical literacy curriculum for non-reading adolescents used the creation of students' literacy history narratives as an example to illustrate the way in which the curriculum employs critical language experience to enable students' critical reflection on their experiences and conditions so that they may read the word and the world. It described a problem-posing process in which questions, centered on the relationship of literacy and power, delved into how not being able to read and write has impacted students' lived experiences and what each student views as causes of their limited literacy abilities. Through teachings that promote this awareness of self and the larger societal forces that have influenced their obstructed literacy process, coupled with textual literacy instruction, students come to see that they may alter their circumstances and develop positive alternatives for countering impediments to their literacy development.

Enabling complex literacy teachings, critical language experience based on students' literacy history stories, thus, delves into intricate social, cultural, psychological, and pedagogical dimensions. Students' narratives about their literacy histories enable an ontological description that has pedagogical implications for the teacher and student. As these student-generated stories center on students' lived-literacy-related-experiences, they unravel individual and collective elements of non reading adolescents' relationships with literacy and its ontological meaning. Student narratives can, therefore, inform educators about such questions as: Who are these students? What is the role of school in their lives? What are their lived experiences in school and outside of school? How can school be transformed into a meaningful experience for them? Additionally, the creation of critical literacy narratives facilitates students' process of critical consciousness. As students critically reflect—through speaking, writing, and reading—on their lived experiences in relation to their literacy abilities, they uncover factors that have contributed to their remedial literacy abilities, examine personal responses to these limiting situations, and envision positive alternatives for action to counter possible obstructions they may experience in the present and future.

Ultimately, in contrast to a positivistic paradigm, the critical-democratic literacy pedagogy for non-reading adolescents described in this book provides these youth humane literacy pedagogy. Operating from a multilogical mindset, among other attributes, it: embraces and values student diversity; understands the complexities of education; takes into account socio-cultural, socio-economic, and socio-political influences on students' educational lives; includes students in the construction of the curriculum; incorporates process-based thinking; centers on rigorous, yet adaptable and child-centered, standards, curriculum, and assessment; promotes each students' academic success through curriculum and teachings geared toward their individual needs and pace; develops students' textual and contextual literacy; and encourages critical reflection and self-actualization.

Future Research

This book generated discourse about non-reading adolescents and promoted the development of a socially just educational system. It exposed long-standing as well as recent inequitable structures involved in the school system's production of a population of non-reading adolescents in New York City and, from this understanding, created a critical literacy curriculum for these youth. However, additional research will be needed to support and continue this transformatory agenda.

Research is needed for examining the type of pre-service and in-service teacher training required so that teachers may have the tools needed for putting in practice the critical literacy curriculum described in chapters five and six. Additional research could also examine this critical literacy curriculum within various school settings to discover what specific policy, administrative, programmatic, or other changes must occur both within each site and the school system on the whole to enable its critical pedagogical goals. As this critical literacy curriculum promotes a deeper awareness of students' own agency in transforming their lives, while exposing students to textual and contextual literacy teachings, these critical studies could also document differences in both students' sense of themselves in the world, their forms of resistance, and their ability to read the word and the world as they engage in critical literacy development.

The political understanding of curriculum and ensuing critical literacy curriculum presented in this book focused on non-reading adolescents who live in urban areas, in particular New York City. However, further research is needed to both (a) produce a critical understanding of curriculum as political text within rural areas where there is a presence of non-reading adolescents and (b) subsequently, create a critical literacy curriculum for non-reading adolescents in these areas. Such analyses would produce knowledge specific to the demographics, experiences, and languages of youth in the rural areas studied. This research could also focus on comparing topics covered within urban and rural critical literacy pedagogy curricula for non-reading adolescents as lessons focus on social and ecological contexts in which students live. Furthermore, politically situated curriculum studies could also compare the similarities and distinctions within and between urban and rural areas to gain a deeper understanding of dynamics involved in the underdeveloped literacy skills of non-reading adolescents in this country, as well as their shared and unique lived experiences.

Since the current educational system does not operate from a critical literacy pedagogical vision, this research is particularly vital for revealing structures that limit non-reading adolescents throughout the country. As such, this knowledge would contribute to a necessary research foundation for encouraging national policymakers to take widespread action to reverse this trend. It could, perhaps, lead to the development of critical literacy curricula for non-reading adolescents throughout the country that takes into account cultural, economic, and political forces specific to the place in which students live and teaching occurs.

In addition to the need for creating multiple critical curricula models that facilitate monolingual English as well as bilingual literacy instruction for non-reading adolescents within both urban and rural mainstream and non-mainstream public schools (such as those within detention centers), supplementary research is important for analyzing the strengths and weaknesses of these literacy programs in practice to promote the highest quality critical pedagogy. Further analysis is also necessary for promoting supportive and inclusive pedagogical practices and policies for struggling readers. These studies, for example, could:

- Explore non-punitive, literacy support structures that could be built into the educational infrastructure, rather than having a separate special education program, to ensure early intervention as well as literacy instruction in every grade that is tailored to struggling readers' particular performance level, regardless of their age

- Compare on-going, authentic assessments grounded in standards of complexity in contrast to high-stakes standardized evaluation methods used with various groups of non-reading adolescents and other struggling readers to look at overall consequences of these two types of assessments—such as variations in students' affective relationship towards learning as well as the tests' ability to accurately measure students' progress and development, meet the students' academic, social, and emotional needs, and incorporate complex aspects of learning and cognition

Studies could also examine the implementation of a critical literacy curriculum with non-reading adolescents within community institutions—such as within youth centers or churches—since the school system reflects and reproduces wider inequities of society that constrict particular groups across class, "race"/ethnicity, and gender categories. This analysis could, furthermore, highlight commonalities and differences with regard to applications and effects of a critical literacy curriculum, such as the one laid out in chapters five and six, within these community-based institutions in comparison to public schools, both mainstream and non-mainstream.

Research questions for this kind of analysis might involve, but not be limited to:

- What are students' affective engagement and motivation toward literacy development?

- Do students have a more positive attitude toward their learning experience within a particular educational setting?

- To what extent are the academic, social, and emotional needs met of youth who are linguistic minorities and/or who have been identified for special education?

- To what degree does the space allow students' and teachers' to critically reflect in order to promote agency?

- Is the depth of critical inquiry stifled due to the educational setting?

- What are the topics covered in critical dialogue?

- What is the nature of material read and written?

- In which type of setting do students feel more empowered?

- How do students perceive their own progress?

- How do teachers perceive students' progress?

- What forms of assessment are used?

- How does assessment impact students' behavior and motivation?

- How does critical literacy instruction inform students' identity formation?

- What are students' self-perceptions as emerging readers and authors?

As this research would produce information about the potential of critical literacy curricula for non-reading adolescents within diverse educational settings, it would provide important knowledge for (a) enriching teacher training programs for critical literacy educators, (b) understanding institutional influences that shape contemporary non-reading adolescents' critical literacy teachings, and (c) reflecing on the benefits and challenges of implementing critical literacy pedagogy for non-reading adolescents.

The above research questions could also be used for comparative studies specifically examining a critical literacy curriculum in mainstream schools and schools within juvenile detention centers. Additionally, in light of the recent expansion of juvenile correctional facilities and the increasing role of public schools within them, studies within the critical tradition can expand their already comprehensive vision to include specific discourse about non-reading adolescents within detention centers. For example, in an effort to reverse societal inequities critical pedagogues could explore from the multiple perspectives of students, parents/guardians, administrators, and teachers the multifaceted social, political, economic, and pedagogical forces involved in, as well as the implications of, non-reading adolescents' disproportionate incarceration across identity categories.

Moreover, qualitative studies that explore non-reading adolescents', including those who are also incarcerated, and their parents'/guardians' views on factors that have contributed to the youths' underdeveloped literacy skills are an essential piece to understanding non-reading adolescents' individual and collective lived experiences. This analysis would serve as a critical resource for improving the schooling they receive and their overall treatment within social institutions. It is imperative that the voices of non-reading adolescents be heard. Research from the youths' perspective that describes what the experience is like to be an adolescent who is identified as a non-reader is very limited. Studies that describe, through the actual voices of these youth, the experience of being a non-reading adolescent who is also incarcerated are even sparser. Research that centers on personal narratives of non-reading adolescents, both those who have and have not experienced incarceration, can provide pedagogical insights to administrators, policymakers, and educators for creating (a) literacy intervention that addresses non-reading adolescents' socio-educational needs, (b) measures that could contribute to the prevention of future populations of non-reading adolescents, and (c) critical literacy pedagogy for all students in every grade level.

In addition to the above phenomenological type of inquiry, critical research could also focus on the resilience of those young adults over the age of 21 who grew up classified as non-readers in high school. This analysis could, for instance, engage these individuals' critical reflections on their schooling years, delve into its impact on their past and present lives, explore their talents and passions, highlight their ideas for improving the educational system, and emphasize ways in which they have negotiated their under-developed literacy during their youth and now in adulthood.

The previous studies discussed in this section are examples of the numerous possibilities for the direction in which further inquiry focused on non-reading adolescents could proceed. Among various benefits, these studies as a whole serve as a means for: generating monolingual and bilingual critical literacy curriculum for non-reading adolescents in various geographic regions as well as educational settings; improving critical literacy curriculum and policy for non-reading adolescents; enhancing teacher training for educators who work with non-reading adolescents; promoting critical literacy teachings for all students; exploring the socio-educational experience of non-reading adolescents from different individuals' perspectives; and understanding, through personal narratives, the existential circumstances of non-reading adolescents and young adults who had been identified as non-readers in school during their adolescence. Overall, such research could provide parents, educators, and other concerned citizens an enhanced research-base for demanding that educational policymakers ensure more just and socially empowering literacy pedagogy for non-reading adolescents.

Conclusion

We must work beyond the confines of current prejudicial practices and policy, which serve as forms of social control, to create pedagogy that instead heightens human consciousness—that of the students, educators, and policymakers. For example, educational procedures must be sensitive to the socio-economic circumstances that shape and constrict the rights and aspirations of non-reading adolescents so as to offer meaningful instruction that encourages self-empowerment and self-efficacy. Democratic literacy pedagogy for struggling readers, especially non-reading adolescents, requires a reconceptualization of the prevailing paradigm driving the existing educational system. Inclusive and empowering literacy pedagogy, which has the potential of both reversing the production of a population of non-reading adolescents and of supporting struggling readers at all grade levels, necessitates:

a.   School infrastructure that provides self-actualizing literacy intervention measures throughout grades pre-kindergarten through 12th—within both mainstream and non-mainstream schools, such as juvenile detention centers—which allow educators to tailor instruction to each student's, particularly struggling reader's, pace and level;

b.   The creation of designated upper middle and high schools specifically for adolescents who are in the emergent reader stages;

c.   Literacy teachings rooted in critical literacy curricula to address the academic, emotional, and social needs of students;

d. Instructional practices that include students in the construction of their own literacy curriculum;

e. The end to the use of high-stakes assessments, and its accompanying test-driven curriculum, which penalize students, as well as their teachers and schools, when students have not acquired predetermined criteria that the dominant culture has deemed developmentally appropriate for each grade level;

f. The implementation of evaluation procedures that, instead of undermining students, enable multiple ways of thinking and learning and promote students' success by assessing them at their actual performance level;

g. An overall pedagogical approach that ultimately views literacy curriculum, instruction, and policies from a socio-political, socio-cultural, and socio-economic perspective that incorporates critical, affective, creative, intuitional, cognitive, and experiential components of learning.

A fundamental shift in underlying assumptions shaping the curriculum, forms of assessment, and policies on the whole could contribute to the creation of a truly liberatory education that enables *conscientization* for all students, even non-reading adolescents and other struggling readers.

Appendix

"Clue Word Chart" Procedure

The details below illustrate how to create a vowel chart, using the vowel "a" as an example. However, to make the consonant and digraph charts the teacher repeats the protocol but changes clue words to correspond with each particular phoneme. The following shows the clue word chart process with the letter "a":

1) The teacher says the name of the vowel, "a," then a clue word, for example, "apple," then the short vowel sound for "a."
   Note: *The teacher says the clue word "apple" slowly so that the student can hear the short vowel sound in the beginning of the word. The teacher explains that the first sound in the clue word "apple" is the short vowel sound that the vowel "a" makes (the teacher then repeats the vowel's short sound). The teacher explains that if the student forgets the short vowel sound for "a" s/he can say the clue word "apple" slowly to remember the sound.*

2) The teacher repeats step 1. Then, the student repeats the same process.

3) Once the student begins to learn the vowel sound, using the vowel chart and clue word, the teacher uses phoneme/sound cards to have the student read *cvc* (consonant-vowel-consonant) words using the particular vowel being taught. (Refer to the *Segmenting and Blending* procedures

provided next for instruction on how to use cards for reading these *cvc* words.)

Segmenting and Blending Using Phoneme/Sound Cards

After teaching consonant sounds and the short vowel sound for "a," the teacher uses the alphabet cards to display *cvc* words, one at a time. With the word "sat," for example, the teacher asks the student what sound the "s" makes and then what sound the "t" makes. Before segmenting each sound to read the word "sat," the teacher has the student say the short vowel sound for "a" again, referring to vowel chart if needed. Having the student say the short vowel sound immediately before segmenting and blending the word, assists the student in reading the word more fluently. The teacher then instructs the student to touch each card and say the sound produced by the letter in the order that each letter is "written" from left to right (i.e., displayed with the cards). For blending, the teacher asks the student to say the same sounds quickly in the order they are "written" from left to right without touching the cards to read the word "sat."

After teaching segmenting and blending, the teacher explains to the student that this is the process of reading (decoding) in that each letter makes a sound and the reader must say the sounds in the order they are written to read the word. The teacher can explain that in English there are "tricks" to how certain letters are pronounced when written together (i.e., letter patterns), but the student will learn these letter patterns as lessons progress. The teacher can also discuss that there are also words in English that do not follow a phonetic pattern and, therefore, these "sight words" must be memorized by sight.

After the student successfully decodes the first *cvc* word, the teacher informs the student that the teacher will change one of the consonant letters to create a new word. The teacher says the new consonant sound and then has the student segment and blend this new word. Before segmenting each sound to read the new word, the student says the sound that the vowel in the word makes. Once the student has decoded the word, the student continues to segment and blend different words as the teacher changes one letter at a time to make new *cvc* words with the phoneme/sound cards. The teacher goes at a slow pace when creating new words with the cards to allow the student time to process the information.

Maintaining a careful balance between challenge and frustration, the teacher monitors the student's comfort level. Once the student has a solid understanding of how to decode *cvc* words, the teacher creates new *cvc* words without building on the previous word (i.e., changes more than one letter at a time) and gradually includes the other vowels. However, if the student is having difficulties, the teacher (a) creates consecutive words that have the same vowel sound and (b) changes only one consonant at a time to foster success.

Spelling Using Phoneme/Sound Cards

As the student learns to decode *cvc* words, the teacher also has the student use the phoneme/sound cards to encode (spell) *cvc* words. The following are the procedures for teaching students to spell using the phoneme/sound cards:

1) The teacher places the particular consonant and vowel cards to be used in separate rows with the vowels in the top row. The teacher leaves space below the rows for the student to place the cards that s/he chooses for spelling each *cvc* word that the teacher says.

2) While the teacher says the *cvc* word, the student watches the teacher's mouth.

3) The student repeats the word.

4) Together, the student and teacher tap the sounds in the word.

5) The student identifies the cards that make the sounds that s/he just tapped and spells the word with the cards. As the student internalizes this process, s/he can continue independently tapping and spelling words.

6) Once the student has created the word, the student must check the spelling by segmenting and blending the word. (This last step helps students catch possible mistakes and reinforces the segmenting part in reading.)

Six Syllable Types

1) A **closed syllable** ends in a consonant and has a short vowel sound. Example: *cat, sit, cup,* etc.

2) A **vowel-consonant-e syllable** has a consonant then a vowel then an "e." The "e" is silent and the vowel before it has a long vowel sound. Example: *like, tape, hope,* etc.

3) An **open syllable** ends in a vowel and the vowel has a long sound. Example: *no, be, she,* etc.

4) A **consonant-l-e** syllable has a consonant and then a "le." The consonant and the "l" are pronounced like a blend, and the "e" is present

because every syllable in English has at least one vowel. Example: *puzzle, little, puddle,* etc.

5) An **r-controlled** syllable has a vowel that is followed by an "r" and the "r" changes the way the vowel is pronounced. Example: *bird, car, burn,* etc.

6) A **diphthong/vowel digraph syllable** has two vowels next to each other and they create their own sound. Example: *cloud, bread, blue,* etc.

Glossary

Agency—is the transformative capacity for an individual to act in the world. It is a person's ability to act independently, making one's own free choices, to shape his/her own life and transform oppressive conditions. Literacy, when taught within a critical perspective, can serve as a vehicle for agency.

Alphabetic principle—is the concept that letters represent sounds, or phonemes.

Banking system—is an educational method in which, as Paulo Freire (1970) describes, the educator deposits knowledge into the students, who are merely "receptacles to be filled." According to Freire, the "banking system" of education serves as a pedagogy of social control and domestication, as it prevents dialogue and inhibits the development of students' critical consciousness. In contrast to the "banking system," Freire presents his problem-posing approach as a means for enabling a liberatory education.

Blending—is the process of *blending* (combining) letter sounds (phonemes) to read a word or a syllable. Blending is how /s/ /a/ /t/ becomes sat.

Conscientization—*See* Critical consciousness.

Consonant blend—In a consonant blend two or three consonants are grouped together and the sound of each consonant is retained. Examples of two and three letter consonant blends: *st, br, nd, str, spr,* etc.

Contextual literacy—a synonym for critical literacy

Controlled texts—are written passages involving pre-selected words that follow phonics patterns already covered in lessons. Controlled texts are used within phonics instruction to reinforce phonics rules that students have already learned.

Critical consciousness (also referred to as conscientization)—is the critical awareness of power relations so that one may intervene against oppressive forces to transform these conditions. Critical literacy teachings nurture a student's critical consciousness, as opposed to a "banking system" of education, which inhibits it. Paulo Freire developed this concept of critical consciousness as a pivotal component of his problem-posing method—a pedagogy that facilitates personal and social liberation.

Critical curriculum theory—is an interdisciplinary study of educational experience placed within a critical analysis to understand overt and hidden socio-political influences.

Critical literacy—involves critical thinking and action. It is the ability to interpret experiences, events, and circumstances within a social and political perspective to encourage self and social transformation. Critical literacy pedagogy enables reading and writing of the word and world. See *Definition of Terms* section in *Introduction*.

Critical pedagogue—is an educator who grounds his/her educational philosophy and practices in critical pedagogy.

Critical pedagogy—is an educational approach that engages students in teachings that analyze power relations to promote students' critical consciousness. Within a critical pedagogical framework, since schooling is viewed as a political sphere, instruction is centered within a social, cultural, economic, and political context. With equality and social justice as its goal, critical pedagogy encourages students to move beyond possible positions of disenfranchisement to attain their fullest human potential.

CVC **words**—In phonics instruction, a *cvc* word refers to a consonant-vowel-consonant word. In other words, the word has a consonant then a vowel and then another consonant. The vowel makes the short vowel sound. Examples: cat, sit, let, etc.

Decoding—is also known as reading. It is the act of matching written letter or letter-clusters to oral sounds in order to read a word. For students to learn how to read, decoding must be taught directly.

Dialogic praxis—is an important component of problem-posing education within the Freirean approach. This praxis is facilitated through critical dialogue within a horizontal teacher-student relationship. It enables the learner to become consciously aware of his/her context and his/her capacity to transform difficult circumstances in order to improve his/her reality. In the words of Paulo Freire, dialogic praxis leads to "an education as the practice of freedom" (Freire, 1970, p. 81) and "education for critical consciousness" (Freire, 1974).

Digraph—Two consecutive consonants that together make one sound (phoneme). Examples of digraphs: *sh, ch, ck,* etc.

Dominant discourse— A "dominant discourse" is the discourse of those who possess power. As such, it embodies their perspective, values, and ways of speaking about a subject. Ultimately, the dominant discourse serves to reflect and perpetuate the power structure.

Encoding—is also known as spelling. It is the act of matching written letter or letter-clusters to oral sounds in order to write a word.

English immersion program—teaches English Language Learners in classes that use only English for the language of instruction. There is no effort to maintain the child's native language.

Functionalist literacy—Functional literacy situates literacy within a technical framework that centers instruction on basic reading, writing, and arithmetic skills needed for the rising everyday demands within modern society and for economic gain. From a critical pedagogical perspective, this focus solely on the technical aspects of literacy prevents critical reflection on society and understanding of power relations. In doing so, it provides a means for transmitting the dominant culture's ideology and maintaining the status quo.

Generative themes—are themes representing a group's reality. They are a vital element of the dialogue of "education as the practice of freedom" (Freire, 1970, p. 81). When generative themes are explored in conjunction with conscientization, it introduces those in subjugated positions to a critical form of thinking about their world. Exploring generative themes facilitates students' reflection on their reality in order to act upon it by opposing limiting forces and creating more positive alternatives.

Graphemes—are alphabetic letters.

Hegemonic—controlling; ruling (see Hegemony).

Hegemony—the process by which the ruling class dominates.

High-stakes testing—is a policy in which a test determines important educational decisions. The practice of preventing the promotion of a student to the next grade because s/he did not pass one standardized test is an example of high-stakes testing.

Instrumentalist literacy—is an approach to literacy that limits teachings to quantifiable mechanical skills and the "banking system." It furthermore directs literacy teachings to the standardization of information and knowledge. Critical pedagogy theorists assert that as an instrumentalist literacy approach inhibits the development of students' critical consciousness, it functions as a means for averting dissent and perpetuating the social order.

Language politics—is a term used to describe issues of power related to linguistic differences between people. Within this political sphere, one language (or one particular way of speaking a language) is positioned in a place of authority over others.

Letter patterns—Groups of letters that represent sounds. This term is used in phonics instruction.

Liberatory education—This type of education, which nurtures one's critical consciousness, challenges the "what is" so that students may understand themselves and the world to enact positive change. Liberatory education is in contrast to what Paulo Freire describes as a "domesticating" education, in which teachings merely reflect and preserve the status quo.

Maintenance bilingual program—is designed to teach English Language Learners English while maintaining and enhancing linguistic abilities in their native language. Both English and the child's native language are used in a structured format as the languages of instruction.

Mechanics of literacy—is the capacity to decode and encode written symbols, which involves such processes as phoneme awareness, comprehension, spelling, punctuation, and grammar.

Multilogicality—is the capability to understand the complexities of the lived world and social inquiry from diverse perspectives. This type of viewpoint contrasts the one-dimensionality of a monological perspective.

Ontology—is the philosophical study of the nature of being or existence.

Pedagogy—is the science and art of teaching and instruction.

Phoneme—is the sound represented by letters.

Phonemic awareness—is the understanding that every word is comprised of a sequence of individual sounds (phonemes).

Phonetics—is a branch of linguistics that studies speech sounds.

Phonics—is a method for teaching reading and writing that focuses on the relationships between the sounds of the spoken language and the letters that represent those sounds. Phonics stresses sound-symbol correspondence.

Positivism/Positivistic framework—Positivism is a philosophy rooted in the belief that natural science, with its use of the scientific method and quantifiable data, represents the only authentic approach to the study of human knowledge. The dominant class has employed positivist science, applying its faulty claim of scientific "objectivity" and erroneous assertion that all knowledge can be measured and quantified, to shape mainstream American culture and preserve the social order. Within a positivistic framework, the ruling class emphasizes technical control to impose and perpetuate its dominance. Therefore, in the culture of positivism, education serves as a means for social engineering, as opposed to intellectual growth.

Praxis—is the ongoing process of critical reflection and action upon the world in order to transform it. It is the dialogue between action and reflection, practice and theory, and experience and knowledge—to encourage *conscientization*.

Problem-posing education—is an educational method in which teachers and students co-generate knowledge through critical reflection. Within the Freirean approach, teachings initially emerge from students' cultural themes and personal experiences, which are presented in the form of open-ended problems. Through critical dialogue, wherein teacher and student are knowledgeable equals, problem-posing facilitates students' understanding of power relations, or their critical awareness (conscientization), in order to transform their reality.

Reductionism—is a philosophical stance in which to understand complex phenomena one must reduce them to their constituent parts and then study these pieces separately. It is not concerned with understanding the interconnections of dispersed information or relational patterns. The positivist methodology relies heavily on reductionism.

Segmenting—is the process in reading and spelling of breaking down a word into its separate sounds.

Social efficiency—is a theory of curriculum development, which started at the turn of the 19th century during the rise of Industrialism. Adapted from Frederick Taylor's initial concept of creating high efficiency in American industry, a group of educational policymakers designed a school structure based on a differentiated curriculum for children depending on their class background. This differentiated curriculum aimed to prepare youth for their specific role within society predetermined by their socio-economic position. The socially efficient paradigm, therefore, served as a means for controlling and perpetuating the social order.

Structural dynamics/structural forces—are dynamics/forces that are built into a social system.

Textual literacy/print literacy—is reading, writing, and comprehending the printed word. See *Definition of Terms* section in *Introduction*.

References

Access Quality Education. (2007). *New York Governor Spitzer proposes major education policy and funding reforms.* Retrieved from http://www.schoolfunding.info/news/policy/2-21-07SpitzerNY.php3

Acoca, L. (1999). Investing in girls: A 21st century strategy. *Juvenile Justice Bulletin, Office of Juvenile Justice and Delinquency Prevention, 4*(1), 3–13. Retrieved from www.ncjrs.gov/pdffiles1/ojjdp/178254.pdf

Advantage Learning Systems. (1997). *STAR Reading.* Wisconsin Rapids, WI: Renaissance Learning.

Advocates for Children of New York. (2001a, Spring). *The new continuum of special education services.* The Advocate.

Advocates for Children of New York. (2001b, Spring). *NYC Board of Education revamps bilingual education.* The Advocate.

Advocates for Children of New York. (2004). *An overview of research on the effectiveness of retention on student achievement for New York City schoolchildren.* Retrieved from schoolchildren. www.advocatesforchildren.org/.../5thgradeRetentionwhitepaper9-27-04.doc

Advocates for Children of New York. (2008a). *What your child needs to be promoted.* Retrieved from http://insideschools.org/index12.php?s=1&sh=1&a=25

Advocates for Children of New York. (2008b). *Stuck in the middle: The problem of overage middle school students in New York City.* Retrieved from http://www.advocatesforchildren.org/Stuck%20in%20the%20Middle(final).pdf

Advocates for Children of New York. (2008c). *Tests and promotion: Graduation requirements.* Retrieved from http://www.insideschools.org/st/ST_gradreqs.php

Allen, W. R., & Farley, R. (1987). *The color line and the quality of life in America.* New York: Oxford University Press.

Allington, R. L. (2002). *Big brother and the national reading curriculum: how ideology trumped evidence.* Portsmouth, NH: Heinemann.

Anderson, P. M., & Summerfield, J. P. (2006). What you don't know about evaluation. In J. Kincheloe & S. Steinberg (Eds.), *What you don't know about schools* (pp. 89–101). New York: Palgrave.

Anyon, J. (1997). *Ghetto schooling: The political economy of urban school reform.* New York: Teachers College Press.

Anyon, J. (2005). *Radical possibilities: Public policy, urban education and a new social movement.* New York: Routledge.

Anzaldúa, G. (1987). *Borderlands/la frontera: The new mestiza.* San Francisco: Aunt Lute.

Apple, M. (1993). *Official knowledge: Democratic education in a conservative age.* New York: Routledge.

Asante, M. K. (1987). *The Afro-centric idea.* Philadelphia: Temple University Press.

Asante, M. K. (1991). The Afro-centric idea in education. *Journal of Negro Education, 60,* 170–180.

Baca, L. M., & Cervantes, H. T. (1989). *The bilingual special education interface.* Columbus, OH: Merril.

Bakhtin, M. (1973). *Marxism and the philosophy of language* (L. Matejka & I. R. Titunik, Trans.). Cambridge, MA: Harvard University Press.

Bakhtin, M. (1981). *The dialogic imagination.* Austin: University of Texas Press.

Balfanz, R., McPartland, J., & Shaw, A. (2002). *Re-conceptualizing extra help for high school students in a high standards era.* Prepared for Preparing America's Future. The High School Symposium, Washington, DC, U.S. Department of Education.

Bartolomé, L. (1998). *The misteaching of academic discourses: The politics of language in the classroom.* Boulder, CO: Westview.

Beautrais, A. L. (2006). *Child youth and family: Practices and processes in managing risks of suicide in residences.* Retrieved from www.chmeds.ac.nz/research/suicide/Practices_process_in_managing_risks_residences_cyf_final_june_2006_4.pdf

Bereiter, C., & Engelmann, S. (1966). *Teaching disadvantaged children in the preschool.* Englewood Cliffs, NJ: Prentice Hall.

Bernstein, B. (1975). *Class, codes and control.* London: Routledge and Kegan Paul.

Bhattacharya, A., & Ehri, L. (2004). Graphosyllabic analysis helps adolescent struggling readers read and spell words. *Journal of Learning Disabilities, 37,* 331–338.

Bohm, D., & Peat, F. D. (2000). *Science, order, and creativity.* London: Routledge.

Brandon, W. (2002). Interrupting racial profiling: Moving pre-service teachers from white identity to equity pedagogy. In J. Slater, S. Fain, & C. Rosatto (Eds.), *The Freirean legacy: Educating for social justice* (pp. 139–156). New York: Peter Lang.

Britton, J. (1970/1993). *Language and learning: The importance of speech in children's development,* 2nd ed. Portsmouth, NH: Heinemann.

Britzman, D. (2003). *Practice makes practice: A critical study of learning to teach,* 2nd ed. Albany: State University of New York Press.

Bruner, J. (1996). *The culture of education.* Cambridge, MA: Harvard University Press.

Building Blocks for Youth. (2005). *No turning back: Promising approaches to reducing racial and ethnic disparities affecting youth of color in the justice system.* Retrieved from http://www.buildingblocksforyouth.org/noturningback.html

Carson, C. (1987). Revolt and repression. In C. Carson, D. J. Garrow, V. Harding, D. C. Hine, & T. K. Levine (Eds.), *Eyes on the prize: America's Civil Right years* (pp. 214–223). New York: Penguin Books.

Chaifetz, J., & Kravitz, R. (2005). *Holding back students damages their educational progress: An advocacy report.* New York: Advocates for Children of New York. Retrieved from www.advocatesforchildren.org/reports.php

Chall, J. S. (1983). *Learning to read: The great debate,* 2nd ed. New York: McGraw Hill.

Chall, J. S. (1996). *Stages of reading development.* New York: McGraw-Hill.

Chall, J. S., & Curtis, M. E. (1987). What clinical diagnosis tells us about children's reading. *Reading Teacher, 40,* 784–788.

Chambliss, C. (1994). *The relationship between mass incarceration and unequal education in the United States.* Retrieved from http://www.fedcrimlaw.com/visitors/PrisonLore/PrisonEducation2.htm

Children's Defense Fund. (2004). *Robin Hood in reverse: Bush administration budget choices take from poor children and give to the rich.* Washington, DC: Author. Retrieved from http://www.childrensdefense.org/site/News2?page=NewsArticle&id=6565

Chomsky, N. (1968). *Language and mind.* New York: Harcourt Brace & World.

Chomsky, N. (1986). *Knowledge of language: Its nature, origin, and use.* New York: Praeger.

Coalition for Juvenile Justice. (2001). *Abandoned in the back row: New lessons in education and delinquency.* 2001 Annual Report of the Coalition for Juvenile Justice. Washington, DC: Author. Retrieved from http://www.juvjustice.org/publications/2001ar.html

Coleman, M., & Vaughn, S. (2000). Reading Interventions for students with emotional/behavioral disorders. *Journal of Behavioral Disorders, 25,* 93–104

Correctional Association of New York. (2004a). *Treating juveniles as adults.* Juvenile Justice Project Fact Sheet. Retrieved from http://www.correctionalassociation.org/juvenile_fact.html

Correctional Association of New York. (2004b). *Juvenile detention in New York City.* Retrieved from http://www.correctionalassociation.org/JJP/publications/detention_fact_2004.pdf

Correctional Association of New York. (2005). *Youth confined in OCFS facilities.* Retrieved from http://www.correctionalassociation.org/JJP/publications/youth_in_ocfs.pdf

Correctional Association of New York. (2009a). *Youth confined in OCFS facilities.* Retrieved from http://www.correctionalassociation.org/publications/factsheets.htm

Correctional Association of New York. (2009b). *Juvenile detention in New York City.* Retrieved from http://www.correctionalassociation.org/publications/factsheets.htm

Council of the City of New York. (2005, May 31). *Making the grade? Understanding the 2005 fourth-grade English language arts assessment.* Retrieved from www.nyccouncil.info/pdf_files/newswire/making.pdf

Crawford, J. (1991). *Bilingual education: History, politics, theory, and practice.* Los Angeles, CA: Bilingual Education Services.

Cummins, J. (1981). The role of primary language development in promoting educational success for language minority students. In California State Department of Education (Ed.), *Schooling and language minority students: A theoretical framework*. (pp. 3–49). Evaluation, Dissemination, and Assessment Center. Los Angeles, CA: California State University.

Cummins, J. (1991). Empowering minority students: A framework for intervention. In M. Minami & B. Kennedy (Eds.), *Language issues in literacy and bilingual/multicultural education* (pp. 372–390). Cambridge, MA: Harvard Educational Review 22.

Darder, A. (2002). *Reinventing Paulo Freire: A pedagogy of love*. Cambridge, MA: Westview.

Darling-Hammond, L. (1996). The right to learn and the advancement of teaching: Research, policy, and practice for democratic education. *Educational Researcher, 25*(6), 5–17.

Davidson, H. S. (1988). Meaningful literacy education in prison? Problems and possibilities. *Journal of Correctional Education, 39*(2), 76–81.

Delpit, L. (1993). The silenced dialogue: Power and pedagogy in educating other people's children. In L. Weiss and M. Fine (Eds.), *Beyond silenced voices: class race, and gender in United States schools* (pp. 119–142). New York: State University of New York Press.

Delpit, L. (1995). *Other people's children: Cultural conflict in the classroom*. New York: New Press.

Denzin, N., & Lincoln, Y. (Eds.). (2000). *Handbook of qualitative research*, 2nd ed. Thousand Oaks, CA: Sage.

Dewey, J. (1963). *Experience and education*. New York: Collier (originally published 1938).

Dewey, J. (1990). *The school and society and the child and the curriculum*. Chicago: University of Chicago Press (originally published 1900 and 1902).

Dewey, J. (1991). *How we think*. Amherst, NY: Prometheus Books (originally published 1910).

Dimitriadis, G., & McCarthy, C. (2001). *Reading & teaching the postcolonial: From Baldwin to Basquiat*. New York: Teachers College Press.

Dobbin, S. A., & Gatowski, S. I. (1996). *Juvenile violence: A guide to research*. Reno, NV: National Council of Juvenile and Family Court Judges.

Drakeford, W., & Garfinkel, L.F. (2000). *Differential treatment of African-American youth*. The National Center on Education, Disability, and Juvenile Justice (EDJJ). Retrieved from http://www.edjj.org/Publications/pub_06_13_00_2.html

Du Bois, W. E. B. (1953). *The souls of black folk*. New York: Fawcett World Library (originally published 1903).

Education Trust. (2003). *Latino achievement in America*. Washington DC: Author. Retrieved from http://www.edtrust.org/dc/resources/archive/publications/2003?page=1

Fain, J., Rosatto, C., & Slater, J. (Eds.). (2002). *The Freirian legacy: Educating for social justice*. New York: Peter Lang.

Ferguson, A. (2000). *Bad boys: Public schools in the making of black masculinity*. Ann Arbor: University of Michigan Press.

Fine, M. (1991). *Framing dropouts: Notes on the politics of an urban public high school*. New York: State University of New York Press.

Fine, M., & Weiss, L. (Eds.). (1993). *Beyond silenced voices: Class, race, and gender in United States schools*. New York: State University of New York Press.

Fordham, S. (1988). Racelessness as a factor in black students' school success: Pragmatic strategy or pyrrhic victory? *Harvard Educational Review, 18*(3), 176–206.

Fossey, R. (1996, May/June). Kidding ourselves about school dropout rates. *The Harvard Education Letter,* 5–7.

Foster, M. (1997). *Black teachers on teaching*. New York: The New York Press.

Foucault, M. (1977). *Discipline and punish: The birth of the prison*. New York: Vintage Books.

Foucault, M. (1980). *Power/Knowledge: Selected interviews and other writings*. New York: Pantheon.

Fraser, S. (1995). *The bell curve wars: Race, intelligence, and the future of America*. New York: Basic Books.

Freire, P. (1970). *Pedagogy of the oppressed.* New York: Herder & Herder.

Freire, P. (1974). *Education for critical consciousness*. New York: Continuum.

Freire, P. (1985). *The politics of education: Culture, power, and liberation*. South Hadley, MA: Bergin & Garvey.

Freire, P. (1996). *Letters to Christina: Reflections on my life and work*. New York: Routledge.

Freire, P., & Horton, M. (1990). *We make the road by walking: Conversations on education and social change*. Philadelphia: Temple University Press.

Freire, P., & Macedo, D. (1987). *Literacy: Reading the word and the world*. South Hadley, MA: Bergin & Garvey.

García, E. (1991). Bilingualism, second language acquisition, and the education of Chicano language minority students. In R. Valencia (Ed.), *Chicano school failure and success: Research and policy agendas for the 1990s* (pp. 93–119). New York: Falmer.

García, O., & Baker, C. (Eds.). (1995). *Policy and practice in bilingual education: Extending the foundations.* Clevedon, England: Multilingual Matters.

Garland, D. (2001). *The culture of control: Crime and social order in contemporary society*. Oxford: Oxford University Press.

Garrow, D. J. (1987). Defining equality: The new legal battles over race and Civil Rights (1970-1986). In C. Carson, D.J. Garrow, V. Harding, D.C. Hine, & T.K. Levine (Eds.), *Eyes on the prize: America's Civil Right years* (pp. 243–246). New York: Penguin.

Gee, J. (1992). *The social mind: Language, ideology, and social practices*. South Hadley, MA: Bergin & Garvey.

Gee, J. (1996). *Social linguistics and literacies: Ideology in discourses*, 2nd ed. London: Routledge/Taylor & Francis.

Gee, J. (2002). Literacies, identities, and discourses. In M. Schleppegrel & M. Cecilia Colombi (Eds.), *Developing advanced literacy in first and second languages: Meaning with power* (pp. 159–175). Mahwah, NJ: Lawrence Erlbaum.

Gersten, R., & Woodward, J. (1994). The language-minority student and special education: Issues, trends, and paradoxes. *Exceptional Children, 60*(4), 310–322.

Gillingham, A., & Stillman, B. W. (1997). *The gillingham manual: Remedial training for students with specific disability in reading, spelling, and penmanship*, 8th ed. Cambridge, MA: Educators Publishing.

Giroux, H. (1988). *Schooling and the struggle for public life.* Minneapolis: University of Minnesota Press.

Giroux, H. (1993). Paulo Freire and the politics of postcolonialism. In P. McLaren & P. Leonard (Eds.), *Paulo Freire: A critical encounter* (pp. 177–188). New York: Routledge.

Giroux, H. (1997). *Pedagogy and the politics of hope: Theory, culture, and schooling.* Boulder, CO: Westview.

Gotbaum, B. (2002). *Pushing out at-risk students: An analysis of high school discharge figures.* New York: Public Advocates for the City of New York. Retrieved from pubadvocate.nyc. gov/policy/pdfs/pushing_out_at-risk_students.pdf

Gramsci, A. (1971). *Selections from prison notebooks* (Q. Hoare & G.N. Smith, Eds. and Trans.). New York: International Publishers.

Gregory, J. F. (1996). The crime of punishment: Racial and gender disparities in the use of corporal punishment in the U.S. public schools. *Journal of Negro Education, 64,* 454–462.

Gresson, A. (2004). *America's atonement.* New York: Peter Lang.

Habermas, J. (1970). *Knowledge and human interest.* Boston, MA: Beacon.

Hakuta, K. (1986). *Mirror of language: The debate on bilingualism.* New York: Basic Books.

Hakuta, K., & Snow, C. (1986, Spring). The role of research in policy decisions about bilingual education. *NABE News, 9*(3), 1, 18–21.

Haney, W., Madaus, G., Abrams, L., Wheelock, A., Miao, J., & Grura, I. (2004, January). *The educational pipeline in the U.S., 1970–2000.* Report of the National Board on Educational Testing and Public Policy. Chestnut Hill, MA: Boston College Center for the Study of Testing, Evaluation, and Educational Policy. Retrieved from www.bc.edu/ research/nbetpp/statements/nbr3.pdf

Harding, S. (1998). *Is science multi-cultural? Postcolonialisms, feminism, and epistemologies.* Bloomington: Indiana University Press.

Haunold, J. (2002). Idle hands are the devil's workshop: A history of American child labor and compulsory education; emancipation or reconstituted oppression? In J Slater, S. Fain, & C. Rosatto (Eds.), *The Freirean legacy: Educating for social justice* (pp. 95–103). New York: Peter Lang.

Hawkins, J. D., Herrenkohl, T. I., Farrington, D. P., Brewer, D., Catalano, R. F., Harachi, T. W., & Cothern, L. (2000). Predictors of youth violence. *Juvenile Justice Bulletin, Office of Juvenile Justice and Delinquency Prevention,* 1–11.

Hellman, D. A., & Beaton, S. (1986). The pattern of violence in urban public schools: The influence of school and community. *Journal of Research in Crime and Delinquency,* 23, 102–127.

hooks, b. (1994). *Teaching to transgress: Education as the practice of freedom.* New York: Routledge.

hooks, b. (2003). *Teaching community: A pedagogy of hope.* New York: Routledge.

Illich, I. (1971). *Deschooling society.* London: Penguin.

Kamil, M. (2003). *Adolescents and literacy: Reading for the 21st century.* Washington, DC: Alliance for Excellent Education.

Kantor, H., & Brenzel, B. (1992). Urban education and the "truly disadvantaged": The historical roots of the contemporary crisis, 1945-1990. *Teacher's College, 94*(2), 278–314.

Katz, M. B. (Ed.). (1983). *Education in American history*. New York: Praeger.

Kerka, S. (1995). *Prison literacy programs*. Eric Clearinghouse on Adult Career and Vocational Education. Columbus, OH. ERIC Digest No. 159. ERIC Identifier: ED383859. Retrieved from www.ericdigests.org/1996-1/prison.htm

Kincheloe, J. (2001a). *Getting beyond the facts: Teaching social studies/social sciences in the twenty-first century*. New York: Peter Lang.

Kincheloe, J. (2001b). Describing the bricolage: Conceptualizing a new rigor in qualitative research. *Qualitative Inquiry, 7*(6), 679–92.

Kincheloe, J. (2002). *The sign of the burger: McDonald's and the culture of power*. Philadelphia: Temple University Press.

Kincheloe, J. (Ed.). (2004a). *Multiple intelligences reconsidered*. New York: Peter Lang.

Kincheloe, J. (2004b). *Critical pedagogy primer*. New York: Peter Lang.

Kincheloe, J., & Berry, K. (2004). *Rigor and complexity in educational research: Constructing the bricolage*. London: Open University Press.

Kincheloe, J., & Hayes, K. (Eds.). (2006). *Teaching city kids: Understanding them and appreciating them*. New York: Peter Lang.

Kincheloe, J., & Pinar, W. (Eds.). (1991). *Curriculum as social psychoanalysis: Essays on the significance of place*. Albany: State University of New York Press.

Kincheloe, J., & Steinberg, S. (1997). *Changing multiculturalism: New times, new curriculum*. London: Open University Press.

Kincheloe, J., & Steinberg, S. (Eds.). (2006). *What you don't know about schools*. New York: Palgrave.

Kincheloe, J., Steinberg, S., & Hinchey, P. (1999). *The postformal reader: Cognition and education*. New York: Falmer.

Kincheloe, J., Steinberg, S., & Tippins, D. (1999). *The stigma of genius: Einstein, consciousness, and education*. New York: Peter Lang.

Kliebard, H. (1995). *The struggle for the American curriculum: 1893-1958,* 2nd ed. New York: Routledge.

Klingner, J. (2006). English Language Learners who struggle with reading. *Journal of Learning Disabilities, 39*(2), 108–128.

Kozol, J. (1991). *Savage inequalities: Children in America's schools*. New York: Harper.

Ladson-Billings, G., & Tate, W. (1995). Towards a critical race theory of education. *Teachers College Record, 97,* 47–68.

Lave, J., & Wenger, E. (1991). *Situated learning: Legitimate peripheral participation*. New York: Cambridge University Press.

Lazerson, M. (1983). The origins of special education. In J. Chambers & W. Hartman (Eds.), *Special education policies: Their history, implementation, and finance* (pp. 15–47). Philadelphia: Temple University Press.

Least Restrictive Environment Coalition. (2001, November). *Still waiting, after all these years…Inclusion of children with special needs in New York City public schools*. Report of the Least Restrictive Environment Coalition. New York: Advocates for Children. Retrieved from http://www.advocatesforchildren.org

Leone, P. E., Mayer, M. J., Malmgren, K., & Meisel, S. M. (2000). School violence and disruption: Rhetoric, reality, and reasonable balance. *Focus on Exceptional Children, 33*(1), 1–20.

Leone, P. E., Christle, C. A., Nelson, M., Skiba, R., Frey, A., & Jolivette, K. (2003). *School failure, race, and disability: Promoting positive outcomes, decreasing vulnerability for involvement with the juvenile delinquency system.* The National Center on Education, Disability, and Juvenile Justice (EDJJ). Retrieved from http://www.edjj.org/Publications/Promoting10_03.htm

Lewin, T. (2004, April 14). In cities, a battle to improve teenage literacy. *The New York Times.*

Lewis, O. (1965). *La vida: A Puerto Rican family in the culture of poverty.* New York: Random House.

Lochner, L., & Moretti, E. (2001). The effect of education on crime: Evidence from prison inmates, arrests, and self-reports. *Join Center on Poverty Research Working Paper # 287.* Retrieved from www.jcpr.org/wpfiles/lochner_moretti.pdf

Lyon, G. R. (1998). Overview of reading and literacy research. In S. Patton & M. Holmes (Eds.), *The keys to literacy* (pp. 1–15). Washington, DC: Council for Basic Education.

Lyon, G. R., & Moats, L. C. (1997). Critical conceptual and methodological considerations in reading intervention research. *Journal of Learning Disabilities, 30,* 578–588.

Lyon, R. (1995). Toward a Definition of Dyslexia. *Annals of Dyslexia, 45,* 3–27.

Lyons, J. (1995). The past and future directions of federal bilingual-education. In Baker, C., & Garcia, O. (Eds.), *Policy and practice in bilingual education.* Clevedon, England: Multilingual Matters.

Macedo, D. (2006). *Literacies of power: What Americans are not allowed to know,* 2nd ed. Boulder, CO: Westview.

Macedo, D., & Bartolomé, L. (1999). *Dancing with bigotry: Beyond the politics of tolerance.* New York: Palgrave.

Males, M., & Macallair, D. (2000). *Justice Policy Institute. The color of justice: An analysis of juvenile adult court transfers in California.* Washington, DC: Building Blocks for Youth. Retrieved from http://www.buildingblocksforyouth.org/colorofjustice/coj.html

McCarthey, S. J., & Moje, E. B. (2002, April/May/June). Conversations: Identity matters. *Reading Research Quaterly, 37,* 228–238.

McCarthy, C., & Crichlow, W. (1993). *Race identity and representation in education.* New York: Routledge.

McFadden, A. C., Marsh, G. E., Price, B. J., & Hwang, Y. (1992). A study of race and gender bias in the punishment of handicapped school children. *Urban Review, 24,* 239–251.

McLaren, P. (1994). *Life in schools: An introduction to critical pedagogy in the foundations of education.* White Plains, NY: Longman.

McLaren, P. (2000). *Che Guevarra, Paulo Freire, and the pedagogy of revolution.* Lanham, MD: Rowman & Littlefield.

Meltzer, J., & Hamann, E. T. (2004). *Meeting the literacy needs of adolescent English Language Learners through content area learning.* The Education Alliance. Providence, RI: Brown University. Retrieved from www.alliance.brown.edu/pubs/adlit/adell_litdv1.pdf

Michelli, N. (2005, May). The politics of teacher education: Lessons from New York City. *Journal of Teacher Education, 56*(3), 235–241.

Michelli, N., & Keiser, D. (Eds.). (2005). Teacher education for democracy and social justice. New York: Routledge.

Moats, L. C. (1999, June). *Teaching reading is rocket science: What expert teachers of reading should know and be able to do*. Washington, DC: American Federation of Teachers. Retrieved from www.aft.org/pubs-reports/downloads/teachers/rocketsci.pdf

Moats, L. C. (2001). When older kids can't read. *Educational Leadership, 58*(6), 36–40. Retrieved from www.scoe.org/reading/docs/older_091103.pdf

Morris, M. (2004). The eighth one: Naturalistic intelligence. In J. Kincheloe (Ed.), *Multiple intelligences reconsidered* (pp. 159–176). New York: Peter Lang.

Mount Sinai Adolescent Health Center. (2002). *Adolescent health services: Improving health & lowering health care costs*. New York: The Mount Sinai Medical Center. Retrieved from www.mountsinai.org/msh/clinical_services/ahcpolicyreport1.pdf

National Center for Education Statistics. (2003). *The nation's report card: Reading 2003*. Institute of Education Sciences: National Assessment of Educational Progress (NAEP). Washington, DC: U.S. Department of Education. Retrieved from http://nces.ed.gov/nationsreportcard/states/

National Center for Education Statistics. (2007a). *Literacy in everyday life: Results from the 2003 national assessment of adult literacy*. Washington, DC: U.S. Department of Education. Retrieved from http://nces.ed.gov/naal/

National Center for Education Statistics. (2007b). *The nation's report card: Reading 2007*. Institute of Education Sciences: National Assessment of Educational Progress (NAEP). Washington, DC: U.S. Department of Education. Retrieved from http://nces.ed.gov/nationsreportcard/pubs/main2007/2007496.asp

National Commission on Excellence in Education. (1983). *A nation at risk: The imperative for educational reform*. Washington, DC: U.S. Department of Education.

National Dissemination Center for Children with Disabilities. (2002, June). *General information about disabilities: Disabilities that qualify infants, toddlers, children, and youth for services under IDEA*. Washington, DC: NICHCY. Retrieved from www.nichcy.org/pubs/genresc/gr3.htm

National Dropout Prevention Network. (2000). *Dropout statistics*. Washington, DC: Author.

National Information Center for Children and Youth with Disabilities. (2002). *General information about disabilities: Disabilities that qualify infants, toddlers, children, and youth for services under the IDEA*. U.S. Office of Special Education Programs. Retrieved from nichcy.org/pubs/genresc/gr3.pdf

National Institute for Literacy. (2002a). *Discipline for children with disabilities*. [As adopted in 64 Federal Register 12405, March 12, 1999, regulations regarding discipline under Secs. 300.121(d), and 300.519 52]. Retrieved from http://www.edlaw.net/service/discipline.html

National Institute for Literacy. (2002b) *Literacy fact sheets overview: Reading facts*. Retrieved from: http://www.nifl.gov/nifl/facts/reading_facts.html

National Reading Panel. (2000). *Teaching children to read: An evidenced-based assessment of the scientific research literature on reading and its implications for reading instruction.* Washington, DC: National Institute of Child Health and Development. Retrieved from http://www.nichd.nih.gov/publications/nrp/smallbook.cfm

National Research Council. (1999). *High-stakes: Testing for tracking, promotion, and graduation.* Washington, DC: National Academy. Retrieved from http://www.nap.edu/html/highstakes/

New York City Department of Education. (2006a). *Summary report of grade 3, 5, and 7 summer success academy 2006 summer test results.* Retrieved from http://schools.nyc.gov/daa/2006_Summer/default.asp

New York City Department of Education. (2006b). *Office of multiple pathways to graduation: Developing and strengthening schools and programs that lead to high school graduation and post-secondary opportunities for overage, under-credited youth.* Retrieved from www.ytfg.org/documents/OMPGOverviewandFindingsBroadDistribution102206.pdf

New York City Department of Education. (2007a). *Program intake analysis 1/31/07.*

New York City Department of Education. (2007b). *2007 yearly principal's report.*

New York City Department of Education. (2009a, May). *Promotion 2009: Training for sso's and community superintendents.* Prepared by Teaching and Learning.

New York City Department of Education. (2009b). *Promotion policy.* Retrieved from http://schools.nyc.gov/RulesPolicies/PromotionPolicy/default.html

New York City Department of Education. (2009c). *Mayor unveils plan to end social promotion in all remaining grades from three to eight.* Retrieved from http://schools.nyc.gov/Offices/mediarelations/NewsandSpeeches/2009-2010/20090810_social_promotion.htm

New York City Department of Juvenile Justice. (2007). *2006 FY population statistics.*

New York State Education Department. (2006). *English language arts learning standards.* Retrieved from http://www.emsc.nysed.gov/ciai/ela/elals.html

New York State Education Department. (2008). *Regulations of the Commissioner of Education relating to general education & diploma requirements.* Section 100.5-100.9 of the Regulations of the Commissioner of Education. Retrieved from http://www.emsc.nysed.gov/part100/opener.html

No Child Left Behind Act. (2001). *Title I—Improving the academic achievement of the disadvantaged.* Washington, DC: U.S. Department of Education. Retrieved from http://www.ed.gov/policy/elsec/leg/esea02/pg1.html

No Child Left Behind Act. (2001). *Reading first.* Washington, DC: U.S. Department of Education. Retrieved from http://www.ed.gov/programs/readingfirst/index.html

Office of Program Policy Analysis and Government Accountability. (1998). *Review of educational services in juvenile justice residential facilities.* (Report No. 98-28). Retrieved from www.oppaga.state.fl.us/reports/pdf/9828.rpt.pdf

Office of Juvenile Justice and Delinquency Prevention. (1999, December). Minorities in the juvenile justice system. *1999 National report series: Juvenile justice bulletin.* U.S. Department of Justice: Author.

Ogbu, J. (1978). *Minority education and caste: The American system in cross-cultural perspective.* New York: Academic Press.

Ohanian, S. (1999). *One size fits few: The folly of educational standards.* Portsmouth, NH: Heinemann.

Oliver, P., & Yocom, J. (2004). *Explaining state black imprisonment rates 1983–1999.* Prepared for the 2004 American Sociological Association Meeting.

Orfield, G., Losen, D., Wald, J., & Swanson, C. (2004). *Losing our future: How minority youth are being left behind by the graduation rate crisis.* Cambridge, MA: The Civil Rights Project at Harvard University. Retrieved from www.civilrightsproject.harvard.edu/research/dropouts/LosingFuture_Executive.pdf

Orton, J. L. (1964). *A guide to teaching phonics.* Cambridge, MA: Educators Publishing.

Otheguy, R. (1991). Thinking about bilingual education: A critical appraisal. In M. Minami & B. Kennedy (Eds.), *Language issues in literacy and bilingual/multicultural education* (pp. 409–423). Cambridge, MA: Harvard Educational Review 22.

Ovando, C. J. (1991). Politics and pedagogy: The case of bilingual education. In M. Minami & B. Kennedy (Eds.), *Language issues in literacy and bilingual/multicultural education* (pp. 503–520). Cambridge, MA: Harvard Educational Review 22.

Paley, A. (2007, April 21). Key initiative of "No Child" under federal investigation: Officials profited from Reading First Program. *The Washington Post.* Retrieved from http://www.washingtonpost.com/wp-gdyn/content/article/2007/04/20/AR2007042002284_pf.html

Pinar, W. (1991). Curriculum as social psychoanalysis: On the significance of place. In J. Kincheloe & W. Pinar (Eds.), *Curriculum as social psychoanalysis: Essays on the significance of place* (pp. 167–186). Albany: State University of New York Press.

Pinar, W., Reynolds, W., Slattery, P., & Taubman, P. (Eds.). (2002). *Understanding curriculum: An introduction to the study of historical and contemporary curriculum discourses.* New York: Peter Lang.

Quinn, M. M., Rutherford, R. B., & Leone, P. E. (2001, December). Students with disabilities in correctional facilities [Eric EC Digest #E621]. Arlington, VA: Eric Clearinghouse on Disabilities and Gifted Education.

Ravitch, D. (2000). *Left back: A century of battles over school reform.* New York: Simon & Schuster.

Reed, J. H., Schallert, D. L., Berth, A. D., & Woodruff, A. L. (2004). Motivated reader, engaged writer: The role of motivation in the literate acts of adolescents. In T. L. Jetton & J. A. Dole (Eds.), *Adolescent literacy research and practice* (pp. 251–282). New York: Guilford Press.

Roberts, P. (1996). Rethinking conscientization. *Journal of the Philosophy of Education of Great Britain, 30*(2), 179–196.

Robertson, P., Kushner, M., Starks, J., & Drescher, C. (1994). An update of participation rates of culturally and linguistically diverse students in special education: The need for research and policy agenda. *The Bilingual Special Education Perspective, 14*(1), 1, 3–9.

Roderick, M. (1995, December). Grade retention and school dropout: Policy debate and research questions. *Phi Delta Kappa Research Bulletin, 15,* 88–92. Retrieved from http://www.pdkintl.org/research/rbulletins/resbul15.htm

Rodríguez-Zamora, G. (1979). Setting the stage for learning: A psychological framework. In H. Trueba & C. Barnett-Mizrahi (Eds.), *Bilingual and multicultural education and the professional from theory to practice* (pp. 204–208). Rowley, MA: Newbury House.

Rogoff, B., & Wertsch, J. V. (Eds.). (1984). *Children's learning in the "zone of proximal development."* San Francisco: Josey-Bass.

Rosenblatt, L. (1978/1994). *The reader, the text, the poem: The transactional theory of the literary work.* Carbondale: Southern Illinois University Press.

Rumberger, R. W. (1987). High school dropouts: A review of issues and evidence. *Review of Educational Research, 57,* 101–121.

Rumberger, R. W., & Rodríguez, G. (2002). Chicano dropouts: an update of research and policy issues. In R. Valencia (Ed.), *Chicano school failure and success: Past, present, and future,* 2nd ed. (pp. 114–146). London: Routledge/Falmer.

Rutter, M., & Giller, H. (1984). *Juvenile delinquency: Trends and perspectives.* New York: Guilford Press.

Sadoski, M., & Paivio, A. (2001). *Imagery and text: A dual coding theory of reading and writing.* Mahwah, NJ: Lawrence Erlbaum.

Schon. D. A. (1983). *The reflective practitioner.* New York: Basic Books.

Semali, L., & Kincheloe, J. (1999). *What is indigenous knowledge? Voices from the academy.* New York: Falmer.

Shannon, P. (1988). *Broken promises: Reading instruction in twentieth century America.* Granby, MA: Bergin & Garvey.

Shaywitz, S. E. (1996). Dyslexia. *Scientific American, 275*(5), 98–104.

Shaywitz, S. E., Fletcher, J. M., Holahan, J. M., Shneider, A. E., Marchione, K. E., Stuebing, K. K., Francis, D. J., Pugh, K. R., & Shaywitz, B. A. (1999). Persistence of dyslexia: The connecticut longitudinal study at adolescence. *Pediatrics, 104*(6), 1351–1359.

Shor, I. (Ed.). (1987). *Freire for the classroom: A sourcebook for liberatory teaching.* Portsmouth, NH: Boynton/Cook.

Shor, I. (1992). *Empowering education: Critical teaching for social change.* Chicago: University of Chicago Press.

Shor, I. (1996). *When students have power: Negotiating authority in a critical pedagogy.* Chicago: University of Chicago Press.

Skiba, R. J., Michael, R. S., Nardo, A. C., & Peterson, R. (2000, June). The color of discipline: Sources of racial and gender disproportionality in school punishment. *Urban Review.* Retrieved from http://www.indiana.edu/~safeschl/cod

Snow, C. E., Burns, S., & Griffin, P. (Eds.). (1998). *Preventing reading difficulties in young children.* Washington, DC: National Academy.

Snyder, H., & Sickmund, M. (2006). *Juvenile offenders and victims: 2006 national report.* Washington, DC: U.S. Department of Justice, Office of Juvenile Justice and Delinquency Prevention. Retrieved from http://www.ncjrs.gov/App/QA/Detail.aspx?id=732&context=5

Stone, D. (2002). *Policy paradox: The art of political decision making,* 2nd ed. New York: W.W. Norton.

Swanson, C. B., & Chaplin, D. (2003). *Counting high school graduates when graduates count: Measuring graduation rates under the high-stakes of NCLB.* Washington, DC: Education

Policy Center, The Urban Institute. Retrieved from http://www.allacademic.com//meta/p_mla_apa_research_citation/1/0/7/5/5/pages107556/p107556-1.php

Swanson, H. (1999). Reading research for students with LD: A meta-analysis of intervention outcomes. *Journal of Learning Disabilities, 32,* 504–532.

Tatum, A. (2000, September). Breaking down barriers that disenfranchise African-American adolescent readers in low-level tracks. *Journal of Adolescent and Adult Literacy, 44*(1), 52–63.

Taylor, D., & Dorsey-Gaines, C. (1988). *Growing up literate: Learning from inner-city families.* Portsmouth, NH: Heinemann.

The Mayor's Task Force on Bilingual Education. (2000, December). *Recommendations for immediate reform.* Report of the Task Force on Bilingual Education to Mayor Rudolph Giuliani. Retrieved from www.nyc.gov/html/rwg/pdf/bilingualedreportfinal-pt1.pdf

The New York Immigration Coalition & Advocates for Children of New York. (2006, November). *So many schools, so few options: How Mayor Bloomberg's small high school reforms deny full access to English Language Learners.* Retrieved from www.advocatesforchildren.org/pubs/2005/ellsmallschools06.pdf

Troike, R. (1978). *Research evidence for the effectiveness of bilingual education.* Rosslyn, VA: National Clearinghouse for Bilingual Education.

Trueba, H. T. (1989). *Raising silent voices.* Boston: Heinle & Heinle.

Trueba, H. T., & Barnett-Mizrahi, C. (1979). *Bilingual multicultural education and the professional: From theory to practice.* Rowley, MA: Newbury House.

Tyack, D. (1974). *The one best system: A history of American urban education.* Cambridge, MA: Harvard University Press.

Tyack, D., & Cuban, L. (1995). *Tinkering towards utopia: A century of public school reform.* Cambridge, MA: Harvard University Press.

UNESCO Education Sector. (2004). *The plurality of literacy and its implications for policies and programmes.* UNESCO education sector position paper. Retrieved from unesdoc.unesco.org/images/0013/001362/136246e.pdf

U.S. Bureau of the Census. (2001). *Current population survey.* Washington, DC: U.S. Department of Commerce. Retrieved from http://nces.ed.gov/pubs2005/dropout2001/tables/table_1.asp

U.S. Department of Education. (1999, July). *Taking responsibility for ending social promotion: A guide for educators and state and local leaders.* Retrieved from http://www.ed.gov/pubs/socialpromotion/index.html

U.S. Department of Education. (2001). *Elementary and secondary education part B—Student reading skills improvement grants section 1208.* Retrieved from http://www.ed.gov/policy/elsec/leg/esea02/pg4.html#sec1208

U.S. Department of Education. (2003). *Elementary and secondary education act, title I, part B—Student reading skills improvement grants, subpart 1—Reading first.* Retrieved from http://www.ed.gov/policy/elsec/leg/esea02/pg4.html

U.S. General Accounting Office. (2002). *School dropouts: Education could play a stronger role in identifying and disseminating prevention strategies.* (Report GAO-02-240). Washington, DC: Author. Retrieved from http://www.gao.gov/new.items/d02240.pdf

Valencia, R. (Ed.). (1991). *Chicano school failure and success: Research and policy agendas for the 1990s* (pp. 93–119). New York: Falmer.

Van Manen, M. (1990). *Researching lived experience: Human science for an action sensitive pedagogy.* Albany: State University of New York.

Varela, F. (1999). *Ethical know-how: Action, wisdom, and cognition.* Stanford, CA: Stanford University Press.

Villanueva, V. (1993). *Bootstraps: From an American academic of color.* Urbana, IL: National Council of Teachers of English.

Voltz, D. L. (1996, Winter). Learning and cultural diversities in general and special education classes: frameworks for success. Council on Exceptional Children. *Multiple Voices,* Vol. Unknown, 1–10.

Vygotsky, L. S. (1978). *Mind in society: The development of higher psychological processes.* Cambridge, MA: Harvard University Press.

Vygotsky, L. (1989). *Thought and language.* Cambridge, MA: MIT Press.

Wacquant, L. (2002, January/February). From slavery to mass incarceration: Rethinking the 'race question' in the United States. *The New Left Review.*

Wang, X., Blomberg, T., & Li, S. (2005). Comparison of the educational deficiencies of delinquent and nondelinquent students. *Evaluation Review, 29,* 291–312.

Weiler, K. (1991, November). Freire and a feminist pedagogy of difference. *Harvard Educational Review, 61*(4), 449–474.

Weiler, K. (1996, Summer). Myths of Paulo Freire. *Educational Theory, 46*(3), 353–371.

Western, B., Schiraldi, V., & Ziedenberg, J. (2005). *Education and incarceration.* Justice Policy Institute. Retrieved from http://www.justicepolicy.org/article.php?id=242

Wilson, B. (1988). *Wilson Reading System.* Milbury, MA: Wilson Learning System.

Wilson, W. J. (1987). *The truly disadvantaged: The innercity, the underclass, and public policy.* Chicago: University of Chicago Press.

Wilson, W. J. (1996). *When work disappears: The world of the new urban poor.* New York: Knopf.

Winzer, M. (1993). *The history of special education: From isolation to integration.* Washington, DC: Gallaudet.

Xia, C., & Glennie, E. (2005). *Grade retention: The gap between research and practice.* Terry Sanford Institute of Public Policy. Durham, NC: Duke University. Retrieved from www.pubpol.duke.edu/centers/child/publications/policybriefs/files/edureform/FlawedStrategy-PartOne.pdf

Young, J. (2003). *Crossing the borderline: Globalization and social exclusion: The sociology of vindictiveness and the criminology of transgression.* Retrieved from http://www.malcolmread.co.uk/JockYoung/crossing.htm

Zentella, A. (1997). *Growing up bilingual: Puerto Rican children in New York.* Malden, MA: Blackwell.

Index

Studies in the Postmodern Theory of Education

General Editor
Shirley R. Steinberg

Counterpoints publishes the most compelling and imaginative books being written in education today. Grounded on the theoretical advances in criticalism, feminism, and postmodernism in the last two decades of the twentieth century, Counterpoints engages the meaning of these innovations in various forms of educational expression. Committed to the proposition that theoretical literature should be accessible to a variety of audiences, the series insists that its authors avoid esoteric and jargonistic languages that transform educational scholarship into an elite discourse for the initiated. Scholarly work matters only to the degree it affects consciousness and practice at multiple sites. Counterpoints' editorial policy is based on these principles and the ability of scholars to break new ground, to open new conversations, to go where educators have never gone before.

For additional information about this series or for the submission of manuscripts, please contact:

> Shirley R. Steinberg
> c/o Peter Lang Publishing, Inc.
> 29 Broadway, 18th floor
> New York, New York 10006

To order other books in this series, please contact our Customer Service Department:

> (800) 770-LANG (within the U.S.)
> (212) 647-7706 (outside the U.S.)
> (212) 647-7707 FAX

Or browse online by series:

> www.peterlang.com